EYEWITNESS COMPANIONS

Sailing

FOREWORD BY ELLEN MACARTHUR

JEREMY EVANS ROD HEIKELL
TIM JEFFERY ANDY O'GRADY

DK

LONDON · NEW YORK
MUNICH · MELBOURNE · DELHI

Senior Editor	Simon Tuite
Senior Art Editor	Susan St. Louis
Production Editor	Sharon McGoldrick
Production Controller	Tony Phipps
Managing Editor	Stephanie Farrow
Managing Art Editor	Lee Griffiths

Produced for Dorling Kindersley by
Schermuly Design Co.

Creative Director	Hugh Schermuly
Project Editor	Cathy Meeus
Designers	Steve Woosnam-Savage
	Lee Riches
Editors	Paul Docherty
	Gill Edden
	Polly Boyd
Picture Research	Will Jones
Illustration	John Woodcock
Commissioned Photography	Gerard Brown

Written by Jeremy Evans, Rod Heikell,
Tim Jeffery, and Andy O'Grady

First published in 2007 by
Dorling Kindersley Limited
80 Strand, London WC2R 0RL

THE PENGUIN GROUP

2 4 6 8 10 9 7 5 3 1

A CIP catalogue record for this book is
available from the British Library

ISBN 978-1-40531-624-8

Colour reproduced by Wyndeham Pre-Press, England
Printed in China by Leo Paper Products Ltd

Discover more at
www.dk.com

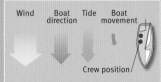

KEY
In this book standard
symbols are used to
indicate the direction
of wind, tide, and
boat, as well as boat
movement and crew
position.

Wind | Boat direction | Tide | Boat movement

Crew position

CONTENTS

CONTENTS (continued)

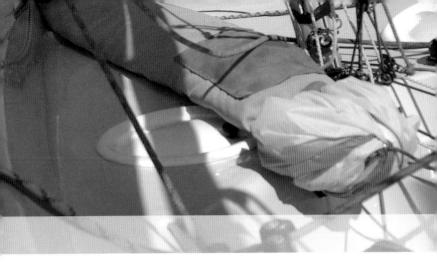

MANY PEOPLE TALK ABOUT MOMENTS THAT CHANGE THEIR LIFE, SOMETIMES PEOPLE EXPERIENCE SOMETHING THAT CHANGES THEIR THINKING, THEIR PERSPECTIVE AND LIFESTYLE, AND EVEN TAKE A NEW DIRECTION.

This can happen at any time in your life, but for me, I was just four.
I stepped onboard the deck of a boat, it was my first time on the water, and it was to be an experience that would change my life forever.

GOING FOR THE RECORD
Ellen MacArthur's trimaran *Castorama/B&Q* is seen here during her record-breaking solo voyage around the world, which she completed on 7 February 2005 in 71 days 14 hours and 18 minutes.

Sailing is an amazing sport for several reasons: firstly it is one of the few sports in the world where men and women can compete on an equal footing; secondly, it is a sport that encourages you to continually learn. I have been sailing since I was four years old and professionally for over ten years, but I know that I still have room to improve and more to learn, not only from my own experiences

ELLEN MACARTHUR
Born in Derbyshire, England, Ellen MacArthur
acquired her first sailing skills in a Topper dinghy,
bought out of her own pocket money. She is now an
internationally renowned yachtswoman.

but the experience of others as well.
For me sailing is a passion that I have
had ever since I can remember; being
out on the water gave me a sensation
of adventure and excitement that
I had never felt before. It is this
excitement that fuelled my dedication
to the sport of sailing.

   The world of professional sailing
encompasses that of solo offshore
sailors, who race across the most
desolate and vast oceans of our
planet, to that of fully crewed boats
racing at record-breaking speeds. The
diversity of the hardware is extensive,
from the elegant and powerful

SMALL-BOAT SAILING
Dinghies and keelboats (such as that pictured above) make a perfect introduction to sailing. Dinghy sailing is also a major international competitive sport.

America's Cup boats that go head to head in a battle of tactics, to the grand prix dinghy and the growing keelboat sector. But there is also another side, the day cruising, the weekend family trips, and the days when you just head out and see where the wind and tides take you! Sailing really does offer something for everyone, a different boat for every level of ability, and every level of participation, whether just cruising or racing at some major regatta on the other side of the world.

Everyone finds their own place; for some the ride is a little rougher than others. One of the questions I am most frequently asked: What is life like out there for months alone, in some of the harshest environments on Earth? The only way I have found to explain this is to imagine driving a car, fast, off-road at night in lashing rain, without headlights! You're forced to hang on to the steering wheel just to stay in your seat, and you have no idea what's coming next. To make matters worse, you have no windscreen and no roof. The wind is screaming in your ears, the spray burning your eyes. That's how it feels sailing fast in the Southern Ocean at night. Although there are many elements in sailing that are beyond our control, to me this is what is the source of the excitement and the challenges that I have not found elsewhere. Sailing can be seen as a complicated sport, inaccessible to many, but it is certainly not all about the yacht clubs and expensive boats. It is about getting out on the water, experiencing the natural world from another perspective, discovering a sense of freedom, and hopefully a feeling of achievement from what you have done. Sailing can teach so many great life experiences, teamwork, determination in the face of adversity, commitment, and, more than anything, confidence in the choices you make.

At the Ellen MacArthur Trust we take young people suffering from cancer and leukaemia sailing.

NECK AND NECK
Yacht racing has for over a century gripped the imagination of sailors throughout the world. Sailing races such as those held at Key West, Florida, USA (pictured right) provide a superb opportunity for experienced competitive sailors as well as keen newcomers to vie for glory.

They are facing the biggest challenge of their life, yet they do it with so much courage. Sailing with them is truly inspiring; they take on a new environment and discipline they have never encountered before and embrace it with a passion and excitement that can't help but change your own perspective on life. These sailing trips offer them a brief escape from the trials of their everyday lives, and enjoying time on the water, no matter what the conditions, lifts their spirits more than we ever hoped for.

After nearly ten years of professional sailing, I continue to be grateful for the opportunities this sport has given me. There are always new challenges to be had, from records and races, to new technology and design, and the challenges on land to making these projects a reality. In every race and every record, you strive to do better and

FAMILY FUN
Sailing is a sport that attracts people
of all ages.It also provides unrivalled
opportunities for families to share the same
recreational activity. Here a father and son
enjoy a fun outing in a Sunfish dinghy.

to learn in a way that will bring more knowledge and understanding of this great sport and the environment in which we race. With passion, drive, hard work, and loyal support, you soon realize that anything is possible.

For everyone who hasn't tried sailing, I hope these pages open up a whole world of possibilities. I hope this book inspires people to learn even more about this amazing sport, to pass this knowledge on to others, and inspire the next generation of sailors. I hope you enjoy this book, and I wish you every success out on the water. If you don't try, you'll never know!

Ellen MacArthur

Ellen MacArthur
Offshore Challenges Sailing Team
www.teamellen.com
www.ellenmacarthurtrust.org

History
of sailing

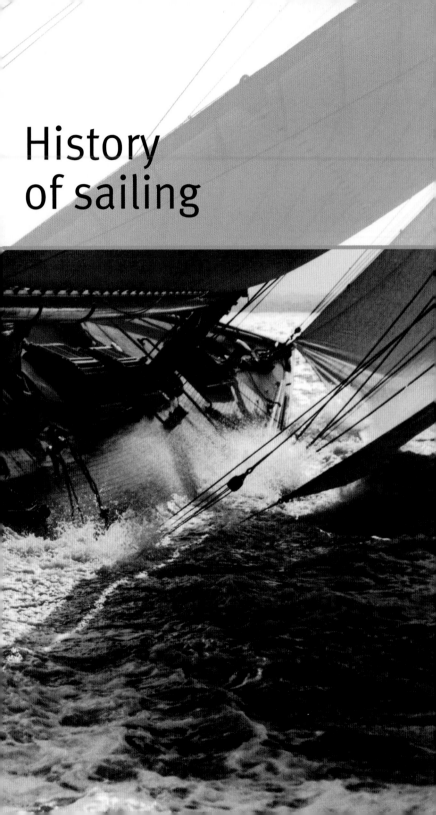

Origins of sailing

Through the 19th and 20th centuries, recreational sailing spread throughout the world. Before that, sailing boats had been used for transport, fishing, commerce, or as warships, for as long as we can trace the history of people living near water.

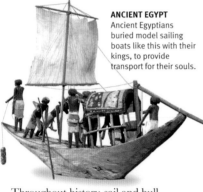

ANCIENT EGYPT
Ancient Egyptians buried model sailing boats like this with their kings, to provide transport for their souls.

Throughout history, sail and hull designs have varied according to coastal conditions and the availability of local materials. A simple square sail rigged before the mast is probably the earliest design, and is found in ancient records from the Mediterranean, the Aegean, the Red Sea, and the Persian Gulf. We know that Roman galleys, powered chiefly by oars, carried square sails for auxiliary power and speed. The Viking ships of the 8th and 9th centuries were square rigged, as were the great three-masted exploration ships of the 15th and 16th centuries. Square sails must be rigged so that the wind blows into only one side of the sail, and they function best when sailing downwind.

The triangular lateen sail, which is set on a yard but rigged fore and aft behind the mast, has greater flexibility. This type of sail can swing from side to side, depending on the direction of the wind and how the sail is trimmed.

The design allows sailing more or less against the wind, as well as before it. The lateen sail was used on early Arab dhows and Polynesian outrigger canoes long before it became common on European and North American boats. The great ocean traders of the 17th and 18th centuries made use of a combination of square and lateen sails.

A variation on these two designs is the lugsail – a four-sided sail that is bent on to a yard but rigged fore and aft. The Chinese junk rig uses a lugsail with multiple battens; about a fifth of the sail is set forward of the mast and complex sheeting allows almost infinite adjustment of the sail.

The Bermudan rig (*see* Rig designs, pp.46–47) is an altogether newer sail shape. This is a triangular sail, set with the luff attached directly to a tall mast. It is the most common sail shape on modern yachts, though by no means the only one. Variations on all the traditional sail shapes are still in use all over the world.

RECREATIONAL SAILING

While work – and survival – came first in ancient times, we do have records of recreational sailing. In Egypt, for example, Cleopatra was carried down the Nile on a luxury vessel that could today be described only as a royal yacht.

VIKING SHIPS
From about AD 700, the Vikings used these high-prowed boats to transport heavy loads for long distances. They were built on a long keel made from a single piece of wood and carried a single square sail.

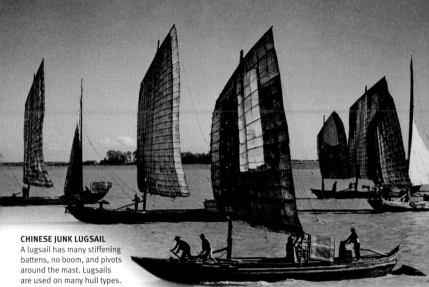

CHINESE JUNK LUGSAIL
A lugsail has many stiffening battens, no boom, and pivots around the mast. Lugsails are used on many hull types.

We know that the Norsemen built slender, swift craft in which to race each other, and that medieval vessels of Venice, at the northern tip of the Adriatic Sea, had embroidered sails quite impractical for working ships. There is also a record of a ship with the off-putting name *Rat of Wight* built in Cowes, in 1588, as a pleasure ship for Queen Elizabeth I of England.

The origin of the word yacht can be traced back to 1599, when a Dutch dictionary used the phrase *jaght schip* to mean a boat used for recreational racing. At that time in the Netherlands, all the right circumstances came together for the pastime to take hold: an economy that produced wealth and leisure time; waters sheltered from both weather and armed raiders; plus shipbuilding skills. Of all the diverse uses for boats in a country built on estuaries and inland waterways, criss-crossed by canals and dykes, waterborne recreation was a natural development.

ROYALTY AND REGATTAS

It is likely that King Charles II took yachting to England following his years in exile in the Netherlands: when he was restored to the throne after the English Civil War, the Dutch East India Company presented Charles with the 16-m (52-ft) yacht *Mary*, complete with gilded fittings, in 1660. She inspired similar vessels, built on the Thames.

The first recorded regatta of sailing boats was in 1720, on the south coast of Ireland at the Water Club of Cork. Rather than race, they took part in waterborne dressage, which involved performing intricate manoeuvres according to signals. So, the sport of yachting was born.

TRADITIONAL BAHAMIAN SAILBOATS
Early contestants of the Bahama Sailing Regatta were fishing and freighting vessels. Now contenders build new, traditional-style boats with the sole purpose of winning races.

EGYPTIAN WORKBOAT
The traditional shallow-draught felucca, on the River Nile, has a centre plate and huge, heavy sails made from natural fibre. Its gentle passage, using light winds and river currents, is popular with tourists.

Gravesend and back for a wager of £100. Other royal races followed.

Through the 18th century, yacht racing gradually took hold among the wealthy and those seeking prestige, primarily across Europe and in North America. Of course, the aristocratic and wealthy did not do all the hard work required on their boats – they employed large numbers of crewmen to handle the heavy sails and spars. The first decades of the 1800s saw the establishment of yacht clubs around the world. By the 1870s, influential clubs had been established in Gibraltar, Stockholm, Hobart, New York, Bermuda, Mumbai, Ostend, Toronto, Nova Scotia, Rotterdam, New Orleans, Auckland, Hamburg, and Genoa among other cities. All of these generated high standards of racing.

In England in 1826, the Royal Yacht Club of Cowes – later (1833) the Royal Yacht Squadron – organized a race that was the start of what became Cowes Week (*see* Cowes Week, pp.322–323). In 1851, the New York Yacht Club's schooner *America* came to England and raced British yachts around the Isle of Wight for the One Hundred Guineas Cup. Out of her victory the America's Cup was born, the oldest continuing international competition in sport.

CRUISING FOR PLEASURE

Racing was for the elite, but the 19th century saw a spreading culture of recreational voyaging. Richard Tyrrell McMullen started cruising in English waters in 1850 and did much to encourage amateur yachtsmen to navigate and exercise sound seamanship. His book *Down Channel* (published in 1869) was the start of cruising literature. By 1880, there were enough serious sailors involved in cruising for the formation of the Cruising Club in England.

Americans were also sailing far afield. Bernard Gilboy crossed the Pacific on his own in 1883; William Hudson and Frank Fitch crossed the Atlantic together in an 8-m (26-ft) boat in 1866. The best known of all is Joshua Slocum, an American, who was the first to circumnavigate the

EARLY RACING

It seems that England's King Charles had "caught the bug" for yachting, for in 1661 we have the first recorded race for racing's sake. This was between *Catherine*, built for Charles II by Christopher Pett, and *Anne*, owned by Charles' brother the Duke of York. They competed on the River Thames from Greenwich to

ROYAL CLUB
Royal patronage often lent prestige to the earliest yacht clubs. This painting of about 1820 depicts a yacht of the Royal Yacht Club of Cowes with King George IV on board.

world alone. He took three years, starting from Boston in 1895 and sailing against the prevailing winds. Of course, cruising yachts were not mass produced then as they are now. Many of the craft chosen for cruising were either very small (and therefore affordable) or conversions of traditional working vessels. Many purpose-built cruising yachts would not have standing headroom below, bunks would be narrow, and sanitary arrangements rudimentary. The option of converting a 15–20m (50–70ft) trawler or barge – with ample room below decks

EARLY YACHT CLUBS

Among the earliest yacht clubs were the Neva Flotilla, St. Petersburg (1717) and the Water Club of Cork, later to become the Royal Cork Yacht Club (1720). Here, keen spectators watch the Corinthian Yacht Club Race, Marblehead Harbor, Massachussetts, 1922.

for several cabins, heads compartments, and a proper galley – was a favoured choice in the early years after World War I. In some areas, notably the Netherlands, the designs of these old working boats have been retained into the modern cruising fleet. For cruisers, sailing remains the ultimate expression of personal freedom.

BARGE RACING
Shallow-draught barges with leeboards are ideal for the mainly shallow waters of the Netherlands. Modern cruising and racing versions of the distinctive Dutch design are common in the area.

The advent of modern racing

Three boats, *America*, *Reliance*, and *Atlantic*, will always be seen as heralding the era of modern racing. Designed for wealthy men, in the mid 19th and early 20th century, each was innovative and successful. They required huge crews and, by modern standards, they seem extreme.

BUILT FOR RACING

Much was expected of the 31-m (102-ft) schooner *America*. Her builder, William Brown, commissioned George Steers to design her for a New York Yacht Club (NYYC) syndicate headed by its founding commodore, John Cox Stevens, who planned to take the vessel to England in 1851 to race the best British yachts.

With fine bows, low freeboard (height above water), raked masts, and beamy hull form, *America* looked fast. The concave bow sections, and maximum beam located halfway along the hull's length, were innovatory and designed according to the theories of the Scots engineer John Scott Russell. However, British designers continued with their

bluff-bowed vessels, while the hull forms pioneered in *America* found more favour in the USA. Steers placed *America's* widest section well aft of Russell's theoretical optimum.

America won the famous race around the Isle of Wight but did not lead to any profound change in yacht design in European waters. One factor was how tonnage was calculated in order to create time allowances for handicapping, so that yachts of different design could race each other. But she was influential: the British cutter *Alarm*, which might have beaten *America* had the race been with handicap, was lengthened and re-rigged as a schooner.

LONG AND FAST

Imagine what was involved in the longest and most daring America's Cup yacht ever built, *Reliance*. Launched by the

AMERICA
The NYYC boat won the One Hundred Guineas Cup at Cowes in 1851. *America* was scrapped in 1945; a modern reconstruction is pictured.

ATLANTIC
This famed three-masted American-built schooner is seen here in 1928 before the start of a transatlantic race to Spain in pursuit of a trophy offered by the Spanish King Alfonso.

famous Herreshoff Manufacturing Company of Bristol, Rhode Island, USA (*see* p.28), she was 43.8m (144ft) overall but only 27.3m (89ft 9in) on the waterline. Nearly 15.2m (50ft) of her total length comprised bowsprit and sensuously long bow and stern overhangs.

Reliance was a pure racing yacht, created for a single reason: to defend the America's Cup in 1903. Interior amenities were negligible save for one stateroom. The crew WC was screened by canvas – unremarkable today, but unusual in luxury yachts at the turn of the 20th century.

She needed a crew of 66. Her topmast sprit was 57.6m (189ft) above water. Her ballast was 100 tons of lead. She had 278.7 sq m (3,000 sq ft) more sail than *Columbia*, the 39.6-m (130-ft) Cup defender that Nathanael Herreshoff had designed two years earlier. Her shallow hull form was made from steel frames, skinned with bronze plates, and decked with aluminium. Shipwrights regularly used hammers and mallets to repair the dimples that appeared in the long bow.

RECORD SPEED
Atlantic was a three-masted 60-m (187-ft) schooner. A record that endured 75 years was the remarkable feat of a time of 12 days 4 hours in the Transatlantic Race of 1905. There were few or no design rules for the race, though propellers were removed. *Atlantic*, designed by William Gardner and built in

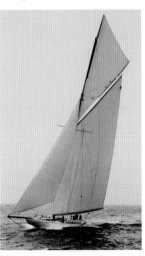

steel by Townsend and Downey, carried 1,719 sq m (18,500 sq ft) of sail. Some of her success was attributable to skipper Charlie Barr, a Scot and three-time America's Cup winning skipper for the Americans. In one 24-hour passage *Atlantic* clocked an astonishing distance of 642km (341 nautical miles).

It took until 1980 and the legendary French yachtsman Eric Tabarly's trimaran, *Paul Ricard*, for *Atlantic*'s time to be bettered, in 10 days 5 hours. Since then, *Phocea* has crossed in 8 days 3 hours (1988) and *Nicorette* in 11 days 13 hours 22 minutes (1996). Robert Miller's giant 44-m (144-ft) schooner *Mari Cha III* set the current record of 6 days 17 hours 52 minutes in 2003.

RELIANCE
Two months after defending the 1903 America's Cup, this notable craft was sold for scrap. But for nearly 100 years, *Reliance* held the record as the world's largest sloop.

THE GOLDEN YEARS

The years either side of World War I were golden times for yacht racing. Around the world, and especially in Europe, clubs were forming and regattas held. But there was no cooperation between clubs and each evolved its own set of rules for racing. This created problems when two or more clubs, especially those from different countries, tried to race against each other.

In 1907, in Paris, France, the International Yacht Racing Union was formed. The IYRU comprised yachting authorities from France, Austria-Hungary, Denmark, Finland, Germany, Great Britain, Holland and Belgium, Italy, Norway, Spain, Sweden, and Switzerland. Together they devised an international rule of measurement for racing yachts, and a common code of yacht-racing rules that was acceptable to all European countries. In 1929, the North American Yacht Racing Union

took steps to align their rules with those of Europe. In 1960 a totally universal code was adopted.

The IYRU continued until 1996, when it became the International Sailing Federation (ISAF). A few of the measurement rules and adapted versions of the racing rules devised in 1907 are still in use today.

METRE CLASS YACHTS

It was at the first conference of the IYRU that the "Metre Rule" was devised, for 6-, 8-, and 12-Metre class yachts. In each case, the Metre class measurement is not a length, but the result of a formula representing a computation of waterline length, beam, draught, freeboard, and sail area, with certain other restrictions also taken into account. These are therefore not one-design classes, but boats built to conform to rules which make racing even-handed without stifling innovative design.

Typically the Metre Class yachts are long, low, beautiful sloops. Boats of this era rarely had a deckhouse, while a cockpit or guardrails

AMERICAN WINNER
In the America's Cup of 1886, near Staten Island, New York, USA, the American sloop *Mayflower* and the English cutter *Galatea* compete over a distance of about 62km (33 nautical miles). *Mayflower* won by 13 minutes 18 seconds.

were unheard of. Racing was an extremely wet experience for the crew. Many Metre class yachts from between the war years are still traceable: some have been restored and race as an International Class alongside modern yachts built to the same measurements.

J-CLASS YACHTS

If any class of yacht epitomized the era it was the J-Class. These boats were also built to a formula, but on a different scale: with an overall length of more than 36.5m (120ft), the waterline length had to be 22.8–25.9m (75–87ft). With a Bermudan rig (*see* Rig designs, pp.46–47), the sail area was not limited, but the draught was limited to 4.5m (15ft). Only ten new J-Class yachts were built, six in the USA and four in Britain: *Enterprise, Weetamoe, Whirlwind, Yankee, Shamrock V, Rainbow, Velsheda, Endeavour I* and *II*, and

J-CLASS IN ACTION
The restored J-Class yacht *Velsheda*, built in England in 1933, dwarfs more modern entrants in the America's Cup Jubilee race around the Isle of Wight in 2001.

Ranger – other racing yachts had been faster and bigger but few had the magic of the Js. Their lines were sensuous, their owners famous, and they had the cachet of being America's Cup yachts. These beautiful, powerful yachts were raced for just eight years between 1930 and 1937 in Britain and the USA, including the America's Cups of 1930, 1934, and 1937. Those that were not scrapped later fell into disrepair. The survivors – *Velsheda, Shamrock V,* and *Endeavour I* – were all restored in the 1990s.

AT THE WHEEL
T. O. M. Sopwith at the helm of the J-Class sloop *Endeavour I* during a heat of the America's Cup race in Newport, Rhode Island, USA, 1934.

EVOLUTION OF BOAT DESIGN

George Lennox Watson was one of the first to set up a drawing office purely to design boats for sport and pleasure, in Glasgow in 1873. His *Britannia* was one of the most successful British yachts of all time. American brothers John B. and Nathanael Herreshoff, who established the renowned Herreshoff Manufacturing Company in Bristol, Rhode Island, USA, in 1863, were also specialists.

Between 1893 and 1914, the Herreshoff company designed seven advanced, powerful racing sloops. Five won the right to defend the America's Cup, and all five vanquished the challenger. Besides these majestic yachts, Herreshoff created a whole range of dayboats and small yachts.

The dominant yacht designer of the 20th century was another American, Olin Stephens. His reputation was established by the 15.5-m (51-ft) yawl *Dorade*, winner of the 1931 and 1933 transatlantic races.

OLIN STEPHENS AND DORADE

The designer helms his new yawl, built in 1930, on a close reach. His brother, Rod, is just behind him. The formal clothing of those on board suggests a demonstration sail on a fine, sunny day.

Influential on two counts, she rated well under the handicap rules used both in Europe and America, and heralded the dominance of the single section Bermudan mast over the two-section gaff rig for offshore boats. Olin Stephens was still designing race winners five decades later, often pioneering ideas that later became the norm.

In the 1950s, Ricus van de Stadt of the Netherlands challenged the accepted wisdom that rudders should be hung on the trailing edge of the keel to reduce wetted surface and boost performance. The combination of separate hydro-dynamically efficient keels and rudders, coupled to the light plywood construction of the 12-m (39-ft) *Zeevalk*, foreshadowed the adoption of the "fin and skeg" hull design. Van de Stadt was one

MIRROR DINGHY

The Mirror, promoted by the British daily newspaper of the same name, was introduced in 1963 and is still going strong, with 80,000 around the world.

of the first to see the benefits of glass reinforced plastic (GRP) as a means of volume production. The 9-m (30-ft) Pionier class was a breakthrough in Europe.

French designers added to the mix of ideas, notably Jean Berret, Jean-Marie Finot, and the Michel Joubert/Bernard Nivelt partnership, who all preferred beamy stern sections. These increased the space inside the hull, leading to cabins under the cockpit where there had been only locker space in the old style of boats. Light displacement meant lower hull weights, which cut material costs. Small jibs meant easier handling as the need to change headsails was much less. Broad sterns (from the French designers) gave more living space.

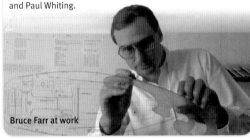

NEW ZEALAND BOAT DESIGNERS

Bruce Farr has enjoyed dominance in the race and production boat market since the 1970s. Farr had considerable success with light displacement boats powered by fractional rigs – so called because the jib is normally only seven-eighths of the mast's height. Meanwhile, New Zealand was producing other noted designers such as John Spencer, Laurie Davidson, and Paul Whiting.

Bruce Farr at work

DINGHY SAILING

Materials and displacement transformed dinghy design too. Plywood speeded up building time, which generated a post-World War II dinghy boom. Flat panels and the simple curvature allowed by just four pieces of plywood were simple to construct. This particularly appealed to the do-it-yourself builder, the best example being the 3.3-m (11-ft) Mirror dinghy, designed by Jack Holt.

Another development has been that of planing hulls. Planing means that the boat is able to rise above the theoretical limitation of its displacement and sail at much higher speeds. In the 1990s, big sail plans,

especially large asymmetric spinnakers, enabled even higher top speeds. Keelboats mirrored this trend with lighter, better mannered hulls able to handle much greater power from their rigs. No dinghy has made a bigger impact than the Laser, a single sail, one person 4.2-m (14-ft) dinghy, conceived in 1969 by Canadian designer Bruce Kirby. Introduced into Olympic competition in 1996, it has since attracted more nations to participate in Olympic sailing events than ever before.

PIONIER 9 UNDER SPINNAKER
Van de Stadt was an innovator in GRP production boats. Small sloops like the Pionier were mass produced and therefore affordable; they dominated the cruiser/racer market in the 1970s.

Long-distance sailing

Long-distance yachtsmen and women sail the lonely oceans to prove they can do it, or do it faster. American Joshua Slocum was the first to sail around the world alone. His inspirational book, *Sailing Alone Around the World*, was published in 1900 and has been rarely out print since.

Slocum's *Spray* was a 10.9-m (36-ft) converted oysterman and was 100 years old before he set sail from Boston, Massachusetts in 1895. *Spray* was modest but she steered well and sailed well in rough seas. Slocum finally reached home after two years and two months at sea. Others, such as the American Harry Pidgeon (*below*), followed. Some cruised in a leisurely way, others claimed "firsts" by choosing the more arduous routes.

SIXTIES CHALLENGES

It was during the 1960s that the record-breaking began. England's Francis Chichester challenged preconceptions about what was possible in terms of time and distance. In 1966–67, Chichester made only one stop on a voyage from Plymouth and back via Sydney, which took a total of 226 days in the 16.4-m (54-ft) *Gypsy Moth IV*. Alex Rose, also British, set off soon after Chichester returned. He stopped twice in the 10.9-m (36-ft) *Lively Lady* and was slower than Chichester. Frenchman Alain Colas was much faster: his St. Malo–Sydney–St. Malo voyage took 168 days and was the first in a multihull, the 20.4-m (67-ft) *Manurewa*.

Briton Robin Knox-Johnston was the first to make a solo non-stop passage, taking 313 days in his 9.7-m (32-ft) ketch *Suhali*. He was

GYPSY MOTH IV
After 107 days at sea, Francis Chichester reached Sydney Harbour, Australia. This was the only stop in his solo circumnavigation, proving that one person could be self-sufficient for extended periods.

HARRY PIDGEON
Inexperienced Harry Pidgeon built his own 10.3-m (34-ft) yawl *Islander* and set off in 1921 to circle the globe alone. Returning in 1925, he repeated the feat in 1932–37.

one of nine starters in the 1968/69 Golden Globe race; only two others completed the course.

While these voyages utilized the eastabout route, proven over the centuries by trading ships to make best use of the prevailing winds and currents, British paratrooper Chay Blyth was successful in going "the wrong way round" on the largely upwind course into the prevailing westerlies. His *British Steel* took 293 days in 1970–71.

FEMALE CIRCUMNAVIGATORS

The first woman around the world was Polish Krystyna Chojnowska-Liskiewicz. She crossed her outward track – which defines a circumnavigation – in 1978, just a few weeks before New Zealander Naomi James completed her voyage with stops in Cape Town and New Zealand. That James's voyage was via Cape Horn means that many regard her as the true first woman circumnavigator. The first woman to complete a non-stop circumnavigation was Australian Kay Cottee. She achieved it in 189 days in 1988. Fast improving sail-handling systems and electrical autopilots, as opposed to mechanical wind vanes, were achieving new efficiencies for solo sailors.

RECENT RECORDS

In 2001, Tony Mowbray became Australia's fastest solo, non-stop, unassisted world circumnavigator. Then 2004–6 witnessed three remarkable journeys. Francis Joyon of France shattered the previous record, held by a monohull, in his 27.4-m (90-ft) trimaran *IDEC* in 72 days 22 hours 54 minutes. A year later, Ellen MacArthur took a day off the record. Then Dee Caffari tackled the upwind westabout route; her 21.9-m (72-ft) steel cutter *Aviva* took 178 days 3 hours 5 minutes.

No one has attempted to better the achievement of Australian Jon Sanders. In 1986–87, he sailed alone around the world three times, a total of 131,535km (71,023 nautical miles). This was the longest distance sailed by any vessel unassisted and solo. Sanders broke 15 records on that voyage, including the longest period spent alone at sea: 657 days 21 hours 18 minutes.

ERIC TABARLY
The renowned French long-distance sailor crosses the line on *Pen Duick II*, winning the 1964 Observer Single-Handed Transatlantic Race.

ELLEN MACARTHUR
In 2005, Ellen MacArthur set a time of 71 days 14 hours 18 minutes in the purpose-designed 22.8-m (75-ft) trimaran *B & Q/Castorama*. Modern satellite communications meant that the world shared much of her arduous journey with her.

Sailing today

Sailing for pleasure or sport is about freedom and experiencing the joy of the open water. In competitive sailing, the freedom remains; the only restraints are the Yacht Racing Rules, developed by the International Sailing Federation, and rules developed for local conditions.

MODERN RACING

Modern racing boats, such as dinghies, smaller and larger keelboats, and multihulls, fall into two broad categories: one-design classes and development classes. Classes specify factors such as hull dimensions, construction materials, boat weight, and crew weight and number.

One-design boats within a particular class have a virtually identical design governed by strict rules. Good examples of one-design boats are the Laser single-handed dinghy, the 49er two-man skiff, the Melges 24 keelboat, and the Farr 40 keelboat. In one-design racing, results depend largely on crew performance.

Development-class boats vary in design and construction within a given class, according to specified parameters, so that

OPTIMIST
A perfect starter dinghy for a small child or an older novice, the Optimist was a ground-breaking new design. This 2.3-m (7½-ft) snub-nosed boat is now competitively sailed in more than 110 countries.

DRAGON RACING
Designed in 1929 by Swede Johan Ankar for a crew of three, the Dragon was an Olympic class boat from 1948 to 1972. It always provides exhilarating sailing.

similar but different boats can race in the same event. The Finn dinghy and the America's Cup Class epitomize classes in which innovative design to produce a faster boat is used to gain an advantage, introducing variables into the race beyond sailing skills alone. Boats of different classes can also be "measured" to fall within broad class groupings, usually for offshore racing.

If popular, and accepted by the International Sailing Federation (ISAF), classes may gain International status. Popular examples are the children's training boat, the Optimist (*see opposite*) and the 8.9-m (29-ft) Dragon keelboat (*see above*), with fleets in more than 26 countries spread over five continents.

CLUB HANDICAP RACES
In club racing, a local handicap system often operates, so that boats from different classes can race together, providing closely contested sport for sailors at all levels. This makes it possible to win the club trophy in the oldest, heaviest boat in the fleet – if you are skilled enough!

ONE-DESIGN RACING
The Laser has a simple, planing hull and a large, single-sail rig. These boats give exciting racing from club to Olympic level. A range of different rigs has been developed for different weights of sailors.

LEISURE SAILING

In the first part of the 20th century, the cost of boat purchase discouraged the spread of sailing as a leisure activity. However, this was perhaps more a problem of perception than of reality. For every boat owner, there is a network of friends and family who can share in the costs as well as the pleasures of going afloat, making it a much more affordable pastime for most people.

Access to the water was also once a problem, as yacht clubs held a grip over both training and mooring facilities. From the 1960s onwards, however, worldwide marina building meant that mooring space could be rented commercially without yacht club membership. This opened up sailing so that it became a pastime enjoyed by people from all walks of life. One of the joys of the sport now is the wide mix of people who participate, sharing their skills and experience for mutual enjoyment.

CHARTERING

The rise of yacht chartering during the 20th century meant

FLOTILLA SAILING
Cruising under the guidance of an experienced skipper, flotilla sailors quickly acquire a taste for the freedom of sailing in sunny climates and the relaxed nature of sailing social life.

that sailors didn't need to own a boat or know a skipper to go sailing. Boats had always been available for hire, but as the chartering industry expanded, yachts for hire became available to an increasingly broad spectrum of people. Today you can hire virtually any kind of boat in many locations around the world.

You can hire a charter yacht and sail it yourself, provided there is a qualified skipper and sufficient qualified crew, or you can hire a skipper. In the early 1970s, a third possibility developed: flotilla sailing. In a group of hired boats, inexperienced crews could sail together under the watchful eye of a mothership. This way of accessing the sport has become particularly popular in scenic areas with many small harbours within short, day-sailing

TAZ AND CHILDREN
The single-sail Taz dinghy is an ideal starter boat for young children. It can be adapted to a two-sail rig if desired.

distance, and where the weather in the holiday season is reliably warm, notably the coasts and islands of the Mediterranean and the Caribbean.

OLD BOATS, NEW USES

Individual craftsmen around the world have done much to keep alive the spirit of local sailing-boat design. Mud and sand both act as good preservers of timber, allowing many neglected old working craft to be rescued and become renovation projects for modern boat enthusiasts. If you acquire an old boat, building and maintaining it will be part of the fun. So, small cargo-carrying coasters or river craft, fishing boats, and lifeboats have all become part of the leisure-sailing fleet.

In addition, as a generation of old, ocean-going sailing ships went out of commercial use, some were saved and have been restored as sail-training vessels, primarily for young people. There are now approximately 300 sail-training vessels in the world, ranging from old to newly built and from small yachts to the mighty, four-masted Russian barques, *Sedov* and *Kruzenshtern*, each about 115m (380ft) long and dating from the last days of commercial sail in the 1920s. Rallies and races among these tall sailing ships sometimes cover thousands of kilometres. They give many people the opportunity to experience the thrills and hardships of going to sea as well as creating fellowship among crews and across nations.

TALL SHIP RACING
A square-rigger sailing off the British Isles in the annual Tall Ships Race. The first race took place in 1956 and had five competitors. It became an annual event around the world and now attracts millions of spectators and more than 100 ships.

Getting started

Sailing environments

The principal ingredients for enjoyable sailing are fair winds, good weather, and a pleasant stretch of water. This provides a huge choice of locations, ranging from inland lakes to your pick of the best places to sail on seas and oceans.

SAILING INLAND

While the wind is free, inland water may be privately owned, which means you may need to pay, obtain permission, or join a club to go sailing, with fees for mooring or launching your boat. Sailing does not necessarily require large expanses of water. Dinghy sailors – particularly those who enjoy regular racing – can pursue their sport on tiny reservoirs and narrow rivers. Any surrounding hills or trees that interrupt the wind can be turned to the sailor's advantage, with shifts in wind strength and direction adding a tactical element.

Bigger stretches of inland water provide opportunities for sailing faster and farther, with the potential for yacht cruising in wonderful places. For variety and interest, seek out new and different locations. Dinghies are easy to carry on a

DINGHY VERSATILITY
Dinghies are ideal for sailing in all kinds of waters, from inland lakes and narow rivers to open coastal locations. They are also easily portable.

car roof-rack or trailer and you can tow small "trailer-sailer" yachts. Sailing on rivers is also enjoyable, but it is best suited to dinghies if the river is narrow or shallow. Watch out for changeable depths, downstream currents, and tidal flow if you are close to the sea.

OPEN SEA
Sailing in the open sea offers freedom that cannot be found inland but requires good knowledge of factors such as local tides.

COASTAL SAILING

Sailing within a mile or two of the coast combines the best of all worlds. You have unlimited space to roam, but are always close to the shore and safe havens. Dinghy sailors can enjoy sailing from a fixed location on the shore, such as a club. Yacht sailors have the option of coastal hopping from port to port, matching the length of their hops to their expertise and prevailing weather conditions. Many coastal areas are tidal (*see* pp.242–243), which provides a navigational challenge, particularly in areas with a large tidal range. In such

URBAN SAILING

Urban waters, such as the Saltsjön in Stockholm, may be busy but the sailing is always interesting. You just need to know who has right of way.

situations, a good understanding of tides is vital. Sailing in a large, natural harbour can offer a good compromise between inland and coastal sailing. You have the protection of surrounding land inside the harbour, but you have the opportunity to venture outside on the open sea in fair weather and, above all, a fresh breeze. Take care, and be aware that tidal flow can have a major effect on water depth and currents inside harbours.

FRESHWATER SAILING

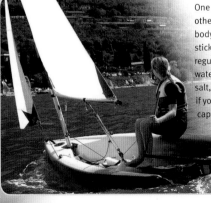

One big advantage of sailing on lakes and other inland waters is fresh water. Your boat, body, and clothing do not get covered with sticky, damp salt, which must be washed off regularly if you sail on the open sea. Fresh water does not sting your eyes as much as salt, and it is certainly more pleasant-tasting if you take an inadvertent gulp during a capsize. On the minus side, fresh water may be considerably colder than salt water and is also far less buoyant.

Lake Garda, Italy, one of Europe's premier inland sailing venues

How do I start?

The days when yachting was an elite sport are now long gone. Today, sailing can be enjoyed wherever there is water and wind. What is more, you can enjoy sailing at many different levels, from the smallest dinghies through to fully crewed yachts.

DINGHY OR YACHT?

A dinghy is a small, open boat that is in very close contact with wind and water. It may tip right over, but it provides an intimate experience of sailing – every movement can have an impact on the boat's performance. A yacht is much larger and can provide very comfortable accommodation for several people on board, with the advantage that it cannot tip over completely, thanks to a heavy keel underneath. But if you have never sailed before, there are many advantages to learning to sail in a dinghy, whatever your long-term ambitions may be. Handling a dinghy provides basic sailing expertise, and you will make quick progress if you move on to sail a yacht, which works on the same principles on a larger scale. Owning a yacht is likely to require a much greater commitment than a dinghy in cost and time.

THE COST OF A YACHT

Berthing and maintenance can make the cost of owning a yacht expensive. Charter or group ownership may be most cost effective for people who are able to use a yacht for only limited periods during the year.

GO FAST!
Catamaran sailing provides great excitement for all ages, so long as the crew don't mind getting wet when a teenager is at the helm!

DINGHY RACING
Racing a dinghy is the best way to improve boat handling and sailing expertise. You don't need to be good to start – you just need the will to join in and make sailing friends.

GO TO SCHOOL

Learning to sail has never been easier, with professionally run courses for both dinghy sailing and yacht cruising now widely available at all levels at sailing schools, clubs, and activity centres, around the coast and at inland locations. Sailing courses are administered by governing bodies of the sport in different countries – for instance, the Royal Yachting Association in Britain or Australia and the Fédération Française de Voile in France. A typical course may last between one and five days, with all necessary equipment and comprehensive safety cover provided. You should expect to get fully qualified instructors, running a carefully structured, standard course.

TAKE A HOLIDAY

Don't risk getting cold and wet on your first outing in a boat – it may well put you off. If you live in a cold climate, it is well worth looking into one of the many specialist sailing holidays, whether dinghy or yacht sailing, that are available around the world, with tuition and equipment provided. Once you have learned to sail in the sun, you are sure to want to pursue this sport back home!

THE FLOTILLA HOLIDAY
The yacht flotilla provides a one- or two-week cruise in company in the sun, with a professionally crewed lead boat acting as pilot and mothership to ensure nothing goes wrong.

Types of boat

There is a massive choice of boats to suit different sailing styles and aspirations. Whatever type you choose, it should provide good performance, safe sailing, and be a pleasure to crew or skipper.

DINGHIES

Dinghies are small, open boats that are very responsive to sail. Unlike a yacht, a dinghy does not have a ballasted keel. Instead, it has a daggerboard or centreboard to prevent it from going sideways, relying largely on crew weight and skill to keep the boat upright when wind is in the sails. That may sound like a challenge, but in reality, most dinghies are stable and very easy to sail.

Most dinghy classes are 4–5m (13–16ft) long and are designed to be sailed single-handed, by one crew, or two-handed. One of the smallest dinghies available is the 2.3-m (7½-ft) Optimist dinghy, for children, which was originally designed by Clark Mills in 1947 and is popular worldwide. Some dinghies are fitted with spinnaker and trapeze wires to enhance performance.

CATAMARANS

Often called "beach cats" or "cats", catamarans are similar to dinghies except they have two hulls separated by a mesh platform. They are more stable and can provide a faster ride than monohulls: the crew is able to counterbalance larger sails and the boat encounters reduced water resistance when lifted on one hull. Cats are a lot of fun to sail, but they

CLASSIC KEELBOAT
Old wooden boats, such as this traditional Dutch design, offer you classic sailing, but cost more time and money to maintain than modern boats.

EASY SAILING
Learners and parent-child crews may find a small two-person dinghy that offers easy handling and good performance, such as the popular Laser 2000, a good choice.

GO FOR SPEED
Small catamarans, such as the SL16, are popular with speed enthusiasts who like to fly and have fun. They are surprisingly easy to sail.

need a good Force 3 breeze to really get going and are not a good choice for light winds.

KEELBOATS

Keelboats are open boats that tend to be slightly larger than dinghies and are fitted with a heavy lead keel that prevents them from capsizing. They range in length from around 6–9m (20–30ft) and typically have two, three, or five crew. Most keelboats are racing classes, led by such popular designs as the Laser SB3 and Melges 24 sportsboats. Despite having a keel, these high-performance boats can give a very fast, challenging ride.

YACHTS

Yachts are keelboats with cabins and accommodation. Cruisers are designed for coastal or even ocean cruising, particularly for holidays with a family or friends on board. Cruiser-racers make a compromise between cruising comfort and racing performance. Racing yachts are designed for optimum performance with few creature comforts. Large multihulls are also available, which fill the same cruising and racing roles with a crew living on board; unlike yachts, they have no ballasted keel.

MAXIMUM PERFORMANCE
A large, asymmetric spinnaker provides this Topper Vibe dinghy with turbo boost. The hull is made from plastic polyethylene and is formed by a process called rotomoulding, which makes it low-cost and extremely robust.

SAILING COMFORT
A modern sailing cruiser about 10m (33ft) long, such as the one shown here, should combine good performance with easy handling and will accommodate up to six crew very comfortably.

"IT WAS THE VOICE OF THE BOW
WAVE: GIVE ME WIND AND I
SHALL GIVE YOU MILES!"

Bernard Moitessier, Cape Horn: The Logical Route

Rig designs

The majority of modern sailboats of all sizes are Bermudan rigged, with a triangular mainsail attached to an upright mast. This ultimate blend of performance and easy handling was reached after centuries of reliance on square-rigged sails.

FROM EARLY TO MODERN DESIGN

Modern rigs developed from the fore-and-aft gaff (four-sided) mainsail rigs. In the search for speed, sail area was extended upwards by topsails, forwards by jibs (triangular headsails) set on a long bowsprit (a spar projecting from the bow), and aft by extending the main boom behind the stern. Nearly all modern yachts have a Bermudan rig, which dates from the early 19th century. This has a single mast and boom and the mainsail provides much

of the power, helped by a headsail – a jib or a genoa (a larger headsail) – overlapping the mainsail. The rig is typically supported by wire cables: forestay (front), shrouds (sides), and backstay on yachts. Horizontal struts known as spreaders help to prevent the mast, which in newer boats is usually made from aluminium or carbon fibre, from bending sideways.

ANCIENT AND MODERN
The Bermudan-rigged ketch (foreground) descends directly from a square rigger (background).

1939

ELEMENTS OF RIG DESIGN

All rig designs, whether old or modern, incorporate one or more masts and one or more sails. Other spars (poles) in the

rig might include booms, which extend the foot of a sail, yards, which support square sails from a mast, and bowsprits, which support a sail beyond the bow.

GAFF CUTTER
This rig has a long bowsprit, two foresails, a large gaff mainsail, and may have a topsail.

GAFF KETCH
A similar rig to the cutter, the gaff ketch has a small mizzen mast and sail forward of the rudder head.

GAFF SCHOONER
A schooner is rigged with fore and aft sails on two or more masts. The rig may include topsails.

CUTTER CLASSIC RIG
The typical cutter has two foresails and a very long bowsprit. Classic cutters are gaff-rigged and have jib-headed topsail for extra power.

SUPERYACHT
This 21st-century "superyacht" has a masthead Bermudan sloop rig. Today's superyachts are much bigger than their forerunners, the J-Class. They rely on modern technology and equipment to manage two massive sails.

SCHOONER CLASSIC RIG
The massive aft rig provides most of the power on this old schooner, while the forward rig helps balance the boat.

BERMUDAN CUTTER (J-CLASS)
J-Class racers, up to 26.5m (87ft) long at the waterline, combined classic and modern rig elements.

BERMUDAN SLOOP
This rig has triangular sails with long, straight luffs. A sloop has one mast and, usually, one headsail.

TWIN-CREW DINGHY
This modern jib-and-mainsail rig has a large roach (outer curve) to increase the size of the mainsail.

Hull and keel design

A boat's forward motion is powered by wind against its sails but is resisted by the water its hull moves through. Modern hull-design solutions to this problem combine light materials with a reduced wetted surface area and a hull shape that is easily handled and adequately spacious.

DINGHIES

Dinghy hulls are flat at the stern with a narrower, V-shaped bow to promote upwind performance and slice through waves. Dinghies do not have fixed keels but moveable daggerboards or centreboards. Unencumbered by the drag of a heavy fixed keel, the typical lightweight dinghy hull is able to start planing in moderate winds. Planing occurs when the hull lifts on to its bow wave and leaves its stern wave behind. As the boat accelerates on to the plane, its bow lifts clear of the water, its wake becomes flat, and it rides on the flattish aft part of its hull. The sailors then enjoy a wonderful sensation of skimming across the water.

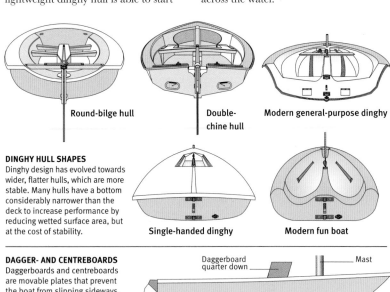

Round-bilge hull

Double-chine hull

Modern general-purpose dinghy

DINGHY HULL SHAPES
Dinghy design has evolved towards wider, flatter hulls, which are more stable. Many hulls have a bottom considerably narrower than the deck to increase performance by reducing wetted surface area, but at the cost of stability.

Single-handed dinghy

Modern fun boat

DAGGER- AND CENTREBOARDS
Daggerboards and centreboards are movable plates that prevent the boat from slipping sideways. A daggerboard drops and lifts vertically and can be taken out of its case. A centreboard swivels from horizontal to vertical and is held inside its case by a bolt.

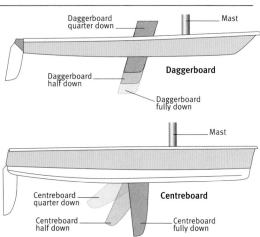

Daggerboard quarter down

Mast

Daggerboard half down

Daggerboard

Daggerboard fully down

Mast

Centreboard quarter down

Centreboard

Centreboard half down

Centreboard fully down

MOVING THE CENTREBOARD
The centreboard is moved by the crew. Gaskets seal the centreboard slot when it is fully retracted.

YACHTS

The typical yacht hull is V-shaped at the bow and round at the stern. To keep it upright, the hull has a heavily ballasted keel bolted to the underside. The keel's weight means that most yachts sail through the water with their top speed limited by the amount of water displaced by the hull and cannot plane as dinghies do (*see opposite*). Instead, the hull sits down in the water and floats to its waterline, unlike the flat-bottomed modern planing dinghy. Classic wooden yachts have long, slim hulls that incorporate a full-length, or long, keel. They tend to heel right over and have very limited cabin space. Modern yachts have much wider hulls, with a high freeboard (height out of water) and a separate fin keel. They have a large cabin space and achieve maximum performance when heeling at no more than around 20 degrees, making them comfortable to sail.

SKEG-HUNG RUDDERS
The red and blue rudders in the foreground are attached to a projection of the hull known as a skeg. As well as supporting the rudder, the skeg also acts as a small keel to balance the steering.

BOW SHAPES
Classic yachts have a narrow hull with a raked (angled) bow to slice through waves. The forepeak is cramped and the boat may be prone to pitching. A more modern bow is almost vertical, with greater volume; it has increased waterline length, resists pitching, and accomodates a forecabin.

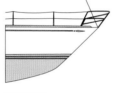

Raked bow

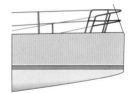

Vertical bow

STERN SHAPES
The classic counter stern provides an extremely elegant hull shape, but the modern scooped stern is much more practical. It provides a "step aboard" entrance as well as acting as a bathing area and diving platform. A scooped stern can also be used to store a life raft.

Counter stern

Scooped stern

KEEL SHAPES
Traditional cruisers have a full-length keel with internal ballast. Modern cruisers have a fin keel bolted underneath and a rudder hung on a skeg (hull projection). Racing yachts have slim fin keels with a ballasted bulb at the bottom and a separate rudder.

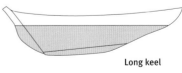

Long keel

Cruising fin keel

Racing fin keel

Anatomy of a dinghy

A dinghy consists of a hull and deck, a rig with spars and sails, fittings and control systems, and foils (*see* Hull and keels, pp.48–49) below the waterline to help guide the boat. These elements range from basic on a novice single-hander to complex on the most high-performance boats.

HULL AND DECK

Most modern dinghy hulls are moulded in some form of plastic, although wooden boats, built mainly from marine plywood panels, are also available. Glass-reinforced plastic (GRP), or fibreglass, is the most popular material. It uses polyester or vinylester resin reinforced with woven glass and covered with a gelcoat to give a tough, shiny finish. The best balance of light weight, stiffness, and durability is given by foam-reinforced plastic (FRP), which uses a thick sheet of lightweight closed-cell foam as the rigid core between a thin inner and outer layer of GRP. More costly materials, such as carbon fibre and epoxy resin, may be used for high-performance boats. Rotomoulded polyethylene is less expensive than GRP, and is used in many of the most popular modern dinghy makes, all of which are very durable and ideal for recreational sailing. The plastic polyethylene granules are heated and rocked inside a mould; they spread over the mould's surface to form the hull and deck, with a foam core to increase stiffness. Rotomoulded polyethylene is relatively heavy, making it less suitable than GRP for high-performance sailing.

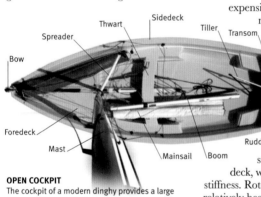

Spreader · Thwart · Sidedeck · Tiller · Transom · Bow · Foredeck · Mast · Mainsail · Boom · Rudder

OPEN COCKPIT
The cockpit of a modern dinghy provides a large open working area for two crew. Built-in buoyancy ensures it is not possible for the boat to sink.

OPEN STERN
Modern dinghies have a self-draining cockpit, so any water drains out through the open transom at the stern.

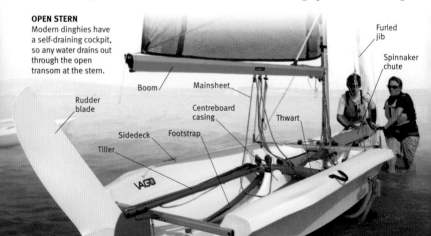

Furled jib · Spinnaker chute · Boom · Mainsheet · Rudder blade · Centreboard casing · Thwart · Sidedeck · Footstrap · Tiller

THE CONTROLS
The crew adjust the angle and power of the sails using sheets and control lines. The boat is steered using the rudder foil.

TOP PERFORMANCE
This high-performance rig features a huge asymmetric spinnaker to maximize downwind performance and a laminate mainsail. Racks on each side of the hull provide the crew with increased leverage on the trapeze.

THE RIG

In modern dinghies, basic masts are aluminium or fibreglass tubes, as used on unstayed single-handed dinghies, such as the Laser. Tapered aluminium masts, supported by a forestay and shrouds, provide superior performance, with carbon (the strongest material) masts for top-level use. Booms are mostly aluminium, although top-performance booms may be carbon. Polyester is the usual sail material for making mainsails and jibs. Laminate materials provide a more stable shape than polyester but tend to deteriorate with heavy use. Lightweight rip-stop nylon is used for spinnakers.

Anatomy of a yacht

Today's cruising yachts are highly developed, providing a great sailing experience that can easily be mastered by a crew of family or friends. The main requirement is to combine the right level of knowledge with the correct equipment, all of which is readily available.

THE MODERN YACHT

Most modern yachts are made from low-maintenance glass-reinforced plastic (GRP), or fibreglass. The main on-deck area for the crew is the cockpit, from where they control the sails. Most cruisers have a cockpit table and comfortable bench seats for relaxation. Forward of the cockpit, the coachroof provides headroom for the main cabin below.

Guard rails run down both sidedecks to the foredeck, passing through vertical stanchions fixed to the deck; they are connected to rigid metal rail structures at each end of the deck – the pushpit (at the stern) and the pulpit (at the bow).

The sails and masts of virtually all modern yachts have a Bermudan rig arrangement (*see* Rig designs, pp.46–47), with two sails and a single mast and boom.

Auxiliary power is generally provided by an inboard diesel engine, which is economical over a long distance at a steady cruising speed. The engine is vital when docking the boat in a crowded marina. It also charges the batteries that power the yacht's electrical systems, enabling sailors to cruise in comfort with services such as hot water, lighting, heating, and refrigeration. Electricity also powers the yacht's navigation and communications instruments.

LOOKING FORWARD

The view forward from the cockpit shows clearly laid out control lines leading back from the mast, with clutches to lock them and winches to wind them in.

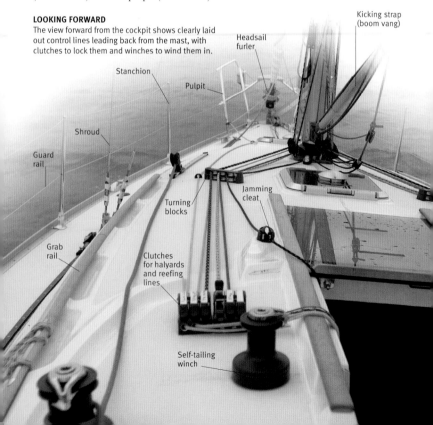

Kicking strap
(boom vang)

Headsail
furler

Stanchion

Pulpit

Shroud

Guard
rail

Jamming
cleat

Turning
blocks

Grab
rail

Clutches
for halyards
and reefing
lines

Self-tailing
winch

Forestay
Headsail
Mainsail
Gooseneck
Topping lift
Spinnaker pole
Boom
Mainsheet
Sunsail Sun Fast 37

MAST SUPPORTS
Full-length wire shrouds support the mast on each side. Struts called spreaders extend between the mast and shrouds to spread the load. Wire "lowers" support the middle portion of the mast.

Headsail sheet block on traveller

PERFORMANCE CRUISER
Yachts range from dedicated racers to pure, blue-water cruisers. A cruiser-racer with a good performance and comfortable accommodation is an excellent multipurpose choice.

Steering compass

Steering wheel

Engine control lever

Binnacle

STEERING
Small yachts are steered using a tiller directly connected to the rudder. Larger yachts use a steering wheel connected to the rudder by cables. A large-diameter wheel provides lighter steering.

Dinghy wear

Modern dinghy wear is designed to keep the sailor as warm, dry, and comfortable as required, using technical fabrics to provide safe and enjoyable sailing in all conditions. For normal dinghy sailing through spring, summer, and autumn, a wetsuit is the top choice.

WETSUITS

A wetsuit is made of neoprene rubber, lined on the inside for comfort and the outside for abrasion resistance. Modern wetsuits are super-stretchy, allowing you to bend, flex, and stretch easily. The main body of a wetsuit is usually made from thick neoprene, for warmth, while the material used on the arms and legs tends to be lighter, thinner, and more stretchy. Neoprene is a windproof and water-

SUMMER GEAR
A rash vest and shorts looks great for summer sailing, but wind-chill means that you may soon get cold without a wetsuit.

proof fabric. However, the seams of a wetsuit will only be watertight on the more expensive types of wetsuit. Also, water will seep in at the neck, wrists, and ankles. On a top-quality wetsuit with perfect fit, this seepage will form a thin layer of water that warms to the temperature of your body,

Long tag allows you to pull up zip with one hand

Protective rash vest beneath suit with high collar to prevent chafing

SHORT WETSUIT
A short wetsuit is a good choice for dinghy sailing on a warm day, but not for catamaran sailing, which requires knee protection.

Trapeze harness worn directly over wetsuit, with buoyancy aid on top

without cooling you down. On a budget wetsuit, large amounts of cold water can flush through, making your body progressively colder.

WETSUIT FEATURES

Most wetsuits have a long zip at the back, with twin neoprene flaps that provide a watertight or water-resistant barrier. Good features to look out for include flatlock stitching to reduce chafing on the inside of the suit, plus anti-abrasive seat and knee panels. A rash vest is often worn under a wetsuit to prevent chafing. Short-arm wetsuits provide excellent upper-body mobility for most sailing conditions; a convertible suit offers the option of removable full-length sleeves.

Neoprene warm-weather wetsuit with stretch and durability

STAY COOL, NOT COLD
It may be hot, but if the wind is up and your boat is fast, wind-chill will cool your body down. Always wear a wetsuit, particularly if there is any chance of capsizing.

EXTRA PROTECTION

While sailing you may be exposed to cold weather and possible injury unless you wear sufficiently protective clothing. Your extremities, such as hands, feet, and head, require particular protection from cold, so warm boots, gloves, and hat are needed in cold weather. Gloves are also useful for avoiding rope burn. A spray top provides extra protection in cold, windy, or wet weather, and special shorts can be worn when hiking (leaning out).

SPRAY TOP
The best spray tops are windproof, waterproof, and breathable, combining loose fit with all-seasons capability.

HIKING SHORTS
Neoprene hiking shorts give extra warmth, wetsuit protection, and support for your legs while hiking, or leaning out.

Battens in back of legs give superior protection

Wetsuit may be worn beneath hiking shorts if desired

Neoprene dinghy boots keep feet warm

Cruiser wear

If you sail in a hot climate, all you may need for yacht cruising is a T-shirt, shorts, sailing shoes, and sunglasses, plus a fleece for cooler evenings. But much sailing takes place where wind chill and cold water are hard to avoid, making purpose-designed clothing vital.

LAYERING FOR TOP PERFORMANCE

All modern cruiser wear is based on the three-layer system of protective clothing. To keep warm in cold or wind, you must stay dry inside wind- and waterproof clothing that retains your body heat. Wet skin gets cold 30 times more quickly than dry skin, so your clothing must be able to transport moisture away from the skin, while holding dry, warm air close to the body and keeping the elements out. For yacht sailing, it must also be durable, reasonably lightweight, and non-restrictive as you move around the boat.

Polyester fabrics are the best choice for a base layer next to your skin. They will wick sweat away from your body without absorbing water. By contrast, cotton, a natural material, can absorb 30 per cent more than its weight in moisture; a wet material will transfer heat away from your body up to 30 times more quickly than dry air. The mid-layer holds warm, dry, insulating air inside your outer protective clothing, while also providing the same level of water transmission away from

COLD-WEATHER WEAR
Contemporary yachting wear teams a water- and windproof jacket with a fleece lining and matching trousers.

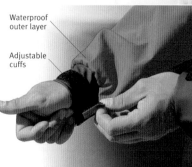

Waterproof outer layer

Adjustable cuffs

CLOTHING COMFORT
Look for adjustable ankles and cuffs, which will provide a comfortable and watertight fit when worn with shoes, boots, or gloves. If conditions are going to be extremely wet, neoprene seals provide a perfect grip round your wrists without constricting blood flow.

your body. Specialist fleece materials are great for this job. The outer layer is wind- and waterproof but also breathable, to allow moisture passing through the base and mid-layers to escape.

WARM AND DRY

Up to 40 per cent of body heat may be lost through the head, feet, or hands. In cold weather, wear thermal socks, boots, thermal gloves, and headgear. Wrist and ankle seals will prevent water seepage into your base layer. Neck closure allows your jacket to be partially open or fully closed. Many jackets have hoods stowed inside the collar that can be accessed when needed.

Inner lining — Zip cover

ADDING CLOTHES
A waterproof jacket can be worn directly over high-cut trousers, to which heavily reinforced knees and seat add durability. In cold conditions, you would need to add a warm fleece under the jacket.

TROUSERS
High-cut waterproof trousers should be a loose fit. Features to look for include a heavy-duty two-way zip, seat and knee patches, hand-warmer fleece pockets, and adjustable ankle closures and braces.

BREATHABLE WATERPROOF FABRIC

The breathable, waterproof, and wicking fabric from which modern cruising wear is made consists of a special membrane laminated between inner and outer materials. This arrangement allows moisture from inside to breathe out, while preventing any sea- or rainwater from getting in. This system was invented in the 1970s and soon helped transform waterproof clothing into a more effective and comfortable method of protection from the elements.

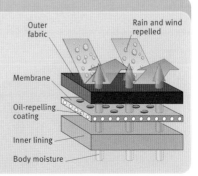

Outer fabric

Rain and wind repelled

Membrane

Oil-repelling coating

Inner lining

Body moisture

Footwear and accessories

Sailing is a technical sport that relies on top-quality equipment and specialist clothing for function, comfort, and safety. Whether you sail on a small dinghy or a large yacht, your feet, hands, eyes, and skin all require the best possible protection.

FOOTWEAR

You should always protect your feet when sailing. Bare feet are vulnerable to knocks, cuts, and other injuries when moving about a boat and they may get cold on a dinghy. Also, it is no fun treading on broken glass when pulling a boat through shallow water! Ideally, you should always wear purpose-designed shoes or boots to protect your feet and provide good grip.

Dinghy shoes and boots are lightweight and combine neoprene uppers for a comfortable, warm fit with a razor-cut rubber sole for maximum grip and flexibility. Boots are warmer and more durable for use throughout the year, with the bonus of ankle protection.

For yacht sailing in moderate conditions, a good-quality pair of deck shoes will provide maximum traction and protect your feet. Features to look for include removable footbeds with breathable mesh construction or leather uppers. For stronger winds or cold weather, invest in a pair of high-quality boots. Leather with a breathable, waterproof lining combines comfort and durability.

A word of warning – the soles of deck shoes, yacht boots, and dinghy shoes and boots are designed to provide maximum grip while sailing, and this requires fairly soft rubber that is more susceptible to wear and tear than normal rubber soles. If you wear them ashore, you will wear them out much more quickly.

DECK SHOES
Deck shoes are suitable footwear when you are yacht sailing. They protect your feet and give you fail-safe grip, combined with maximum flexibility.

YACHT BOOTS
In harsher conditions, rubber boots are the most inexpensive but leather boots are more stylish and durable and allow your feet to breathe.

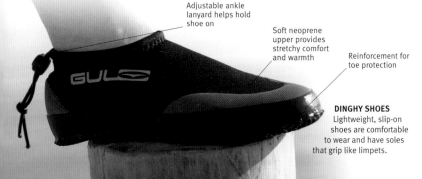

Adjustable ankle lanyard helps hold shoe on

Soft neoprene upper provides stretchy comfort and warmth

Reinforcement for toe protection

DINGHY SHOES
Lightweight, slip-on shoes are comfortable to wear and have soles that grip like limpets.

GLOVES

Since virtually all types of modern rope are synthetic and relatively slippery, you need sailing gloves in order to pull rope hard, particularly in the case of narrow-diameter control lines. Gloves also protect against rope burn. All-round gloves for sailing combine an elasticated back with a durable, grippy, quick-drying padded material for palms and fingers.

The gloves should be easy to pull on and off using tabs and should provide the best possible comfort and dexterity. Many sailors favour short-fingered gloves, which make tasks such as tying knots and undoing shackles easier; some gloves feature a combination of long and short fingers, with heavier-duty construction using neoprene or fleece for cold weather.

SUMMER GLOVES
These short-fingered gloves are hard wearing and comfortable to wear, ensuring you can get a hold on ropes of all sizes and pull or hold that rope with ease. Note the wrist cuffs and elasticated backs combined with imitation leather material.

HEADGEAR

Your face, and any other exposed skin, and your eyes are susceptible to damage from the ultraviolet rays in sunlight, so make sure to wear an effective sunscreen (*see below*). Sunglasses with polarized lenses, which filter out UV rays, are also essential to protect your eyes. You can also wear a hat to prevent sunburn and sunstroke. In cold weather, a hat helps prevent heat loss through your head.

SUNSCREEN PROTECTION

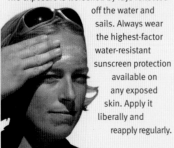

A cooling breeze may lead you to think the sun's rays are weak. In fact, you are exposed to damaging UV rays even in cloudy weather. The exposure is worsened by rays reflected off the water and sails. Always wear the highest-factor water-resistant sunscreen protection available on any exposed skin. Apply it liberally and reapply regularly.

EYE PROTECTION
Good-quality sunglasses are vital when sailing. Desirable features include a close-fitting, floatable frame with glare-free, polarized lenses.

"KNOWLEDGE DISPELS FEAR."

Chay Blyth

Safety equipment

Buoyancy aids, lifejackets, and harnesses are key to sailing safety and every crew should wear them. Dinghy and yacht sailing involve different safety considerations, equipment, and standards. The focus in either case is on staying onboard and, if you do fall over the side, staying afloat.

DINGHY SAFETY

Wearing a buoyancy aid is strongly recommended for dinghy sailing. As its name suggests, it helps flotation in the water should the crew capsize. Buoyancy aids are recommended only for use by swimmers in sheltered waters when help is close to hand. Unlike lifejackets, they are not guaranteed to turn a person from a face-down position in the water. Flotation is measured in Newtons (N): 10N = 1kg (2.2lb) flotation. You should always get professional advice when fitting a buoyancy aid, but as a rule of thumb 50N is the minimum recommended for sailors weighing more than 70kg (154lb); 45N for 60–70kg (132–154lb); 40N for 40–60kg (88–132lb); and 35N for up to 40kg (88lb). Features to look for include closed-cell foam construction, which is light and will not deteriorate, a secure pocket with room for a whistle and knife, a waist belt to prevent the buoyancy aid from riding up, and a crotch strap for junior sizes.

PULL-ON BUOYANCY AID
Pull-on buoyancy aids with side-entry zips are favoured by dinghy racers. The sailor's upper body and arms are unrestricted, with elasticated sides, shoulders, and hem for a snug fit. The buoyancy aid is worn over the trapeze harness with the hem pulled in tight well above the hook.

FRONT-ENTRY ZIP
Waistcoat-style buoyancy aids are slightly bulkier than pull-on buoyancy aids, but they are easier to put on and a great choice for recreational sailing. Adjustable shoulder straps are a useful feature for a perfect fit.

CRUISER SAFETY

The skipper should instruct the crew when they need to wear a harness and lifejacket – always in poor conditions or at night. The harness should be worn under the lifejacket and waist and shoulder straps need to be adjusted to ensure a good fit. All lifejackets should be equipped with a whistle, light, and retro-reflective strips.

KEEPING IT ON
The lifejacket has a waist belt to ensure it cannot ride up. A crotch strap can provide extra security.

INFLATION
Air-only lifejackets are far less bulky than foam-only or air-foam buoyancy. The CO_2 cylinder, which inflates air lifejackets, may be activated automatically on entering the water or by pulling a toggle. It also has an oral inflator.

CLIPPING ON
A safety harness is the most important piece of safety equipment at sea as it keeps you on the boat. The harness may be built in to a waterproof jacket or a lifejacket (as here), or it may be separate. (*See also* Crew comfort and safety, pp.188–189 and Rough weather procedures, 260–261.).

CARRY A KNIFE

All dinghy crew should carry a purpose-designed safety knife, which must be accessible during a capsize. This is to cut through rope or cord if a crew member gets trapped under the boat or sail.

Multi-purpose tool stored in buoyancy-aid pocket

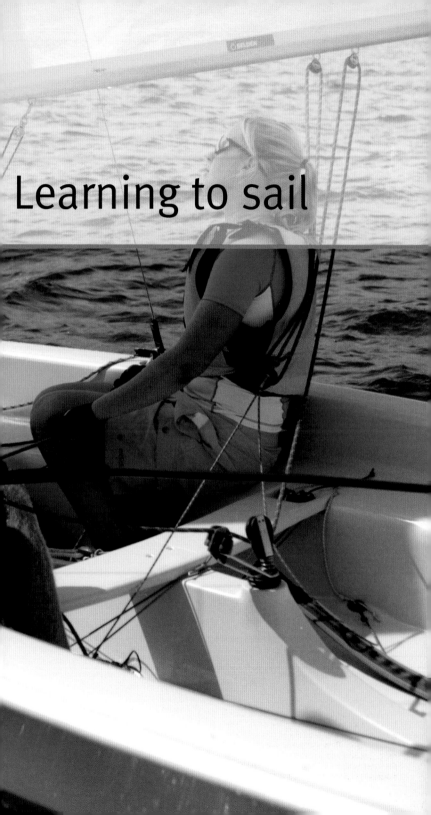

Learning to sail

Wind and sail

If the dinghy or yacht designer has done a good job, learning to master a modern sailing boat should be straightforward. However, it does require some understanding of the aerodynamic forces involved.

ROLE OF THE CREW

To drive a boat forwards using wind and sails, the crew must achieve a balance between trimming the sails correctly, resisting the sideways force on the rig, and counteracting the heeling force on the boat. Whether there is one crew, two, or several, they must work with the wind and the boat, as a unit.

UPWIND SAILING

All modern sailing boats can sail at an angle of about 45 degrees to the direction from which the wind is coming (upwind). Their sails are designed to drive the boat straight ahead, but on an upwind course there will also be a powerful sideways force on the sails that will push the boat sideways through the water. This is known as "leeway".

HIKING TO WINDWARD
Sailing a Solo class dinghy in a moderate Force 4 breeze, the helmsman sheets the sail in tightly and has the centreboard fully lowered. He hikes out (leans out) over the side of the dinghy, using his weight to counteract the heeling force on the sail.

A sailing boat therefore has a foil (*see* p.68) under the hull, which resists leeway, allowing the sails to drive the boat forwards instead of sideways. On a dinghy, the foil is a centreboard or daggerboard, while a yacht has a ballasted keel.

However, the resistance from the foil will make the dinghy or yacht heel, or lean over, with the sideways force of the wind, rather than slipping sideways. On a dinghy this heeling force is counteracted by the weight of the crew leaning out over the side, or "hiking"; on a yacht, the keel is weighted with ballast to help prevent the yacht heeling right over, while the crew weight has limited effect.

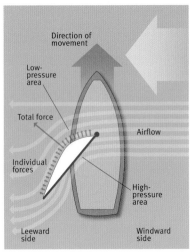

WIND POWER
Wind separates over both sides of the sail, creating high pressure on the windward side (closer to the wind) and low pressure on the leeward side (away from the wind). These pressures blow and suck the sail respectively, driving the boat forwards through the water, while a centreboard or a keel resists the sideways pressure exerted on the boat by the wind.

DOWNWIND SAILING

When the wind is blowing from behind the boat, sailing is described as "downwind". In this situation, there is less sideways force on the sails, and less heeling force on the boat, than when sailing upwind. With more concentrated forward drive, and less leeway, the boat should be able to sail faster. This may be helped by increased sail area from a spinnaker, which helps to blow the boat downwind at speed.

In moderate or strong winds, sailing directly downwind may not be the best course. With no sideways force on the sails, the boat may be inclined to roll from side to side, making it difficult to steer, and creating the danger of an involuntary gybe (in which the boom swings uncontrolled across the boat), if the wind catches the wrong side of the mainsail. It is more comfortable to turn towards the wind, and sail "on a broad reach" – that is, with the wind blowing towards the stern of the boat at an angle. On a broad reach, there is enough sideways force to keep the boat stable, and airflow over both sides of jib and mainsail drives the boat at higher speed.

TRUE AND APPARENT WIND

"True wind" is the wind speed and direction when you are in a fixed position. If you are moving, the wind speed will appear to change. Heading into a true wind of 10 knots at a boat speed of 10 knots, the "apparent wind" would be 20 knots. Heading away from a true wind of 10 knots at a boat speed of 10 knots, the apparent wind would be zero knots. It therefore feels windier when sailing upwind. As the boat goes faster, the angle of the apparent wind moves farther towards the bow.

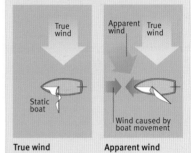

True wind   **Apparent wind**

TRAPEZING DOWNWIND
Sailing on a broad reach, this 420 dinghy is fully powered in Force 4 wind. The crew stands out on a trapeze to achieve maximum leverage on the rig.

Side forces and leeway

The sails that drive a dinghy or yacht have a direct relationship with the centreboard or keel underwater. It is this that prevents the boat being blown sideways, and transforms wind force into forward drive. Boat designer and crew must keep the relationship in balance.

THE UNDERWATER FOIL

In wind, a flat-bottomed boat slips sideways in the water, known as "making leeway", unless the wind blows directly from behind. An underwater foil provides lateral resistance to this sideslip. On a dinghy, the foil is a centreboard or daggerboard; on a yacht it is a ballasted keel. In either case, various shapes are available. The foils on a Hobie 16 catamaran (*see* pp.140–141), for example, consist of a flat outside edge on each hull, with sharp edges along the bottom.

A centreboard or keel reduces the sideways movement created when the wind blows against the sails.

This increases the tendency to heel over, which in turn is balanced by the crew's weight (on a dinghy) or a ballasted keel (on a yacht). The underwater foil also creates hydrodynamic lift to windward, which is transformed into forward motion. Sophisticated foil design and construction are used for high-performance sailing boats, with precise profiling of the leading and trailing edges.

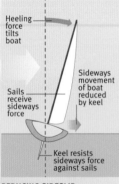

Heeling force tilts boat

Sideways movement of boat reduced by keel

Sails receive sideways force

Keel resists sideways force against sails

REDUCING SIDESLIP
A keel prevents a boat being blown sideways and partly transforms side forces into forward drive. The sideways force on the sails and the keel's resistance combine to produce a heeling (tilting) force.

SAILING UPWIND
Yacht crews are too light to prevent their boats from heeling. This yacht is sailing upwind, where side forces on the sails are greatest, and has achieved its maximum angle of heel for efficient performance.

HOLD IT LEVEL
If a boat heels when sailing upwind, it will tend to turn into the wind. Rather than pull on the tiller, as here, let out the mainsail until the boat is upright.

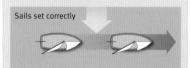

LEEWAY
Even with a centreboard or keel, any boat will be driven sideways by the wind. The helmsman must compensate by changing course slightly.

BALANCED BOAT

The "centre of effort" (CE) corresponds to the fulcrum of all side forces on the rig created by wind blowing across the sails. For the boat to sail correctly, this centre of effort must be balanced with the "centre of lateral resistance" (CLR), which is mainly provided by the underwater foil.

A boat's designer has primary responsibility for ensuring that it is balanced but, however well-designed the boat is, the balance will be affected by other factors. For example, the way the boat is rigged – if the mast is raked too far back, the CE will move behind the CLR. Balance is more likely to be affected by the way the boat is sailed and the way the sails are trimmed (*see* pp.78–79); the aim of the helmsman should be to keep the boat level and balanced.

BALANCED SAILS AND HELM

With perfectly balanced sails, the boat will sail straight ahead with a neutral or balanced helm. If the sails are out of balance, with too much drive from the mainsail, the boat will turn towards the wind with "weather helm". If the sails are out of balance with too much drive from the jib, the boat will turn away from the wind with "lee helm".

Sails set correctly

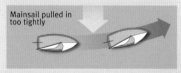

Balanced helm

Mainsail pulled in too tightly

Weather helm

Mainsail let out too far

Lee helm

"NOT BOUND TO ALLEGIANCE TO

ANY MASTER, WHEREVER THE

WIND TAKES ME, I TRAVEL

AS A VISITOR."

Horace, Epistles

Points of sailing

The angle of a boat relative to the wind is its "point of sailing". You can sail at any angle of the 360-degree circle, except in the "no sail zone", where your boat heads directly into the wind. Points of sailing for catamarans differ slightly (*see* pp.144–145).

SAILING COURSES

Various terms are used to describe the course (direction) and action a boat takes in relation to the wind. Luffing, or luffing up, is turning the bow of the boat towards the wind; bearing away is turning the bow of the boat away from the wind. On upwind courses (close hauled and close reach), the boat is turned towards the wind; on downwind, or offwind, courses (broad reach and run), the boat is turned away from the wind. You are on starboard tack when the boom is on the port side of the boat; you are on port tack when the boom is on the starboard side of the boat. Close hauled, or beating, to windward is sailing as close to the true wind direction as possible, with the wind blowing diagonally across the bow; reaching is sailing with the wind blowing from the port or starboard side; running is sailing with the wind blowing from behind.

Close haul

Close reach

Beam reach

Broad reach

CLOSE HAULED
This yacht is beating to windward, with mainsail and headsail sheeted in tightly so it can sail as close to the wind as possible.

CLOSE HAULED
Sailing close to the wind, sails pulled in, centreboard down; crew sitting out to balance the boat.

CLOSE REACH
Bearing away slightly, sails eased a little, crew sits out; boat sails slightly faster.

BEAM REACH
Bearing away until wind is directly across side of boat, sails eased; centreboard may be partly lifted.

POINTS OF SAILING

Each time a boat alters its point of sail, the set of the sails must be adjusted and, in dinghy sailing, the crew's weight must be distributed in a specific way.

NO SAIL ZONE

No sail zone

Sails cannot fill

If a boat sails too close to the wind it risks entering the "no sail zone", where the sails cannot fill. The closest most boats can sail towards the wind is about 40 degrees off the true-wind angle. High-performance boats may be able to "point" a little higher; cruising yachts may "point" quite a lot lower. Progress towards the wind is made by sailing close-hauled to windward, on a zig-zagging course.

No sail zone

Run

Run (goosewinged)

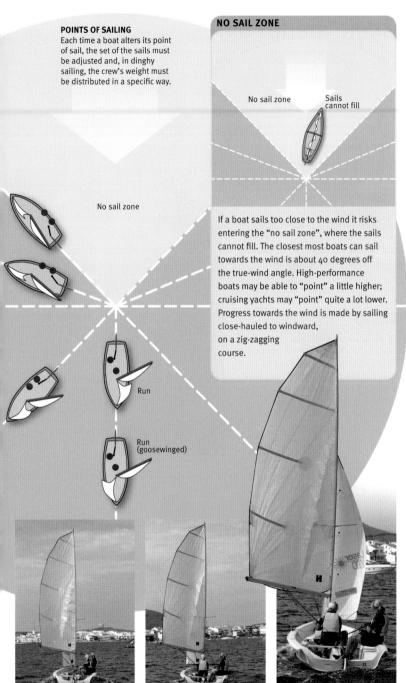

BROAD REACH
Wind blows diagonally from behind, sails eased, centreboard partly lifted; crew sits in.

RUN
With the wind directly behind, sails eased, centreboard lifted; crew sits on centreline.

GOOSEWING
Running directly downwind, sails eased; jib can be "goosewinged" to windward side.

Basic manoeuvres

Learn the difference between getting "stuck in irons", "heaving-to", or just drifting with sails flapping and wind on the beam. Then practise moving off with the sails sheeted in to power the boat, and changing direction both upwind and downwind. You will then be in control.

HEAD TO WIND

One of the simplest ways to stop the boat is to turn directly into the wind. The boat will then be "head to wind" or "in irons". To get out of this situation, pull in the jib on one side, so that the wind blows on to the back of the sail – known as "backing the jib". This will help to push the bow round until the wind is blowing on to the side of the boat. Then let go of the jib and pull it in on the new leeward side.

HOVE-TO

A safe way of stopping with the wind abeam (from the side) is to heave-to. In the hove-to position, the jib is sheeted to windward, the mainsail is let right out, and the rudder is pushed over. The boat will then drift slowly and safely to leeward. To continue sailing, pull in the jib on the leeward side, straighten the rudder, and pull in the mainsheet.

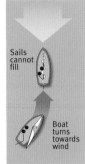

Sails cannot fill

Boat turns towards wind

GOING HEAD TO WIND
If you attempt to steer directly into the wind, the boat will stop and you will find yourself "in irons" with the sails flapping. The boat will then begin to blow backwards, reversing in the direction in which the rudder is pointing.

Tiller to leeward

Mainsail flapping

HEAVING-TO
To heave-to, sheet in the jib on the windward side, let out the mainsail completely, and push the tiller to leeward.

LYING-TO

Another manoeuvre you can use to stop the boat is to lie-to with the wind blowing from just forwards of abeam and both sails loosened. In this position, the sails will be flapping and the boat will be blown sideways. The speed with which the boat drifts will depend on the wind strength; and some of the wind force will be converted into forward movement by the centreboard. However, it is not advisable to allow sails to flap hard for long periods because they will become damaged.

To get underway after lying-to, pull in the mainsail and jib until they stop flapping. With the wind from ahead, both sails will need to be pulled in tightly.

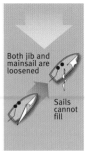

Both jib and mainsail are loosened

Sails cannot fill

LIE-TO
To lie-to, sail close to the wind on a port tack, with the wind blowing on to the port side of the boat. Loosen both sails and allow the boat to drift.

THE BASICS OF CHANGING DIRECTION

When changing direction under sail, you will need to adjust both sails and rudder, and only small rudder adjustments will be needed. On a dinghy, the mainsail provides most of the power: pulling it in helps turn the boat towards the wind; letting it out helps the boat bear away. The crew should adjust the jib sheet as the boat settles on to the new course.

WATCH WHERE YOU GO
Always keep a good lookout and check the surrounding water before changing course. If the view to leeward is blocked by the sails, helm and crew should look under the boom and round the front of the jib.

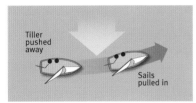

Tiller pushed away

Sails pulled in

HEADING UP
When turning towards the wind, push away the tiller and pull in both sails until they stop flapping. Only a slight change in rudder direction is needed.

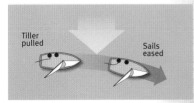

Tiller pulled

Sails eased

BEARING AWAY
When bearing away from the wind, pull the tiller and let out the mainsail, then the jib. The boat may not be able to bear away until the mainsheet is eased.

Using the rudder

Changing direction on a dinghy or yacht bears little resemblance to steering a car. The rudder is likely to be the primary control when you want to change direction, but it must be used with secondary controls, such as the sail trim, and the boat has to be balanced.

STEERING A DINGHY

A dinghy rudder assembly has four main parts: the rudder blade, rudder stock, tiller, and tiller extension. The blade is attached by hinges to the stock, which is in turn attached to the transom of the dinghy. The tiller is attached to the stock and enables you to turn the blade from side to side. The tiller extension lets you steer while sitting on the sides of the boat. Turning the blade causes it to act like a brake as turbulent water builds up in front of it. Most of the time, only small rudder movements are needed to change direction, and the faster the boat moves, the more sensitive the rudder becomes.

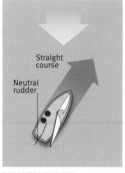

BALANCED RUDDER
If sailing a straight course, balance the boat and sails so the rudder feels neutral (*see opposite*). Rectify any excess weather helm (*see p.69*) by lowering the rudder

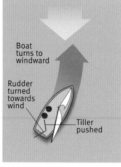

STEERING TOWARDS THE WIND
To steer into the wind, push the tiller away only slightly. You can help the boat to turn by pulling in the mainsail and letting the boat heel to leeward.

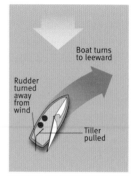

STEERING AWAY FROM THE WIND
To turn to leeward, pull the tiller very slightly so that the rudder does not act as a brake. To help the turn, let out the mainsail and let the boat heel to windward.

GENTLY DOES IT

The rudder blade is vertical when sailing, but it can be lifted for bringing the dinghy ashore. The rudder stock holds the blade in place and allows it to swivel from the up position to fully down.

Tiller

Tiller extension

Rudder stock

Rudder blade

WATER FLOW
You can enhance rudder
effectiveness by reducing
heeling and making sure the
sails are correctly trimmed.

STEERING A YACHT

Most larger yachts use a wheel connected
to the rudder by cables to control steering.
Unlike a dinghy rudder, the blade is sited
beneath the hull and often sits behind
a fixed fin called a skeg. This helps direct
water flow over the rudder blade, helping
to keep the yacht balanced when the
blade is turned.

The response of a rudder depends on
the speed of water flow over the blade.
At slow speeds, a yacht may lose steerage;
if it stops altogether, the rudder will have
no effect at all. When motoring, the
phenomenon known as "prop walk"
(*see* Manoeuvring under power, pp.192–
193) can have a major effect on the
rudder when going astern.

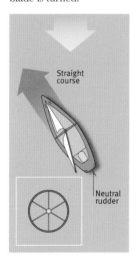

Straight
course

Neutral
rudder

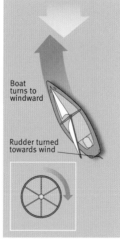

Boat
turns to
windward

Rudder turned
towards wind

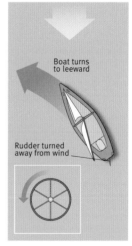

Boat turns
to leeward

Rudder turned
away from wind

NEUTRAL RUDDER
Sailing straight ahead in very light
winds, the wheel can be centred.
If the boat is heeling, it will tend to
head into the wind and you need
to steer slightly away from it.

STEERING TOWARDS THE WIND
Turning the wheel to the right
turns the boat to starboard, which
here is towards the wind. Pulling
in the mainsheet will encourage
the boat to turn.

STEERING AWAY FROM THE WIND
Turning the wheel to the left turns
the boat to port, which here is
away from the wind. If the boat
is heeling, let out the mainsail
to allow the boat to turn.

Sail trim

Trimming sails to the correct angle to the wind is a principal skill
of good sailing. If a sail is let out too far (under-sheeted), it will flap,
reducing forward drive. If pulled in too tight (over-sheeted), airflow
over both sides will be disrupted, stalling the sail and slowing the boat.

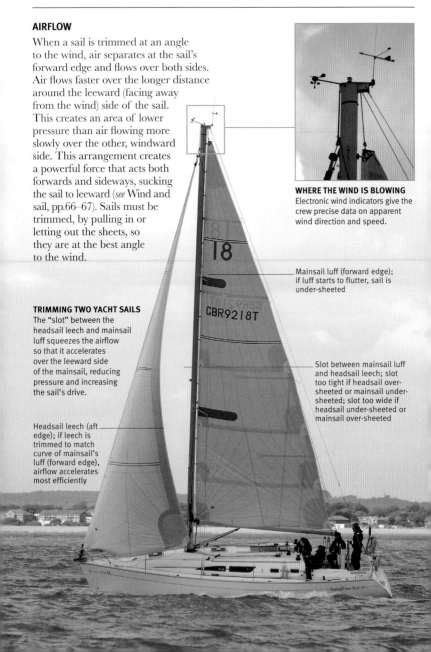

AIRFLOW

When a sail is trimmed at an angle
to the wind, air separates at the sail's
forward edge and flows over both sides.
Air flows faster over the longer distance
around the leeward (facing away
from the wind) side of the sail.
This creates an area of lower
pressure than air flowing more
slowly over the other, windward
side. This arrangement creates
a powerful force that acts both
forwards and sideways, sucking
the sail to leeward (*see* Wind and
sail, pp.66–67). Sails must be
trimmed, by pulling in or
letting out the sheets, so
they are at the best angle
to the wind.

WHERE THE WIND IS BLOWING
Electronic wind indicators give the
crew precise data on apparent
wind direction and speed.

Mainsail luff (forward edge);
if luff starts to flutter, sail is
under-sheeted

TRIMMING TWO YACHT SAILS
The "slot" between the
headsail leech and mainsail
luff squeezes the airflow
so that it accelerates
over the leeward side
of the mainsail, reducing
pressure and increasing
the sail's drive.

Slot between mainsail luff
and headsail leech; slot
too tight if headsail over-
sheeted or mainsail under-
sheeted; slot too wide if
headsail under-sheeted or
mainsail over-sheeted

Headsail leech (aft
edge); if leech is
trimmed to match
curve of mainsail's
luff (forward edge),
airflow accelerates
most efficiently

18

GBR9218T

TRIMMING A SINGLE SAIL
For maximum performance, the sail is trimmed so the lower part of the luff (just above the sailmaker's logo in the lower corner) just starts to "lift" due to wind blowing on the leeward side.

TELL-TALES

Tell-tales are lightweight tape streamers that can be positioned either side of the headsail or mainsail, near the forward edge or the aft edge, to indicate the behaviour of airflow and how well the sail is trimmed. On a correctly trimmed sail, the tell-tales on either side will fly straight backwards, in parallel. If windward tell-tales fly higher, pull in the sheet; if leeward tell-tales fly higher, let it out.

Tell-tale starting to lift upwards

Tell-tales streaming in parallel

Top panel; panels twist in line with wind as it increases, reducing heeling moment and making mainsail easier to control

Batten; helps support rigid shape of sail when air flows over both sides

Mainsail; sail almost fully powered with airflow over both sides

Crease in sail; creases do not necessarily impair performance; they may be removed using cunningham tension control line

Jib trimmed to match mainsail

Mainsheet; helmsman may need to ease the sheet to sail through gusts

TRIMMING TWO DINGHY SAILS
The slot between jib and mainsail accelerates airflow over the leeward side of the mainsail, creating more suction to drive the boat forwards. The jib is trimmed to match the mainsail, unless the helm lets out the mainsheet to keep the dinghy upright in a gust.

Trimming the boat

Lightweight dinghies and high-performance racing keelboats are extremely responsive to the position of the crew. Weight needs to be moved fore, aft, and sideways to ensure the boat is correctly "trimmed" for changes in direction, wind strength, and conditions on the water.

CREW POSITION

The hull of a dinghy has to be trimmed so it does not drag or sink. All modern dinghies perform best if they are sailed upright. If you let them heel, the side of the boat will dig in the water, the centreboard will lose grip, and there will be an increased tendency for the boat to experience weather helm.

The first job of the helmsman and crew is to move their weight outboard as the wind increases, eventually hooking their feet under the toestraps and "hiking out" over the side. They should keep their bodies close together – this weight distribution will help prevent the bow from pitching in waves. For best performance, a boat must also be trimmed fore and aft. When sailing into the wind, the crew should move their weight forward to lift the stern. In a dinghy they should sit right next to the shroud, but may need to move back a little to help the bow lift over waves. As the boat bears away on to a reach and gathers speed, the crew should move back over the flattest part of the hull.

Trimming is less critical in yachts, due to their greater weight and tolerance for heeling. In a race, however, distributing the crew's weight correctly may make a significant difference to performance.

SAILING UPWIND
When changing course to sail upwind, both crew move forward, close together, ensuring the stern does not drag in the water and slow the boat down. Always sail the boat upright for maximum performance.

Crew and helmsman sit out at centre of boat

Laser 2000

22

SAILING ON A BROAD REACH
When the bow lifts and the hull starts to plane on its stern on a broad reach, both crew move back. However, the boat must be kept flat to maintain control. If crew weight is insufficient, let out the mainsheet to bring the boat upright.

Crew and helmsman sit out towards back of boat

TRIM BY FEEL

All boats respond differently according to the power of the rig, the hull's shape and weight, and prevailing conditions. With a little experience, you start to make intuitive decisions on the spot to keep the boat under control in different situations. Sliding fore and aft along the sidedecks becomes second nature as you learn when weight is required towards the bow or over the stern in order to avoid heeling over.

STRONGER WIND
In stronger winds, move your weight outboard and lean out to hold the boat upright. The boat should not heel any more than the angle shown here – if it does, bear away. Keep well forward when sailing upwind and move back when sailing downwind.

Vertical axis

Crew and helmsman keep to windward side

Vertical axis

Crew moves to leeward side

LIGHT WIND
Keep crew forward in light wind to push down the bow and lift up the stern. The boat should be upright, although you may need to heel slightly to leeward to keep the sails filled.

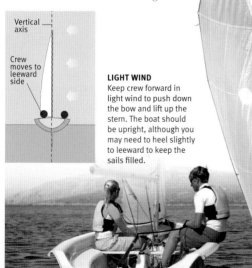

"THERE'S NOTHING... HALF AS WORTH DOING AS SIMPLY MESSING ABOUT IN BOATS."

Kenneth Grahame, The Wind in the Willows

Rules of the road

Avoiding collisions is a priority afloat. The rules of the road are simple and straightforward to put into practice, ensuring that all types of sailing boats, powercraft, and commercial shipping can share crowded areas of water in complete safety.

HOW NOT TO COLLIDE

There are various rules you must be familiar with before you sail. First, boats under sail generally have right of way over boats under power. However, boats under sail should give way to commercial vessels engaged in fishing or those constrained by draught or restricted in their ability to manoeuvre for whatever reason.

WHO GOES FIRST?
As a general rule, starboard tack has right of way over port tack. However, starboard must avoid a collision if port is clearly out of control.

When sailing, port tack should give way to starboard tack. For boats on the same tack, the windward yacht must keep clear of the other boat. When motoring, the boat to starboard has right of way. In practical terms, if you can see the other boat's red navigation light you must give way; if you can see their green light, you have right of way.

On a head-on potential collision course, both boats should turn to starboard to prevent the collision from occurring. When overtaking another boat, you must maintain a considerable distance from it.

If you are sailing in a narrow channel, you must keep to the right side; if crossing in a channel is essential, you should do so at 90 degrees.

It is the skipper's responsibility to do everything possible to avoid a collision, so keep a proper lookout at all times. When you alter your course to avoid a collision, make your intentions clear so the skipper in the other boat can understand what is happening.

RULES FOR RACING
Rules for racing are complex, but the main requirement is to avoid collisions. Rounding a mark, the helmsman of the inside boat can request room by calling "Water!" only if it overlaps the outside boat within two lengths of the mark.

Although the rules of the road are important, do not always stick blindly to them. For example, it may be much easier for the crew of a starboard-tack dinghy to tack out of the way of a larger port-tack yacht. Finally, do not assume other people will understand or abide by the rules of the road. It obviously makes more sense to get out of the way than be run down by a powerboat!

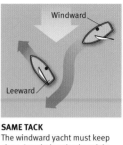

SAME TACK
The windward yacht must keep clear. A yacht beating has right of way over a yacht reaching or running on the same tack.

YACHT'S RIGHT OF WAY
Sailing boats have right of way over powerboats. In this case, neither boat is under sail but the motoring yacht has right of way because it is on the starboard side of the powerboat, with a clear view of its green light.

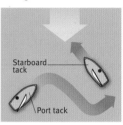

DIFFERENT TACKS
Starboard tack has right of way over port tack. The port-tack boat should bear away, tack, or stop until the other boat has passed.

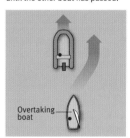

OVERTAKING
The overtaking boat must keep clear of the boat being overtaken, irrespective of whether it is driven by power or sail.

KEEP TO THE RIGHT
The ferry must maintain its speed in order to manoeuvre in a narrow channel. The yacht must keep to the right side of the channel, well out of the way of the larger ship.

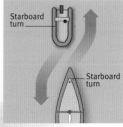

HEAD-ON COURSE
When two boats under power are on a head-on course, they should both turn to starboard to avoid collision.

Ropework

Ropes of all kinds are vital for sailing and securing a boat. Ropes for different purposes on the boat all have different dimensions and requirements, with the coloured outer core of modern synthetic rope helping to identify its use in the cockpit or on deck.

BRAIDED ROPE
A core of twisted or braided strands is encased in an outer braided sheath for protection and extra strength.

ROPE CHOICE

The strength of rope depends on the materials, construction method, and diameter. Lightweight braided ropes are exceptionally strong, with minimal stretch, and can be used for narrow-diameter halyards, control lines, and sheets. Be aware that thinner rope is harder to hold and pull with your hands. It is advisable always to wear sailing gloves for handling rope – as well as providing considerable extra holding power, gloves will help prevent rope burn if a synthetic rope slips through your hands.

Polyester three-strand rope can be pre-stretched for use as sheets or halyards and is also useful for mooring. Nylon three-strand rope stretches too much for halyards or sheets, but is a popular choice for anchoring or mooring. Polypropylene three-strand rope is the least expensive option for mooring and will float, but it has very poor stretch qualities.

ROPE WEAR

Synthetic rope cannot rot but it will deteriorate through abrasion, often caused by rubbing against a fairlead (rope guide) or block, which may destroy one of the strands or the outer casing. If any part of a rope appears to have deteriorated, change the whole rope.

THROWING A ROPE

To ensure that a thrown rope reaches its target, make sure it is coiled with enough length to reach well past the target and allow extra for tying round a cleat or bollard. When you throw, there needs to be enough weight to carry across the distance, which is why it's necessary to throw a fairly tightly packed coil and ensure the rest of the rope will run free without snagging. Be careful who you choose to throw to on the dock. People are often enthusiastic to help, but may have no experience of catching a rope or securing it on a cleat.

1 **Coil the rope,** allowing plenty of length. Divide the coil into two, holding one coil in each hand.

2 **Throw one of the coils** at the target. If you need extra length, unwind as much of the second coil as required.

COILING A ROPE

Loose rope that is not in use should be coiled so it can be stowed out of the way but is accessible and ready when needed.

If you leave rope lying around – particularly a long, thick rope such as a mooring warp – it will invariably become tangled and difficult to unravel when you need it in a hurry, as often happens when berthing a yacht. Rope tends to twist when it is coiled. To avoid kinks, coil three-strand rope in the same direction as the strands are twisted. Braided rope may need to be coiled in figure-of-eight loops which follow the way that the rope naturally wants to twist and turn.

TWISTING THE ROPE
Twist the rope between thumb and forefinger each time you make a loop to ensure that the coils lie flat.

1 **Starting from the end** of the rope, make large loops with one hand and gather the coils with the other.

2 **Keep the coils of rope** evenly sized by paying out an arm-span length for each loop you make.

3 **Leave plenty of rope** to secure the coils. Take a horizontal turn round the top of the coils.

4 **Continue wrapping** the rope around the coils with at least two more tight turns to lock the coils together.

5 **Bend the rope** into a loop and push it through the centre of the coils, above the horizontal turns.

6 **Holding the loop firmly in place**, pull the free end of the rope up and insert it through the centre of the loop.

7 **Pull tight** to secure the coil. When you need to use the rope, pull the free end out of the loop and unwind.

Basic knots

You need only a few knots for sailing, but those knots must be fail-safe and also easy to untie. You should practise all the knots shown until you know for sure that you can tie them securely every time – whether you are in a hurry, in the dark, or on a boat that is rolling and pitching.

FIGURE OF EIGHT

This is the basic stopper knot used for sailing, which ensures that the end of a rope cannot run out through a block or fairlead. Simple and effective, it is typically used for securing the end of a sheet.

1 First, make a small loop by crossing the working end over the standing part of the rope.

2 Holding the loop in one hand, use your other hand to twist the working end under the standing part of the rope.

3 Feed the working end of the rope down through the loop so that it makes a figure of eight.

4 Pull the end tight to ensure the figure of eight is secure. The knot should take only a few seconds to tie.

BOWLINE

This is the key knot for sailing – secure under tension but quick and easy to untie. The bowline (pronounced bow-lynn) is particularly useful when mooring or tying a sheet to the clew of a sail. It is a useful skill to be able to tie it one-handed.

1 Make a loop with the working end on top, hold it in place, and pass the end through the centre of the loop.

2 Holding the crossing turn in place, take the working end under and over the standing part of the rope.

3 Still holding the crossing turn in place, feed the working end of the rope back through the loop.

4 Pull the bowline tight with both hands, ensuring there is not an excess of rope at the working end.

CLOVE HITCH

This knot provides a quick and easy way to secure a rope to a bollard or ring, typically for short-term use when mooring a small boat or inflatable tender. The clove hitch is also useful for tying a fender to a rail, or two clove hitches can be used to tie the post of a traditional burgee to a flag halyard.

1 **Make a turn** with the working end of the rope, passing it over the standing part of the rope.

2 **Make a second turn** with the working end of the rope in the same direction as the first turn.

3 **Feed the working end** of the rope under the standing part of the rope, as shown.

4 **Pull the clove hitch together** by pulling on both the working end and the standing part of the rope.

5 **Leaving a long working end**, the tightened clove hitch is reasonably secure and very quick to untie.

ROUND TURN AND TWO HALF HITCHES

As a mooring knot for a ring, post, or rail, the round turn and two half hitches is considerably more secure than the clove hitch. The principal advantage over the bowline is that it can be untied more easily when the rope is under heavy load.

1 **Make a round turn** by looping the working end of the rope twice round the mooring ring, post, or rail.

2 **Pass the working end** over the standing part of the rope. Ensure the working end is long enough for this knot.

3 **Feed the working end** around the standing part of the rope – this is your first half hitch.

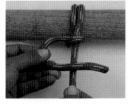

4 **Repeat to tie** the second half hitch, which must loop round in the same direction as the first.

5 **Pull the working end** of the rope tight to close up the second half hitch and lock the knot.

6 **Always leave plenty of length** for the working end when you tie this knot. This will keep the half hitches secure under load, but allows you to untie them quickly and easily when required.

REEF KNOT

~~The original purpose of the reef~~
knot was to tie the reefing lines of the
mainsail securely together. Modern
reefing systems mean that reefing lines
are obsolete on the majority of yachts

nowadays, but the reef knot still serves
~~a useful purpose when you need to tie~~
the ends of two ropes or cords of equal
diameter together – for example, when
using sail ties to secure a lowered
mainsail on the boom.

1 Cross the two working
ends of the rope, with
the left end (red) over the
right end (blue).

2 Take the left working end
(red) and, with forefinger
and thumb, bring it under the
right working end (blue).

3 Cross the left working
end (red) over the right
working end (blue) and bring
it up to create a loop.

4 Pass the left working end
(red) down through the
loop and back towards you to
form a reef knot, as shown.

5 Pull both ends taut to
close the knot. If in doubt,
always remember to tie the
reef knot "left over right,
then right over left".

MANAGING ROPES AND LINES

It is vital to keep ropes tidy
and ready for immediate use.
If they are not correctly coiled,
the rope may snag or tie itself
in knots, the halyard may jam,
or you may be unable to
throw a mooring line to
the shore. Using the
right rope for the job

Coiled halyard   is vital. Ensure that
mooring ropes of
different lengths are neatly laid out in
the mooring locker and never allow them
to get mixed up with other equipment. Check
ropes regularly for abrasion; replace them as
soon as possible if worn. Wash them occasionally
in warm, soapy water to remove salt residue.

**Correctly coiled and neatly
stowed ropes are ready for
instant use.**

SHEET BEND

The sheet bend is a simple and secure way of tying two separate pieces of rope together. It can provide a quick and effective solution to extending the length of a mooring line – for example, if the crew is rowing the line ashore in the tender and the rope suddenly runs short. When the two ropes to be joined are of different diameter, always use the double sheet bend (*see below*), as this knot will be more secure.

1 **Make a loop** in the end of one rope (red). Pass the working end of the other rope (blue) through the loop.

2 **Continue to feed** the working end (blue) around the back of the initial loop (red), as shown.

3 **Bring the working end** (blue) up under itself, while crossing over the loop of the other rope (red).

5 **Despite its simple** appearance, the sheet bend is a surprisingly secure knot, particularly under tension.

4 **Pull both** pieces of rope (the working end and the initial loop) tight in order to close the sheet bend.

DOUBLE SHEET BEND

Taking an additional turn around the loop produces a double sheet bend. This provides extra security when tying two ropes together. This knot is particularly recommended for ropes of different diameter, as shown here.

1 **Follow steps 1, 2, and 3** for the single sheet bend (*above*), with the thicker rope (green) forming the loop.

2 **Continue by taking a** second turn around the initial loop (green) with the thinner rope (white).

4 **Pull the ends** of both the thin and the thick rope tight in order to close the double sheet bend.

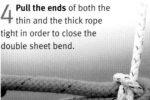

3 **Cross the working end** of the thinner rope (white) over the loop of the thicker rope (green) and tuck it under itself.

Sailing a dinghy

Types of dinghy

There is a huge range of different dinghy designs and classes from which to select the boat that will best suit you, each offering a particular sailing experience for varying ages and abilities. The first decision to make is whether to sail single-handed or with a crew.

DOUBLE-HANDERS

Double-handers are sailed by a helmsman and one crew, who have both a mainsail and jib to drive the boat, with the option of a spinnaker for use downwind. It is rewarding to work as part of a team in which the crew plays an important role, and you may be glad of the company while you sail. Larger dinghies used for recreational sailing may have sufficient space and buoyancy to carry four or five people, making them ideal for family sailing (*see* Types of keelboat, pp. 96–97).

SINGLE-HANDERS

Sailing a single-hander has the advantage that you do not need to find a crew. Single-handers tend to be smaller and lighter than double-handers, making them easier to handle on land and possibly more responsive under sail.

Popular single-handers, such as the Laser, Pico, Topper, and Open Bic, are extremely simple dinghies with just one sail and an unstayed rig. This makes them cheap to own and maintain, quick to assemble, and easy to store. When sailing a single-hander, the crew is captain and in complete charge of the boat. This puts beginners

HIGH-PERFORMANCE SKIFF
The 29erXX, designed for trapezing, provides a dramatic, high-speed dinghy-sailing experience for two skilled crew.

on a steep learning curve that is hard work but very productive in terms of acquiring sailing skills.

Being alone on the boat should not mean you are alone on the water. Always sail in company, with coach support or safety cover close to hand.

DINGHIES FOR RACING

Dinghy racing is the most effective way to improve your sailing techniques. The crew has to practise and master certain

BALANCING ACT
The Musto Skiff provides a great ride for those who combine agility on the trapeze with sailing skills.

TWIN HULLS FOR SPEED
The Hobie 16 Spi (equipped with a spinnaker) provides a fast, fun ride and is raced as the official world championship youth catamaran.

manoeuvres, such as quick tacks and gybes, while learning to maximize speed on all points of sailing. Any dinghy can be used for racing if competition is available – for example, the Laser is the world's most popular racing dinghy, providing enjoyment for almost all ages across a wide range of ability levels.

PERFECT FOR CHILDREN
The Open Bic is a fast, modern dinghy designed for young children to learn to sail, go racing, and, most importantly, have fun.

hull shape. The best-known skiff is the 49er, which is raced in the Olympics. Other dinghy classes raced at the Olympic Games (*see* pp. 338–339) include the Laser and Finn single-handers for men, the Laser Radial for women, the 470 two-person dinghy for both men and women, and the Tornado catamaran class for men.

HIGH-PERFORMANCE DINGHIES

Dinghies designed for high performance may feature: trapezes to provide extra leverage for the crew; an asymmetric spinnaker to optimize downwind sailing; lightweight hull construction using materials such as carbon fibre; lightweight carbon spars; and sails made from materials such as Mylar and Kevlar for maximum stability.

Dinghies known as skiffs provide ultimate high performance. They have a very high power-to-weight ratio and employ an oversize rig on a small, flat

CATAMARANS

A catamaran consists of two narrow hulls joined by two aluminium beams, with a trampoline providing a "deck" in the centre, stretched between the hulls. With the hulls spread wide apart, the crew can obtain more leverage than a dinghy crew, allowing them to sail with a bigger and more powerful rig. The result is that catamarans are not only stable but also tend to be faster than most dinghies – they can be a lot of fun to sail. Disadvantages may include extra cost, and poor performance in light winds.

Types of keelboat

Small keelboats with a ballasted keel or centreplate tend to be considerably more stable than dinghies. Depending on the size of the boat, the cockpit may provide comfortable space for as many as five crew, with a choice between traditional or modern cruisers and racers.

CRUISING KEELBOATS

A small keelboat may prove to be the best choice for cruising. It will be stable enough to be left at a mooring or be anchored overnight. Unlike dinghies, keelboats cannot capsize because a heavy keel or ballasted centreplate will hold the boat steady if the wind blows against it. The worst that can happen is that the boat will round up into the wind, indicating to the skipper and crew that the sails should be reefed to bring the boat under better control.

Keelboats tend to be larger than dinghies. At the smaller end of the range is the 4.94-m (16-ft) Laser Stratos, which provides a very stable sailing experience in an open cockpit. At the upper end is the 7.64-m (25-ft) Folkboat, which has a small cabin and a traditional design and claims to have the largest fleet of cruiser-racers in the world, having originated in Scandinavia in 1942.

Compared to a bigger yacht, a small keelboat is likely to be cheaper and easier to maintain and sail, and two crew may be able to manage the rig. With a

shallow draught keel or centreplate, the small cruiser may be able to explore areas where yachts cannot sail. Accommodation may be cramped but can be extended with a cockpit tent. The fittings may be spartan, with no yacht luxuries such as pressurized water or electric lights, but should provide enjoyable camping in fine weather and make a splendid refuge for children when afloat.

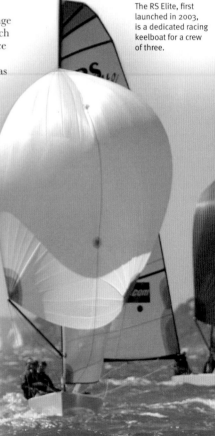

ELITE RACING
The RS Elite, first launched in 2003, is a dedicated racing keelboat for a crew of three.

WORKING DESIGN
The Cornish Shrimper is an example of a small, traditional working keelboat adapted for modern recreational sailing.

SMALL RACER
The J24 is one of the world's most popular small keelboats. It is used as a day-racer for five crew, with a tiny cabin providing shelter inside the hull.

RACING KEELBOATS

Many small keelboats are used exclusively for racing. Classic designs include the long, slim, and extremely beautiful Dragon, which was designed in 1929 and is raced by a crew of three, and the Star, which is raced by two crew and is the oldest Olympic class. The Star was originally designed in 1911 but has recently been considerably updated with a modern rig.

Many modern racing keelboats are categorized as sportsboats, such as the Melges 24 or the Laser SB3. These are comparable to big, ballasted, high-performance dinghies, their oversize rigs providing plenty of adrenaline for the four or five crew struggling to keep them upright. Unlike traditional keelboats, sportsboats are designed to be sailed upright on a flat-bottomed hull that can plane across the surface of the water, instead of heeling over and slicing through the water on a long, narrow hull. These superfast keelboats cannot capsize like a dinghy, but they may get flattened if their crews lose control racing downwind with a spinnaker.

Rigging a two-handed dinghy

Every dinghy is rigged in a slightly different way and you should familiarize yourself with the manufacturer's instructions for the dinghy you are handling. The rigging sequence shown here is an example of how to rig a typical two-handed dinghy.

PREPARING THE MAST

Select a flat location with the dinghy parked securely on its trailer and sufficient space all around. Check for overhead cables and other obstructions. Lay out the mast, boom, and rigging components. The mast may be fitted with a separate wire forestay to attach to the bow; on dinghies with roller furling systems the forestay is provided by a luff wire built into the jib. If there is no conventional forestay, attach a rope temporarily. Ensure that each wire is led separately to the base of the mast with no kinks or tangles. Cover securely with tape any pins and rings which could catch on the spinnaker. Halyards for mainsail, jib, and spinnaker should all be fitted and secured by knots, along with a burgee or wind indicator, before raising the mast.

1 **Prepare the dinghy** for rigging on its trailer or trolley, with clear working space all around. When possible, choose a day with light wind. Two people are needed to rig the boat.

2 **One person lifts** the mast vertically and locates it in the mast step, while the other person is ready to attach the two shrouds that support it.

RAISING THE MAST

In light wind, a small aluminium mast can be lifted to a vertical position by one person. On some dinghies, before raising the mast, it is normal to attach the shrouds to the shroud plates on the hull with the mast laid horizontally along the boat. The mast is then lifted so that the base fits into the mast step, letting it lean forward, while you attach the forestay to the bows. On the Laser Vago shown here, one person lifts and supports the mast in its final position, while the other person fixes it into the mast step and attaches shrouds and forestay to their fixing points on the hull.

MAST STEP
The heel of the mast fits into the mast step, where it straddles a bolt that holds it securely in position.

CLEVIS PINS
A clevis pin and split ring are used to secure shrouds and other fittings. Beware that split rings can be fiddly. They are easily dropped and lost.

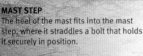

3 **Shroud plates** attached to the hull allow shroud length to be adjusted with a pin and ring system. A dinghy's rigging manual will recommend which hole to use.

4 **A length of rope** secures the wire forestay temporarity to the roller-furler mechanism. This is removed when the jib is rigged.

RIGGING THE JIB

Many modern two-handed dinghies have roller-furling jibs, which can remain rigged throughout the sailing season. The jib luff wire forms the forestay that supports the mast. A cover can be used to protect the furled sail from damage from sunlight when the dinghy is not in use. Wind the furling line fully on to the drum, before attaching the tack of the jib, and lead the line back to the cockpit. Attach the furling swivel firmly to the end of the halyard with a shackle. Have the rolled jib ready for hoisting, neatly laid along the boat, tack foremost.

1 **With a rope forestay** holding the mast, attach the tack of the jib to the roller furling drum. Attach the head of the jib to the roller furling swivel on the jib halyard.

2 **Pull the wire jib halyard** down from the back of the mast. When it is fairly tight, hook the tensioning block on to the wire loop.

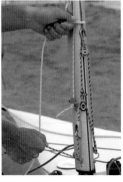

3 **Pull down** on the halyard tension control rope until the luff of the jib is taut. On some dinghies, a lever is used to apply final tension to the luff of the jib.

4 **With the luff wire of the jib** now providing the forestay, stow the temporary forestay alongside the mast. Attach the sheets to the clew of the jib using stopper knots.

STOPPER KNOTS
Attach sheets to the clew with figure-of-eight knots (see p.88) on either side of the cringle (reinforced eye).

FITTING THE BOOM

The boom provides longitudinal tension in the mainsail, with an adjustable outhaul pulling the clew towards the end of the boom. To prevent the boom lifting when the wind fills the sail, in most boats there is a multi-purchase adjustable line or aluminium strut called a kicking strap ("kicker") or boom vang. A gnav is an upside-down strut, on top of the boom. Pulling forward the base of the strut presses the boom down.

GOOSENECK
An articulated joint connects the swinging boom to the mast.

1 **Two people are required to** fit the boom and gnav to the mast. Despite the extra fiddling, a gnav has the advantage of freeing up space under the boom, with less danger of the crew getting trapped by the kicker during a tack or gybe.

2 **Articulated joints link the gnav** between the mast and a slider on the boom. A multi-purchase control line pulls the slider forward to push down the boom and tension the mainsail.

MAINSHEET BLOCK AND CLEAT
A figure-of-eight stopper knot (*see* p.88) is tied at the end of the mainsheet.

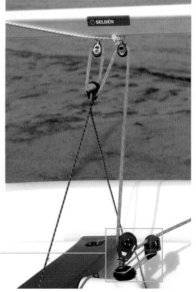

3 **The mainsheet** (red) is threaded through blocks to the main jamming cleat, which allows you to lock or unlock the mainsheet. The top blocks are attached to a bridle rope (blue) which lets them move from side to side.

PREPARING TO HOIST

Hoist sails with the dinghy head to wind.

Always hoist the mainsail with the bow of the dinghy facing into the wind. A sail flapping in a sideways breeze is both dangerous and very difficult to hoist. Do it as close to the water as possible, so you don't have to push the boat too far on its trolley with the mainsail raised. If you have to alter direction and get side-on to the wind, the boat may blow over. If you are sailing where there is no beach, launch the dinghy and moor it alongside the pontoon with the bow into the wind. If the wind is moderate or fresh, postpone hoisting the mainsail until you are ready to go sailing and intend to launch almost straightaway. The mainsail can be hoisted ahead of time in light winds, but you should not leave the boat unattended in case of changes in wind direction or strength.

1 **Fit the tack slider** into the outer end of the groove in the boom and pull it all the way along the boom towards the mast.

2 **Feed the clew** outhaul line through the cringle to control tension in the foot of the sail. Then lead it forward along the boom and cleat it.

3 **Attach the halyard** to the head of the sail. Push the rope through the cringle to form a loop and lock it in place with the bobble.

LUFF GROOVE
One person should feed the bolt rope into the luff groove at the base of the mast. It may be quite tricky to slide it in.

4 **For the hoist,** two people need to work together. One pulls on the halyard while the other feeds the bolt rope into the luff groove.

FITTING THE RUDDER

The rudder stock is fitted to the transom "gudgeon" with a "pintle"; these together form a hinge by which the rudder can be raised or lowered during sailing. To prevent the rudder falling off during a capsize, a spring clip or retaining split pin (as shown here) is fitted to hold it in place.

1 **Align each pintle** with a gudgeon on the transom. This can be tricky to do if the boat is afloat.

2 **With the pintles in place,** make sure the rudder is locked on to the transom by a clip or retaining pin.

REEFING THE MAINSAIL

If the wind is strong, you may choose to reduce the size of the mainsail by reefing. This is not possible on all dinghies, but the system shown here is known as "slab reefing", with an equal amount of sail pulled down at the luff and the leech.

READY TO GO
The boat is fully rigged and ready to go. This is the time to make a decision about whether it's necessary to reef the mainsail.

1 **Reefing must be done** with the bow of the boat facing into the wind. Start by attaching a reefing line to the reefing cringles at the luff of the sail, then lead it down to a cleat on the boom.

2 **You will find** parallel reefing cringles at the leech of the sail. Fit another reefing line here and lead it down to the boom.

3 **Ease off the** halyard and secure it loosely while you pull luff and leech reefing cringles down on to the boom, then re-tension the halyard.

4 **Here, a single reefing line** pulls down both sides of the sail simultaneously. The excess sail is gathered neatly on the boom.

Rigging a single-handed dinghy

Popular single-handed dinghies such as the Laser, Topper, and Pico all have similar rigging, which is simple and quick to assemble. With practice, you should be able to get one of these boats rigged and ready to sail in about 15 minutes, though you may need help lifting the mast.

UNSTAYED RIGS

The principal feature of all these dinghies is that they have no shrouds or forestay to support the mast. Instead, the mast is self-supporting, with the lower part fitting into a tubular mast step in the foredeck. The unstayed mast does not provide the same level of control as a fully stayed rig. It will bend and flex with the wind, but it maintains sufficient stability for the helmsman to manage the sail. Most of these dinghies have aluminium or fibreglass masts that sleeve together in two halves, which is ideal for storage or roof-rack transport. Instead of being pulled up a track in the mast, the sail has a luff sleeve that slides over the mast.

SIMPLE SYSTEMS
A line is stretched across the rear deck, to form a traveller connecting the mainsheet top and bottom blocks, while allowing the boom to swing.

1 **Thread the traveller line** through fairleads on either side of the boat, then through the small block attached to the mainsheet bottom block.

2 **Feed one end of the traveller** through a loop in the other end and lead it to the cleat just behind the cockpit. The traveller is now complete.

3 **The upper half of the traveller** forms an upside-down V for the tiller to pass through when it is held up by the boom.

1 **Rig the boom** with the outhaul control line, which will be attached to the clew of the mainsail at the back and runs through a turning block at the front.

RIGGING THE BOOM

Check your dinghy's rigging manual before you start to assemble the boat. Identify all the hardware, which should include: hull, with a bung to close the drain hole; lower mast; top mast; boom; sail with sail numbers; battens; daggerboard; rudder; tiller and tiller extension. Rope sets and equipment should include: mainsheet and blocks; traveller line and blocks; kicking strap (boom vang) line and blocks; outhaul line; cunningham line and blocks; daggerboard restraining shockcord.

2 **Place the boom on the deck** ready to be rigged. Make sure it is the right way round, with the gooseneck fitting at the front where it attaches to the mast and the mainsheet fitting at the back.

3 **The outhaul line is led down** to a turning block on the deck and back through a jamming cleat by the cockpit. It can be loosened to allow a fuller sail shape when sailing downwind.

4 **The mainsheet is led aft** from a ratchet block in the centre of the cockpit to two blocks at the transom, connecting the outer end of the boom to the traveller line across the back of the boat. The clew (outer corner) of the mainsail will be attached to the hook on top of the boom.

TOP BLOCK
The end of the mainsheet is secured in the top block with a simple figure-of-eight knot.

Face the boat head to wind before rigging the sails.

RIG ASSEMBLY

Rig with the bow of the dinghy facing into the wind. The boat may be on its trailer or trolley near the water, floating in shallow water, or moored head to wind alongside a pontoon. Assemble the mast by slotting the two sections firmly together.

Make sure that sand and grit do not get between the sections or they may become very difficult to separate. Ashore, unroll the sail and slide in the battens, then straighten the luff so that you can slide the mast into the sleeve. Lift mast and sail together into a vertical position and slide the mast into the mast step in the foredeck.

1 **Assemble the two parts** of the mast. Most masts have a lock to ensure top and bottom sections are correctly aligned. Make sure the sections are firmly engaged.

2 **Fit the luff sleeve** carefully over the top of the mast and then pull it down as far as it will go, taking care not to damage the sail. This may be easier with two people.

3 **Slide the sail battens** into the batten pockets. Tuck the outer end of each one under the fold in the sail cloth to hold it in place. Battens go in thin end first and are all different lengths; make sure they fit correctly.

4 **Lift the mast** and sail, and push the mast base right down into the tubular mast step. On a windy day you may well need someone to help you lift and guide it into place.

5 Attach the boom to the mast by sliding in the gooseneck pin. Check your manual for the position of the gooseneck for the sail you are using.

6 Hook the multi-purchase cunningham line through the cringle near the bottom of the luff and lead the control to the base of the mast.

7 Lead the clew outhaul line, which tensions the foot of the sail, via a series of blocks along the boom and at the base of the mast, to a jamming cleat on the foredeck.

8 Attach the hook fitting at the end of the clew outhaul on the boom to the cringle in the clew. Tighten the outhaul to tension the foot of the sail.

RUDDER AND DAGGERBOARD

Fit the rudder to the transom with the rudder blade lifted, pushing the rudder case down until the pintles are locked by the safety clip – this ensures the rudder cannot fall off. Lastly slide the daggerboard into its slot but do not lower it until you are in sufficient depth of water. Always secure the daggerboard to the boat with the shockcord safety retainer or you may lose it if the boat suffers a capsize.

1 Secure the tiller to the rudder case and make sure the tiller goes through the V of the traveller, so that the mainsheet is free to move.

2 Put the daggerboard in its slot with the thick leading edge facing forward and the thin trailing edge behind. Secure it with shockcord.

"ONCE YOU HAVE DONE ALL IN YOUR POWER TO WIN… YOU'RE GOING TO BE HARD TO BEAT."

Dennis Conner

Launching from a beach

Getting afloat requires careful planning and preparation. Your target is to find the safest and easiest place to launch off the beach, make final adjustments to the dinghy in shallow water, get the crew on board, and set off with minimum disturbance to anyone nearby.

BEST LAUNCH SITES

When possible, always choose a gently shelving beach with a sideshore wind. An onshore wind may create waves and make getting off the beach difficult. An offshore wind will get progressively stronger as you sail further away from the shore. If you are in a tidal area, check the state of the tide. The beach may shelve gently at low water and steeply at high water, which could make conditions difficult. Or you may return at low water and find the dinghy has to be dragged over an expanse of mud.

1 **Pull the dinghy** into the water on its trolley. Keep clear of swimmers and other beach users. If other boats are launching or landing, keep to leeward or give them plenty of space.

2 **Make sure the boat** is facing into the wind if the mainsail is hoisted. There is no need to go in deep; the dinghy will float in water just below your knees. Check everything in the cockpit is ready.

3 **When the wheels are underwater,** slide the dinghy off. One person returns the trolley to the beach, while the other holds on to the dinghy by the bow or sidedeck just forward of the mast.

4 **Fit the rudder**, making sure it is locked on to the transom. Lining up the pintles may be tricky if the boat is moving about – the other crew needs to hold it as still as possible.

5 **The helmsman holds the boat** as the crew gets on board. Keep it at a slight angle to the wind so the boom is clear of the cockpit. The wind will help to balance the crew's weight.

6 **The crew lowers the centreboard** as far and as quickly as possible. Without any centreboard, the boat would go sideways instead of forwards.

7 **The helmsman steps on board** holding the tiller, with the rudder partly lowered in the water. The crew unfurls the jib and sheets in, making the boat bear away from the wind.

DON'T FORGET!

Before you set off in your dinghy, always check the bung or plug, which is used to drain the hull of the boat. Make sure it is done up hand-tight. Check any hatches – make sure they are secure and cannot leak, and ensure the tiller is locked into the rudder and cannot come adrift. Make sure the rudder is properly attached so it cannot fall off if the boat capsizes.

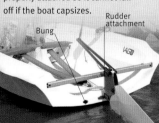

Rudder attachment

Bung

8 **The crew watches** for any obstructions on the way out from the beach. As soon as it is deep enough, the helmsman heads into the wind to slow the boat and drops the rudder to the full-down position.

Returning to a beach

When you head back in to the beach, the basic essentials are to control the speed of your dinghy on the approach, before bringing it to a dead halt in water that is shallow enough for the crew to jump out and hold on, without grounding the boat.

STOPPING THE BOAT

Leave the rudder and centreboard fully down for as long as possible to maintain steerage as you approach the shore. Moderate your speed by rolling the jib or letting it flap, with the mainsheet eased to depower the mainsail. As soon as the crew starts lifting the daggerboard, steer the dinghy into the wind and raise the rudder. The boat should stop when it approaches head to wind, allowing the crew to get out over the windward side and grab the side of the bow.

In stronger onshore winds, it may be easiest to come head to wind to drop the mainsail, then approach the beach under jib alone. Never stand between the beach and the boat if the wind is blowing onshore.

1 **As you approach the beach,** roll up the jib to moderate your speed. Keep a look out for swimmers and other possible obstructions and watch the depth of water.

2 **In shallow water,** half lift the centreboard to prevent grounding and steer the boat into the wind to bring it to a stop. Release any lock-down mechanism on the rudder blade.

3 **The crew jumps out** over the windward side and holds the boat forward of the shroud or by the bow. The helmsman may choose to drop the mainsail before leaving the boat.

4 **The helmsman ensures** the centreboard and rudder blade are both fully up to prevent damaging the foils when the boat is pulled ashore.

5 **The helmsman fetches the trolley** from the beach and points it into the wind, with the cradle just submerged so the dinghy can slide on easily.

6 **Pull the boat by the bow** on to its trolley, then start to push it ashore while keeping the bow pointing into the wind if the mainsail is still hoisted.

7 **Facing head to wind,** there is no need to drop the mainsail before you push the trolley ashore. If you are at an angle to the wind, drop the mainsail first.

TWO APPROACHES

The landing sequence is slightly different, depending on whether the wind is blowing on- or offshore.

You must be head to wind to lower the mainsail so you need to adapt the route of your approach to ensure that you are able to do this safely.

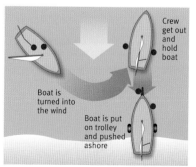

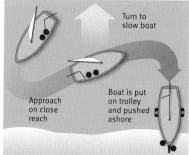

LANDING – ONSHORE WIND
Time your turn into the wind so it is shallow enough for the crew to get out and hold on to the boat without difficulty. Beware of breaking waves.

LANDING – OFFSHORE WIND
Turn into the wind to depower the sails and stop before the bow hits the beach. Roll the jib, but keep rudder and centreboard down as much as possible.

Launching and landing solo

Single-handed sailors can launch and land without assistance in most conditions, though you may need help to park or retrieve the trolley if there is an onshore wind. Plan the launch or landing carefully.

LAUNCHING

Get the boat fully rigged, facing into the wind with the mainsheet slack, the rudder blade lifted, and the daggerboard lying flat in the cockpit. Avoid dragging the dinghy to the water – this may scratch the hull. Instead, use a trolley or ask for help. On the water, keep the dinghy pointing into the wind. Put the centreboard into its slot, push the rudder partly down, and place the tiller extension and mainsheet on the windward side. Push the bow downwind, step into the cockpit, sheet in, and sail slowly until the water is deep enough to push the daggerboard and rudder right down.

1 **Make sure the mainsheet** will run free. In stronger winds, let off the kicking strap to fully depower the mainsail. Walk the boat into water just below your knees.

2 **With the daggerboard and rudder halfway down,** push the bow downwind, step into the boat, and push off with your foot.

3 **Sheet in carefully** so the boat moves slowly away from the shore. Steering will be relatively unresponsive until the rudder is fully down.

4 **As soon as the water** is deep enough, let out the sail. Lean over the transom to push the rudder blade and lock it in the fully down position.

5 **Push the daggerboard fully down.** Make sure the kicking strap is tensioned, then sheet in and sail away.

LANDING

Plan in advance where on the beach you are going to land and at what point you will get out of the boat. Choose an area of shallow water, where you have plenty of space to come head to wind, catch the boat, and get ashore. Look out for swimmers and other obstacles. On the approach, make sure the daggerboard is lifted and the rudder downhaul is undone. If the boat has a self-bailer in the bottom, it should be retracted.

1 **In a fresh wind,** let out the mainsail to slow down. Pull the daggerboard halfway up in plenty of time – never sail it into the ground, which could damage the hull. Lean back to release the rudder downhaul line.

2 **As you approach the shore,** lift the daggerboard. Be on the lookout for obstacles as you near the shore, and choose your approach carefully.

3 **Turn the boat into the wind** and step out on the windward side. Pull out the daggerboard and the rudder to upright. Fetch the trolley or ask for help.

The roles of helmsman and crew

The helmsman and crew work closely together when sailing, managing different parts of the boat or deciding strategy. If you are sailing single-handed or flying a spinnaker, there will always be more than enough to keep you busy, particularly when it is a windy day.

DOUBLE CREW

When there are two or more sailors in a dinghy, the helmsman is likely to act as skipper, deciding whether to tack, gybe, or head back to the shore. However, the crew may be equally able to take on this responsibility, particularly if coaching Wa less experienced helmsman.

The helmsman will steer the boat with the tiller extension (*see below*) – note the downward grip in front of his body, close to the hand holding the mainsheet. This enables him to bring both the tiller and mainsheet hands together for optimum control when sheeting in the sail. The crew is responsible for the centreboard and sheeting the jib on both sides. He or she may also adjust control lines for the outhaul, cunningham, and kicking strap ("kicker" or boom vang), which modify the mainsail's shape. In light or moderate winds, a small amount of kicker tension will power up the mainsail by increasing curvature and reducing twist. In stronger winds, pulling down maximum kicker and cunningham tension will bend the mast and flatten the top of the sail so it twists off, similar to a flat cloth with no power, enabling both crew to keep the boat flat on the water. Raking the centreboard aft may also make sailing upwind easier in stronger winds.

THE MAINSHEET
The helmsman controls the mainsheet in the front hand and tiller in the back hand, with the extension held across the body.

Helmsman

Crew

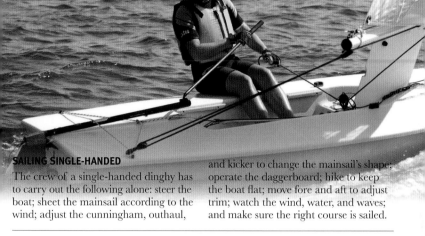

SAILING SINGLE-HANDED

The crew of a single-handed dinghy has to carry out the following alone: steer the boat; sheet the mainsail according to the wind; adjust the cunningham, outhaul, and kicker to change the mainsail's shape; operate the daggerboard; hike to keep the boat flat; move fore and aft to adjust trim; watch the wind, water, and waves; and make sure the right course is sailed.

THE JIB SHEET
The crew has responsibility for controlling the jib sheets on both sides as well as the spinnaker sheets, if fitted.

THE CENTREBOARD
The crew manages the centreboard, which needs to be pulled back to enable it to pivot to the full-down position.

TEAM SAILING
Hiking over the side while sailing to windward, the crew sit close together so their weight is over the widest and most buoyant part of the boat.

Sailing upwind

For sailing upwind you need an instinctive sense of the boat's capabilities. You need to feel that the boat is well balanced, sailing fast, and heading in the right direction, rather than heeling right over, slipping sideways, or pointing too close to the wind.

BEATING TO WINDWARD

Sailing as close as possible towards the wind is known as beating to windward. The sails are pulled in tight to the centreline, with the centreboard or daggerboard fully down to prevent wthe boat from sliding sideways. The helmsman steers a course that compromises between sailing at reasonable speed and pointing as high as possible, which slows the boat down, using telltales on the windward side of the jib as an indicator of when to head up and when to bear away. Both crew members should sit well forward to lift the stern. If necessary, use the toe straps to hike over the side and keep the boat as flat as possible – letting it heel reduces speed and makes steering heavier owing to increased weather helm (*see* Side forces and leeway, pp.68–69).

REACHING

Bearing away on to a close reach or beam reach greatly increases speed. It is important to keep the hull flat to promote planing, which is the moment when the boat starts skimming over the surface of the water on its bow wave. Both crew should slide their weight back to lift the bow as soon as the dinghy starts planing, but be ready to move forward again if the stern sinks.

BEATING IN LIGHT WINDS
The crew sit well forward on either side of the dinghy, ensuring the stern is not dragging. Do not attempt to point high in light winds – just concentrate on keeping the boat moving.

BEATING IN MEDIUM WINDS
The crew hike out to keep the boat as upright as possible, still sitting well forward to lift the stern. Full sails with tight leeches will provide power and enable the dinghy to point high into the wind.

Use both hands to pull in mainsheet

UPWIND POSITIONS

When sailing upwind, both helmsman and crew should sit well forward on the windward side. The helmsman's view may be blocked, so the crew should make it their job to keep a lookout for other boats or obstacles to leeward.

BEAM REACH

When the dinghy starts to plane, move crew aft. Keep the boat as upright as possible. Letting it heel will increase weather helm and slow it down. Pulling down maximum cunningham will help to depower the top of the sail. Sheet the jib to ensure the telltales are streaming.

CLOSE REACH

Easing the sails will increase forward drive. The helmsman can ease the mainsheet to help keep the dinghy upright in gusts. Kicker and cunningham can be used to flatten the sail and open the leech.

Tacking a dinghy

When you tack, you turn the bow of the boat through the eye of the wind and then continue sailing, changing your direction from starboard to port tack (shown here) or vice versa. This basic manoeuvre must be used to sail to any point directly upwind.

TACKING TECHNIQUES

If sailing a two-handed dinghy, the crew has a simple role – keeping the jib sheeted in until the wind catches on the other side, causing it to "back", which helps push the bow round. As soon as it is clear, the boat will complete the tack and the crew should let go of the old sheet, cross over the boat (facing forwards), and pull in on the new side.

The helmsman's role is more difficult and requires practice to achieve a fluid, controlled movement from one side of the boat to the other (*see below*). The helmsman steers into the tack with the mainsheet slightly eased. As the boom crosses the boat, he or she twists around to cross the boat without letting go of the tiller or mainsheet. The helmsman then adjusts the mainsheet.

Experienced sailors use a technique called "roll tacking" if they need to tack frequently in light and gusty winds. Body weight is used to turn the boat with a dynamic movement that drives air into the sails as the boat is rolled on to the new tack, heeling from side to side. The crew stays down on the leeward side as the boat spins round, then moves across quickly to the new windward side to help flatten the boat.

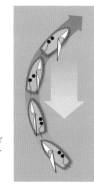

BOAT MOVEMENT
When tacking, the boat changes direction across the wind so that the sails set on the other side.

PRACTISING HELMING TECHNIQUES

The technique for crossing the boat while holding the mainsheet and tiller varies according to the length of the tiller extension and how it fits through the space between boom, mainsheet, and helm. Practice is the only way to work out the most effective routine. The other technique that requires practice is how to change hands on the tiller and mainsheet while keeping control throughout the manoeuvre. The usual method is to hold the tiller behind your back before starting the tack as, shown below.

1 **Practise helming** while holding the tiller behind your back in your front hand and the mainsheet in your back hand. In light winds you may cleat the mainsheet.

2 **Grab the tiller extension** with your back hand while still holding the mainsheet (which can run through your fingers). Then bring your front hand around your body.

3 **Grab the mainsheet** with your front hand and flick the tiller extension into the sailing position across the front of your body without moving the rudder.

1 **When sailing** flat and fast upwind, the helmsman instructs the crew "Ready about!" The crew replies "Ready!" The helmsman says "Lee-oh!" while pushing the tiller to leeward with the mainsheet slightly eased and uncleated.

2 **Letting the boat** heel to windward can help the turn. If you push the tiller further than shown here you may stall the boat in a head-to-wind position. In this case, you will need to back the jib on the windward side.

3 **The jib "backs"** when wind starts to fill it from the new windward side, helping to push the bow on to the new tack. When the bow has passed through the eye of the wind, the crew lets go of the old jib sheet and ducks under the boom to cross to the other side, ready to sheet in the jib on the new side.

4 **Having flicked** the tiller extension to the new side, the helmsman pivots to cross the boat facing forwards, holding both sheet and tiller during this manoeuvre and sliding his or her hand along the extension.

5 **Both crew sheet in** to power up the boat on the new tack, ensuring it stays flat. The helmsman moves the sheet to the front hand and tiller extension to the back hand. Tacking like this requires a lot of practice to achieve a smooth transition.

Sailing downwind

When you bear away from a reach, you are "running" downwind with the wind blowing from behind. Reduced airflow over both sides of the sail slows the boat down as apparent wind (the difference between your boat speed and the true wind speed) is reduced.

WIND BEHIND
When sailing with the wind blowing from behind the boat, let out the mainsail and pull up the daggerboard (or centreboard).

KEEP THE BOAT BALANCED

As the boat bears away to a downwind course with the wind right behind, the crew can balance the boat by sitting on either side. The daggerboard or centreboard can be fully lifted when sailing on flat water, or leave it part down for increased stability if the boat starts to roll. Let the mainsail out as far as possible, without letting it press hard against the shroud, which may distort and possibly damage the sail.

DOWNWIND ALONE

Balancing a boat when sailing single-handed downwind can be more difficult in stronger winds, with the boat tending to roll due to the crew being on only one side. You will go fastest with the mainsheet let right out at 90 degrees, but be more stable if you pull it partly back in. The cunningham and outhaul can be let off to provide a fuller shape. The daggerboard or centreboard can be lifted halfway on most single-handed dinghies, but should be left fully down to maintain

BROAD REACH
Here, with the wind blowing diagonally across the stern on the windward side, the dinghy is on a broad reach. With air flowing on both sides of the sails, the boat can achieve good speeds.

balance on a dinghy with an asymmetric spinnaker. Move your weight far enough back to prevent the bow from burying and be ready to shift your weight from side to side if the boat rolls. Keep steering movement to a minimum. The boat will tend to bear away if it rolls to windward and head up if it rolls to leeward. Unless you are "goosewinging" (*see below*), avoid sailing "by the lee" with the wind blowing across the stern from the leeward side, which may cause an unexpected gybe. If you are not sure of the exact wind direction, turn slightly into the wind.

GOOSEWINGING
On a direct downwind course the jib is blanketed by the mainsail. The solution is to "goosewing" it on the windward side (*see* p.73). It may be necessary to sail slightly by the lee with the crew holding the boom out to prevent an accidental gybe, while the helmsman holds the jib sheet.

ON A RUN
Here, the wind is blowing almost directly from behind. With air pushing rather than flowing over the sails, the boat sails more slowly than on a broad reach.

Gybing a dinghy

When you gybe, the stern turns through the eye of the wind, changing your downwind direction from starboard to port gybe (shown here) or vice versa. The mainsail swings in a wide arc across the boat and is always fully powered, so gybing is challenging in strong winds.

TROUBLE-FREE GYBES

The object of gybing is to change course from one tack to the other (from starboard to port tack in the picture sequence here) while sailing downwind. This requires precise control of the tiller, ensuring a smooth turn with the wind behind. As soon as the wind is on the lee side (blowing over the port side of the stern in the photo, *right*), the helm or crew should help pull the boom across the boat. Don't wait until the wind catches the mainsail on the leeward side and blows it over, which may send the boat in to an uncontrolled gybe. With poor rudder control and the momentum of the boom crossing from side to side, there is a tendency to let the boat round up into the wind and heel over, which is an excellent way to capsize. Keep the boat running deep downwind during the gybe.

GYBING
During a gybe the boat turns across the eye of the wind while sailing downwind.

1 **The helmsman says** "Ready to gybe!", the crew replies "Ready!" and the helmsman instructs "Gybe-oh!" as he or she bears away into the gybe.

2 **The helmsman moves the tiller** to steer into the gybe and then flicks the tiller extension over to the new side while swivelling to face forward. The boat is allowed to heel slightly to windward to help the turn.

3 **As the boat approaches a dead downwind course**, the helmsman grabs the falls of the mainsheet with his front hand and keeps steering round into the gybe. The crew is ready to duck when the boom crosses the boat.

4 **Once the stern has turned through** the eye of the wind, the helmsman pulls the mainsail and boom firmly across to the new side, keeping the boat level. Both helmsman and crew duck as the boom comes across.

5 **The helmsman then changes sides,** making sure to keep hold of both the mainsheet and the tiller extension all the time, in order to maintain control of the boat's balance and direction throughout the gybe.

7 **The helmsman adjusts his hands** on the mainsheet and tiller and corrects the course on the new side. A successful gybe is one where the boat has remained stable and moving smoothly throughout the manoeuvre.

6 **The helmsman** straightens out the course on the new gybe, while the crew sheets in the jib on the new windward side.

GYBING SINGLE-HANDED

Many single-handed dinghies are sensitive to gybe. During the turn, you need to keep the dinghy fairly level and the daggerboard should be halfway up to prevent it from tipping over. As the boat bears off into the gybe, take hold of the mainsheet (as shown) to pull the boom in a controlled way across to the new side. Duck as the boom comes over, crossing the boat to face forward, with the tiller behind your back on the new side.

Simple capsize drill

Capsizing is all part of the fun of learning to sail dinghies – you capsize, then you flip the boat upright again. The simple one-person technique shown here can easily be adapted for two people. If you have difficulties, the golden rule is "always stay with your boat".

KEEP IT SIMPLE
When a capsize is past the point of no return, let go. Clinging on may pull the boat right over and make recovery more difficult.

DRY CAPSIZE

The standard "dry" capsize happens when sailing upwind and the boat is blown over to leeward. This type of capsize should happen slowly enough for you to face forward, swing your front leg over the side of the boat and step smartly on to the daggerboard as the dinghy turns over at 90 degrees. Make sure the mainsheet is running free, then grab hold of the gunwale and lean back to pull the boat slowly upright. As the rig lifts off the water, the bow will spin into the wind. When the daggerboard starts to go underwater, slide into the cockpit and prepare to hold the boat level.

WET CAPSIZE

If you fall into the water – a wet capsize – push the daggerboard fully down and uncleat the mainsheet. Hold the end of the mainsheet, while you swim round the stern. Let go the mainsheet once you have a firm grip on the daggerboard. In windy conditions, swim to the bow and hang on, letting the boat pivot around you until it is head to wind. Then go to the daggerboard and start righting.

CAPSIZE TO WINDWARD

When sailing downwind, you may capsize to windward, with the boat rolling on top of you. Hold the mainsheet as the boat goes over to ensure you do not become separated from it. If the mainsail comes down on top of you, think calmly and swim from underneath. As in a wet capsize, before righting, push the daggerboard fully down and uncleat the mainsheet.

Pushing the daggerboard

1 **A dinghy on its side** can blow downwind quite quickly. Make sure you are connected to the boat when you swim round the stern. Uncleat the mainsheet and hold the end, but take care not to become entangled in it.

2 **Fully lower the daggerboard** and pull down on it to start lifting the rig off the water. If necessary, you may need to climb on to the daggerboard to give extra leverage. Don't worry, the daggerboard is stronger than it looks.

3 **As the rig lifts** the dinghy will turn steadily towards the wind, which will start to blow under the rig and help lift the boat back upright. Don't exhaust yourself by struggling; let the wind do most of the work for you.

4 **Grab the gunwale** as soon as you can reach, to help pull the dinghy upright, still keeping one hand on the daggerboard. At this point the dinghy has almost turned head to wind and should be more or less stationary in the water.

5 **Pull yourself on to the side** deck and into the cockpit. The boat will rock as your weight moves about, so be prepared to balance it, and ensure the mainsheet is running freely. Get your breath back and start sailing!

Inverted capsize drill

In a capsize sometimes the boat becomes inverted, making righting more complicated. The scoop method is a way of helping a two-person crew back into the boat. This reduces the effort needed and helps to prevent the boat blowing over into a capsize on the other side.

SCOOP THE CREW

In a two-person dinghy after a simple capsize, follow steps 3 to 5 of the procedure outlined on these pages.
In the case of a full inversion you will first need to bring the boat on to its side, as in steps 1 and 2.

Following a capsize when there are two crew, the helmsman swims round to the underside of the boat, holding the end of the mainsheet so that he or she cannot become separated from the boat. The helmsman should reach up and grab the centreboard, which will prevent the dinghy inverting. If the centreboard is not fully down, the crew can swim into the cockpit area and make sure it is fully lowered, also checking that the

mainsheet and jib sheets are uncleated and will run freely. Many modern dinghies have a righting line on each side. If not, the crew should throw the top jib sheet over to where the helmsman can catch it. The helmsman can then lie back in the water, with both feet on the gunwale, and pull down on the righting line or jib sheet. The alternative is to clamber on to the centreboard, which will provide more righting moment.

As the boat comes upright, the crew should be able to roll into the cockpit without pulling that side of the boat down. The helmsman can step from the centreboard into the cockpit or, if in the water, over the transom.

1 **If the boat has turned upside down,** first check that you are both safe. Swim to the middle, where you can both hold the gunwale or centreboard. A smaller crew can stand on the gunwale to reach the centreboard.

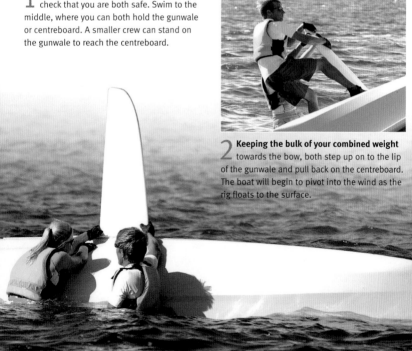

2 **Keeping the bulk of your combined weight** towards the bow, both step up on to the lip of the gunwale and pull back on the centreboard. The boat will begin to pivot into the wind as the rig floats to the surface.

WAITING FOR HELP

If you are unable to get the boat upright, do not leave it and swim for shore. You are much safer hanging on and waiting for help. A capsized dinghy will continue to float, even with two crew on the upturned hull, and is easily spotted by a rescue team. Do not become separated from the boat when it capsizes. Hold on to whatever you can reach – the dinghy will probably blow downwind faster than you can swim.

3 **In the normal righting** position, the helmsman stands on the centreboard while the crew stays beside the cockpit, forward of the centre mainsheet position, without putting any weight on the hull.

4 **The helmsman leans back** on the righting line to pull the boat upright, which "scoops" the crew into the cockpit as the helmsman steps in over the other side.

5 **Both crew should be** ready to stabilize the boat as it comes fully upright. Then sheet in on to a reach to drain out excess water. If self-bailers are fitted, they will need to be opened.

Rigging a spinnaker

The spinnaker is a powerful sail that provides plenty of downwind sailing fun. The asymmetric spinnaker shown here is the spinnaker of choice for all modern dinghy classes, having taken over from the traditional and more complex symmetrical spinnaker.

RIGGING A SPINNAKER

When not in use, a modern spinnaker is stowed, ready rigged, in a chute that runs the length of the foredeck and back towards the cockpit. The spinnaker halyard is a continuous loop of rope led through the spinnaker chute to the bow of the dinghy, diagonally up to a fixed block on the mast, down the mast, and back round a turning block inside the cockpit. Pulling the halyard backwards hoists the spinnaker up the mast; pulling the halyard forwards pulls the spinnaker back inside its chute.

Choose a quiet day for rigging, put the boat where there is plenty of space, and lay the spinnaker out flat beside it. First of all, look carefully at the shape of the sail to identify the three corners.

The tack (bottom forward corner) is secured to the forward end of the spinnaker pole; the head (top corner), is attached to the uphaul end of the halyard; the clew, or outer corner, is attached to sheets. There are patches supporting rings on the vertical mid-line of the sail, through which the downhaul is led. These help to gather the sail into the chute when it is lowered.

After rigging, do a test hoist before you go on the water. Face the boat into the wind and pull up the halyard slowly to ensure that there are no twists in the sail or sheets, and that you have the three corners of the sail the right way round. Then retrieve it carefully into the chute, keeping it well clear of anything that might snag the sail.

1 **Tie the spinnaker tack** to the tack line on the end of the spinnaker pole with a bowline. Double over the continuous spinnaker sheet in the middle and push the loop through the cringle on the clew; pull the sheet ends through the loop to knot firmly in place.

TYING THE BOWLINE
When tying a bowline on to the tack or head of the sail, pull it tightly on to the stainless steel cringle. This will help the sail to set correctly

2 **Pass both spinnaker sheet ends** outside the jib luff and outside the shrouds. Ratchet blocks work in one direction only – the sheet should "click-and-lock" under tension.

3 **Tie the two free ends** of the spinnaker sheets together in the cockpit. When the crew grabs the sheet, it can be pulled either way.

4 **The downhaul end of the halyard** passes through a tack ring to a patch further up the sail. This helps gather the sail when you pull it down.

5 **Check that the downhaul** pulls the whole sail inside the chute, with just the head and clew protruding. The spinnaker is now ready for hoisting.

HANDLING THE SPINNAKER

To hoist, drop, or gybe the spinnaker, the helmsman must bear off downwind until sideways force on the rig is reduced to a minimum. This ensures that both crew can work safely from the centre of the boat, with the mainsail blanketing the spinnaker area.

1 **To hoist the spinnaker,** pull the halyard hand over hand as fast as possible to ensure that the sail does not catch on the bow.

2 **As the crew continues to hoist the spinnaker,** the helmsman maintains a steady downwind course to prevent the spinnaker filling too soon.

3 **With the spinnaker fully hoisted** and the halyard cleated, the crew sheets in as the helmsman luffs on to a broad reach to power the sail.

Sailing with a spinnaker

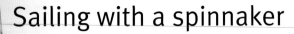

The popular asymmetric spinnaker shown here is easy to use and provides boost when sailing downwind on a broad reach and responds to the slightest of breezes.

PLANING
The powerful spinnaker quickly lifts the dinghy on to a plane

STEERING WITH A SPINNAKER

The technique for sailing with an asymmetric spinnaker relies on sailing the boat flat at full speed on a broad reach, bearing away when a gust hits so that the boat stays level with less sideways pressure on the sails, then luffing as the gust passes to keep the boat flat with increased sideways pressure. This means that unless the wind is absolutely steady, you will never sail in a perfectly straight line towards your target. Instead, you will keep steering in a series of smooth curves to port or starboard to ensure the boat stays flat and fully powered. Never sail low and go slow with a spinnaker. Always head up and sail fast, then bear away on the apparent wind.

DROPPING A SPINNAKER

Bear right away for the drop, so that the spinnaker is blanketed and the crew can work from the centre of the boat. To control the drop, the crew can stand on the sheet or pass it to the helmsman, then take up all slack on the retrieval line before uncleating the halyard. Pull the spinnaker back into its chute as quickly as possible.

BALANCING THE BOAT
Helmsman and crew should work together to keep the boat as level as possible on the water for maximum speed. The crew constantly trims the spinnaker to make the most of the wind.

SAFE SPINNAKER WORK
There is least pressure on the spinnaker when the wind is directly astern of the dinghy. As soon as the boat luffs on to a broad reach, you move into a "power zone" where the spinnaker will catch the wind, power up, and make hoisting or dropping the spinnaker less safe.

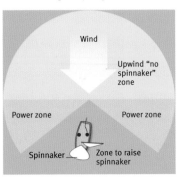

Wind

Upwind "no spinnaker" zone

Power zone

Power zone

Spinnaker

Zone to raise spinnaker

GYBING WITH A SPINNAKER

Dinghies with asymmetric spinnakers sail a direct downwind course by gybing from side to side on a series of broad reaches. When gybing with a spinnaker, the helm should steer a gentle curve from broad reach to broad reach, matching the speed of the turn to the ability of the crew to cross the boat and sheet in the spinnaker on the new side. The boat should stay flat and keep moving at speed throughout the gybe, rather than slowing right down and getting knocked over by the apparent wind.

While concentrating on the spinnaker, don't forget that the mainsail is also gybing, with the boom swinging across the cockpit.

QUICK GYBE
Keep speed up throughout the gybe. Sailing fast reduces load on the rig as the mainsail comes across and the crew sheets in on the new side.

1 **The crew gets ready for** the gybe by moving into the cockpit and taking up slack on the new sheet.

2 **Bearing off downwind,** the crew pulls on the old sheet to flatten the spinnaker in mid-gybe.

4 **The helmsman** straightens the boat out on the new course. The crew trims the spinnaker so the luff is just starting to curl, which provides maximum power.

3 **The crew pulls in the new** sheet and lets the old sheet run free, while moving on to the side deck.

"A GOOD HELMSMAN... USES ALL

HIS SENSES – EVEN HIS SENSE

OF SMELL!"

Arthur Knapp

Simple trapezing

A trapeze allows the crew to stand on the side of the boat, suspended from a wire attached to the mast. This provides a lot more leverage and is less tiring than hiking out, as the crew's lower back is fully supported by the trapeze harness. It is also enormous fun.

CLIPPING ON

If necessary, adjust the length of the trapeze wire so it's easy to get hooked on while sitting on the side of the boat (see p.137). When you attach the trapeze ring, use the adjustable straps of the trapeze harness to pull the hook tight to your body, The hook mounted on a bar helps spread the load to the sides and back of the harness. The shape of the ring ensures it will not fall off the hook if you keep it under tension.

1 **Hold the ring up** when you pull it on to the hook. If necessary adjust your harness so that the hook is near your centre of gravity at around hip level.

2 **Slip the hook on to the ring** as the boat starts to heel. Lean back in a hiking position to put the trapeze wire under tension. Hold the handle on the wire with your front hand, and use your feet to start pushing yourself out.

3 **The front foot goes out first** on to the sidedeck, with your weight on the wire. Keep hold of the jib or spinnaker sheet with your other hand, to help balance your position and keep the sail trimmed.

4 **Follow immediately** with the back foot, and relax into the pull of the harness in a crouching position.

5 **Straighten your legs** and let go of the handle. Face forward with the front leg supporting your weight and the back leg providing balance. Flex your knees with the movement of the boat, and enjoy the sensation of flying over the water.

TACKING ON THE WIRE

During a tack, the helmsman must give the crew sufficient time to come in off the wire, unhook, and then get out on the new side, with good communication throughout the manoeuvre. At the same time, the crew has to keep control of the jib, to help the bows of the boat round. Experienced crews might try a faster tack, going "wire to wire". This is done by catching the handle to go right out on the new side before hooking on.

1 **Here, the crew is trapezing low** for maximum leverage on starboard tack. When the helmsman asks, "Ready about?" she prepares for the tack and replies, "Ready!", pulling in the sheet as necessary.

2 **The helmsman steers carefully** into the wind while the crew bends both legs to come in off the wire, reversing the procedure for going out. At the same time she will need to hold the sheet to control the jib.

3 **The crew moves just ahead** of the helmsman during the tack, ducking under the boom, grabbing the new trapeze ring, then turning forward and hooking on.

4 **The crew starts to go out** on the wire, trimming the jib sheet on port tack. With experience, a crew can be out on the trapeze before the helm has sat down on the new side.

5 **Get into a relaxed position** on the wire with your feet close together and knees slightly bent. If necessary, grab the shoulder strap of the helmsman's buoyancy aid to steady yourself.

Advanced trapezing

On high performance skiff-style dinghies and catamarans it has become normal for both helm and crew to use trapezes, with the helm steering the boat "on the wire". This provides double leverage and double fun.

HELMING ON THE WIRE

It is a challenge to be able to go out on a trapeze and helm at the same time. The first skill to master is going in and out on the wire without moving the tiller and changing course. A good method of achieving this is to "lock" the tiller extension by holding it down in position against the side of the boat.

Once out on the wire, the helmsman has to keep the boat fully powered. If the boat loses power and rolls over to windward, it may be difficult for the helmsman to get inboard. In this situation it is easier for the crew to move, and he or she should react quickly to provide the necessary counterbalance.

In winds above Force 3, both crew are likely to get out on the wire when sailing upwind, with their bodies close together. The helmsman may go out on the wire or stay in on the boat sailing downwind on a reach. This depends on whether progress is improved by sailing out on the wire or in on the side.

SINGLE-HANDED ON THE WIRE
The Musto Skiff is for experts only, with a powerful mainsail and a huge spinnaker operated by a solo helmsman on the trapeze.

1 **The crew goes out first** on the wire, with both feet on the rack. The helm is hooked on, swinging out with both feet on the sides of the boat. Note that the tiller extension is "locked" on to the rack.

2 **The helmsman steps out on to the rack** with his front foot, then follows with his back foot, keeping the tiller extension "locked" so that the boat sails in a straight line. Note that an extra long tiller extension is required.

3 **With two people on the wire,** the crew should trapeze at a slightly lower angle so that the helmsman has a clear view forwards. Both crew "walk" to tack, skiff-style.

COMING IN

Coming in from the wire, either because conditions change or you need to tack, requires coordination between helmsman and crew to maintain boat balance. Having the tiller to manage as well, the helmsman's task is challenging.

KEEPING CONTROL
Both crew bend their knees to come in off the trapeze wires. Holding tiller extension and mainsheet in his back hand, the helmsman grabs the trapeze handle to stand up and unhook. The crew maintains a firm grip on the sheet.

ADJUSTING HEIGHT

Most systems have adjustable height rings so you can alter the trapezing angle. This is useful when moving back along the side of the boat for a fast reach, or if it is necessary to lift your body higher to clear waves. A jamming cleat allows the crew to raise or lower the hook while on the wire, with weight temporarily supported by one arm.

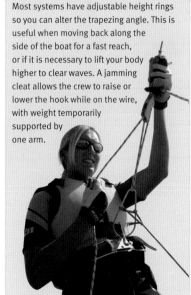

Introduction to catamarans

Small "beach cats", such as the Hobie 16 featured in this section, require slightly different techniques from sailing a dinghy. While all the principles of wind, balance, and trim are the same, "Go for speed!" is always the golden rule for catamaran sailors.

ANATOMY OF A CATAMARAN

Look at the photographs on this page, and it will become clear why catamarans can sail so fast. Both crews are flying the windward hull, with just the leeward hull in the water. That super-slim hull has much less wetted surface area than any dinghy, which means there is far less drag. In addition, each of these catamarans has a beam of 2.43m (8ft), which is wider than any conventional dinghy hull (although not as wide as some high-performance dinghies fitted with wings or racks). The beam of a catamaran gives a crew with twin trapezes a huge amount of leverage, which allows them to sail with a bigger rig than a similar length monohull.

FULL SPEED UPWIND
This Hurricane 5.9 is beating upwind. It will not point as high as a dinghy but will sail a lot faster. Here the crew hit full speed sailing to windward.

KEEPING A CATAMARAN UP TO SPEED

Catamarans perform best in moderate to fresh winds of Force 3–5. They rely on being able to lift the windward hull to sail fast. In lighter winds they tend to stick to the water, and can be frustrating to sail. In stronger winds, the speed of a catamaran can make it difficult to control, with a spectacular cartwheel capsize known as "pitchpoling" likely to catch less experienced sailors.

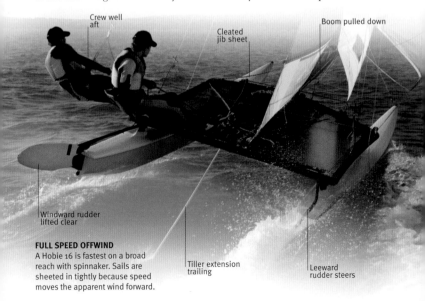

Crew well aft

Cleated jib sheet

Boom pulled down

Windward rudder lifted clear

FULL SPEED OFFWIND
A Hobie 16 is fastest on a broad reach with spinnaker. Sails are sheeted in tightly because speed moves the apparent wind forward.

Tiller extension trailing

Leeward rudder steers

RIGGING

The rigging procedure of individual makes of catamaran vary. Catamaran novices are advised to familiarize themselves with the manual and, ideally, to practise rigging with someone experienced with this type of boat. The steps below indicate some of the key stages of rigging a Hobie 16. Most catamarans have full-length battens in the mainsail, which create rigidity at speed; the jib may also have battens to help stabilize the sail. Loads on the sails are extremely high. Most have a halyard lock at the top of the mast, which is designed to stop the halyard stretching.

Hoist sails with the catamaran head to wind.

1 **Clip the jib on a Hobie 16** to the forestay with plastic "hanks". Other catamarans have a full-length zip up the jib luff.

2 **The mainsail headboard** withstands heavy loads. The bolt rope fits into a slot in the mast, and a double purchase on the halyard makes it easier to hoist.

3 **When the mainsail is pulled** to the top of the mast and the halyard is locked, insert the boom fitting into the mast slot and pull it down firmly.

4 **Rig the multi-purchase mainsheet,** which controls the mainsail. It is combined with a traveller control that allows the mainsheet to slide across the width of both hulls.

5 **Pull down the luff of the mainsail tightly.** The downhaul controls the distribution of power in the sail.

Catamaran launching and landing

Two hulls mean that a special technique is needed to launch or retrieve a catamaran on its trolley. Once on the water, the catamaran provides the crew with an extremely stable platform as they prepare to leave the beach or come in from sailing.

LAUNCHING A CATAMARAN

As with any dinghy, you should rig the sails of a catamaran as close to the water as possible. A catamaran trolley has two wheels on a central axle, with supports for the twin hulls. To put the trolley in place, one crew lifts a bow while the other pushes the trolley underneath.

The trolley supports should be pushed as far back as the balance point of the hulls, usually just behind the front beam. Oversize tyres make it possible to wheel the boat on its trolley, even across soft sand or loose shingle.

1 **A catamaran is rigid enough** for the whole boat to be lifted by one bow. Raise the rudders, and protect the sterns from the ground – two old tyres are suitable for this.

2 **With sails uncleated, and the trolley under** the balance point of the twin hulls, push the catamaran into the water until it is deep enough to float. Then remove the trolley.

3 **If the wind is sideshore** or onshore, the crew can hop on and sail away. In an offshore wind they can "reverse" away from the beach, sitting on the bows with the sterns lifted.

4 **The leeward rudder** must be locked down before the helmsman can power up the mainsail. If the rudder blade is partly lifted, there will be marked weather helm.

COMING ASHORE

Landing a catamaran is usually simple – if the sand is soft you can even sail up the beach. Control your speed as you come ashore, and watch for swimmers. Keep the rudders down to maintain control; if you do not lift them in time, they will knock up on impact with the ground. In more difficult situations, such as a strong onshore wind pushing waves on to the beach, it is good practice to drop the mainsail offshore, roll it on the trampoline, and sail in under jib alone. If approaching a slipway, stop the boat by turning head to wind as you reach the slip, but do not let it ground.

1 **Lift the rudders** when the water is shallow enough to bring the catamaran to a halt by turning head to wind, then jump over the side to hold the boat. Release the downhaul and mainsheet to depower the mainsail.

2 **Most catamarans have a rudder** system that locks the blade up or down and also ensures it will release on impact with the ground. The Hobie rudders are raised or lowered by pulling or pushing on the tiller.

3 **With rudders lifted,** a catamaran will float in very shallow water. Pull it in close to the beach before collecting the trolley. Use the bridle wire (connecting the hulls to the forestay) as a firm point by which to pull the boat.

4 **Line the trolley up.** Then, with one crew holding each hull, push the trolley back with your feet until it is in the correct depth of water to slide underneath without the tyres floating out of position when you start to pull.

Sailing a catamaran

If the wind is strong enough to lift the windward hull, a catamaran will always sail on the apparent wind – meaning that speed forwards through the water tightens the angle of the wind so that it always appears to be blowing from ahead, irrespective of the course sailed.

SAIL FREE AND FAST

The principal requirement of catamaran sailing is to build up apparent wind. When beating upwind, do not try to sail as close to the wind as possible, as with a conventional dinghy. Instead, bear off a few degrees to power up the rig's forward drive. Increased speed will more than compensate for lack of pointing.

Like any boat, a catamaran is at its fastest on a reach. On a run, with airflow over one side of the sails only, and both hulls down in the water, a catamaran is slow. To compensate, catamaran sailors should "tack downwind". Start on a beam reach and head up towards the wind to build up power, lift the windward hull, and increase speed. The result is that the apparent wind direction moves ahead and the helmsman can bear away downwind, still sailing at speed and keeping the hull flying. If the speed decreases and the windward hull drops, he will head up towards the wind, then bear away again, with a succession of gybes taking the boat to a point dead downwind. A catamaran that "tacks" downwind will sail considerably farther than one sailing on a dead run, but owing to far greater speed will always reach a downwind point first.

FULL BORE
Sailing downwind on a three-sail reach, the mainsail is sheeted almost on the centreline due to the apparent wind angle and the speed of the catamaran. The helmsman keeps maximum control by holding the tiller bar and letting the tiller extension trail.

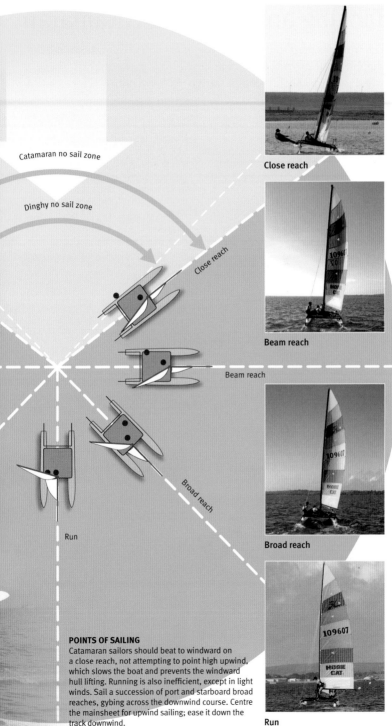

Catamaran no sail zone

Dinghy no sail zone

Close reach

Beam reach

Broad reach

Run

Close reach

Beam reach

Broad reach

Run

POINTS OF SAILING
Catamaran sailors should beat to windward on a close reach, not attempting to point high upwind, which slows the boat and prevents the windward hull lifting. Running is also inefficient, except in light winds. Sail a succession of port and starboard broad reaches, gybing across the downwind course. Centre the mainsheet for upwind sailing; ease it down the track downwind.

Tacking and gybing a catamaran

Catamarans tend to tack and gybe more slowly than monohull dinghies, but provide better stability. This is particularly noticeable when gybing, which is comparatively easy to control. The technique for both manoeuvres is very different from a centre mainsheet dinghy.

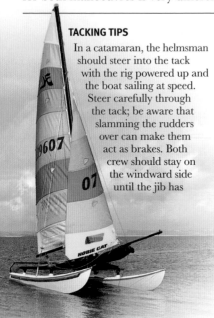

TACKING TIPS

In a catamaran, the helmsman should steer into the tack with the rig powered up and the boat sailing at speed. Steer carefully through the tack; be aware that slamming the rudders over can make them act as brakes. Both crew should stay on the windward side until the jib has backed. This will help to lift the leeward hull, so that the catamaran pivots on the inside hull. Keep both the mainsheet and jib sheet pulled in tight until the jib starts to back and the bows bear away on the new tack. The helmsman should face aft while moving across the boat, easing the mainsheet to help "pop" the battens into their new position and accelerate the catamaran on to the new tack.

TACKING
Crossing the eye of the wind to windward is essentially similar for catamarans and dinghies, but usually you are tacking from a close reach instead of a close hauled course.

1 **As you start to tack,** keep the jib backed in order to help turn the bows, as catamarans are often slow to turn through the wind. High-performance catamarans with daggerboards can pivot more quickly through the turn.

2 **The helmsman faces aft** as he crosses the boat, easing the mainsheet before ducking under the boom. The crew watches the mainsail carefully, waiting until the mainsail has filled on the new side.

3 **When the mainsail has filled** on the new side, the crew pulls in the jib on that side. The helmsman and crew take up their new positions, ready to accelerate on the new tack before luffing to the new close reaching course.

GYBING TIPS

Catamarans are easier to gybe than monohull dinghies because they are more stable, and are unlikely to capsize when both hulls are on the water. As with any sailing boat, gybing becomes more challenging in stronger winds. Be aware that if you steer a catamaran into a gybe at high speed and then slow right down, the apparent wind will swing behind the boat and power up the rig midway through the gybe. Keeping the boat at a steady speed throughout the turn is the surest way to maintain control. As with tacking, the helmsman should steer carefully and progressively through the manoeuvre to avoid turning the rudders into brakes and halting part way through the turn.

GYBING
Crossing the eye of the wind on to a downwind course you are usually gybing from broad reach to broad reach.

1 **The catamaran is at maximum speed** as it bears away into the gybe. In light winds especially, the crew weight should be kept forward so the sterns do not dig into the water and slow the boat.

2 **The helmsman faces aft** while the crew faces forward as they cross the trampoline. At the right moment, the helmsman must flip the tiller extension past the boom end, on to the new side.

3 **The helmsman takes hold of the falls of the mainsheet** to pull the mainsail over to complete the gybe, while at the same time steering through the downwind point on to the new course.

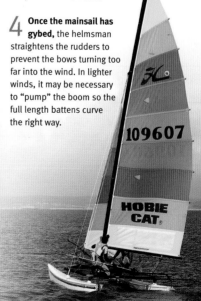

4 **Once the mainsail has gybed,** the helmsman straightens the rudders to prevent the bows turning too far into the wind. In lighter winds, it may be necessary to "pump" the boom so the full length battens curve the right way.

"WE HAVE SALT IN OUR BLOOD,

IN OUR SWEAT, IN OUR TEARS –

WE ARE TIED TO THE OCEAN."

John Fitzgerald Kennedy

Catamaran capsize

When a catamaran capsizes, the crew
need good technique in order to pull it
up. This may include righting from
a pitchpole or from total inversion.

GOING OVER

A catamaran can capsize by being blown
over sideways, or by driving the leeward
bow into the water and "pitchpoling"
(nose-diving), as shown here. If you are
out on the trapeze, try not to fall into
the mainsail as this could break
battens or push the boat upside
down. Beware also of being thrown
forward in a pitchpole, when the
crew may swing round the bows
as the boat suddenly decelerates.
A catamaran floating on its side
may be blown downwind faster
than you can swim, so grab
something as soon as you are
in the water, to maintain
contact. You can climb
on to the lower hull of
a capsized catamaran,
or the underneath of the
trampoline if it is upside
down. Both are secure
positions while you
prepare to right.

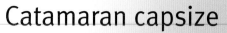

PITCHPOLING
Catamarans have a tendency
to dig the leeward bow into the
water when unbalanced, resulting
in a head-first capsize.

KEEP CLEAR
If the catamaran starts to invert, swim clear
of the trampoline to ensure you are not trapped
underneath the boat.

1 **If the catamaran is upside down,** the crew should scramble on to the bottom hull, standing forward so that the bows swing round into the wind. The boat will then be under control as it rights.

2 **With both crew standing** on the bottom hull, lead the righting line (normally in a pocket close to the mast base) over the upper (windward) hull. Pull to lift the windward bow, helping the rig float to the surface.

3 **Make sure all sheets are uncleated** and pull again on the righting line to lift the rig out of the water. Once the wind can blow under the rig, giving additional lifting power, righting should be easy.

4 **A lightweight crew may have** insufficient leverage to lift the rig. One solution is for the crew to "piggyback" on the helmsman. If that does not work, a rescue boat may be needed to help lift the mast.

5 **The catamaran will accelerate as it rolls** upright. Both crew should drop into the water by the front beam, ready to hold the boat steady as the hull comes down, and prevent another capsize.

6 **Climb back on board** from the side. Climbing over the front beam can be difficult; clambering over the rear beam risks bruises or, more seriously, a bent tiller bar.

Dinghy racing

There is nothing like dinghy racing to improve sailing and boat handling skills. It not only shows you how to sail as quickly and efficiently as possible, but also how to manoeuvre and avoid problems when sailing close to other boats.

RACING GOALS

Sailing is a sport which should always be enjoyable. After you have mastered the basics of sailing around the bay, where do you go next? More wind will certainly entertain you, because that's when all boats become more exciting but also more difficult to sail. Even there you may eventually reach a limit where it seems easy to go screaming up and down, posing the problem that too much of a good thing will inevitably get boring. The solution is easy. Go dinghy racing and you will discover that there is a lot more to learn about sailing after all.

Racing has many virtues. It teaches you to sail the dinghy quickly and efficiently in all conditions and is fantastic for improving boat handling skills, as well as excellent mental training for tactics. It provides a timetable and a goal. For instance, you could arrange

RACING IS FOR ALL AGES
Children learn fastest through racing in junior international classes, such as the Optimist or Cadet, or in a beginner boat such as the Pico shown here.

to go racing every weekend through the main season with the ambition of advancing from the back to the front of the fleet. Competitive sailing allows you to sail in close proximity to more experienced sailors – just watching them on the water and asking questions onshore is a great way to improve skills and make a whole crowd of new friends.

ROUND THE MARK
Young people can perfect their racing skills at smaller events. Here, they beat up to the windward mark at an event on Lake Garda in northern Italy.

RIGHT BOAT, RIGHT EVENT

Dinghy racing is for all ages. Children may start competing in the tiny dinghies from around the age of six, although many enthusiasts come into both sailing and racing a few years later. Adults may take longer to learn and may not be quite so agile, but there are plenty of relatively stable boats in which to enjoy racing. The first two things you need to decide are where you will race and in what boat.

Wherever there is suitable wind and water, you can be sure to find sailing clubs with fleets of dinghies. The national sailing authority for each country will keep a database of clubs that organize regular racing and coaching for specific dinghy classes. Many of the popular classes are "one-design", in which all boats are of the same make and design, while some allow an open choice of construction, sails, spars, or fittings, which generally leads to a more complex and expensive style of boat.

FIND YOUR LEVEL

Entry-level racing is provided by local events. In most countries with an established sailing tradition, active dinghy classes have their own associations, run by members for members, which organize an annual series of events that may include weekend events for racing or training at different venues, a national championship held over several days for each country, plus international championships for the better-known classes. The top level of dinghy racing, which is now contested only by full-time professional sailors, is the Olympic regatta held every four years (*see* Olympic Racing, pp.338–339).

RACING FOR FUN

A local racing event often provides great fun and close finishes. The thrill of participation rather than quest for lavish prizes is the draw.

MAJOR EVENT

The windward leg is a crucial test in any race. This close-fought beat is at Kiel Week, one of the world's major regattas (*see* p.326), on Germany's Baltic coast.

Dinghy racing courses

All dinghy races have the same elements and rules, designed to ensure that everyone enjoys safe sailing while battling for position around the course. Marker buoys ("marks") indicate where to turn, with start and finish lines marked by a committee boat.

START TO FINISH

Most races have a start line laid at 90 degrees to the wind direction on the day. A committee boat at the starboard end of the start line manages the countdown to the start. The object is for boats to cross the line as soon as possible after the starting signal. The first leg is normally a beat to the windward mark. On a windward-leeward course (*below*) the boats have a short beam reach to a spreader mark, then sail downwind to the leeward mark close to the start line. Classes with symmetrical spinnakers will sail directly downwind; classes with asymmetric spinnakers and catamarans will sail downwind on a series of broad reaches. The race may continue with more circuits of the course, usually finishing close to the windward mark at the top of the course.

RACING AROUND THE WORLD
Wonderful scenery near Cape Town, South Africa, provides a superb backdrop to a race between Dabchick dinghies.

RACING RULES

Rules in dinghy (and yacht) racing are used to prevent collisions and provide fair racing. They are often based on the standard rights of way. For example, if boats are on opposite tacks, starboard has right of way, but if boats are on the same tack and overlapped (the bow of one boat is ahead of a straight line drawn across the other boat's stern), the windward boat must keep clear. If boats are on the same tack and not overlapped, the boat clear astern must keep clear. The penalty for breaking a racing rule is a 360- or 720-degree turn (decided by the organizers before the race), which must be completed as quickly as possible.

If a crew breaks a rule but does not do a penalty turn, another crew may lodge a protest, which is decided upon by the organizers at the end of the race.

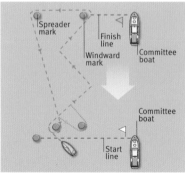

WINDWARD-LEEWARD COURSE
The basic format is several laps of a direct upwind and downwind course. The fleet is "spread" by a short beam reach at the top of the course

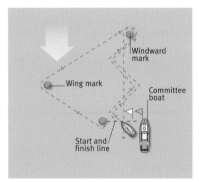

TRIANGLE COURSE
The classic Olympic course combines upwind and downwind legs with two broad reaches forming a triangle. These are run in various combinations.

INTERNATIONAL FLAG SIGNALS

A sound, and preparatory flag signals, are used in the countdown to the start. If a boat starts too early, there is an extra sound signal and the individual recall flag is hoisted. If many boats start early, the general recall flag is hoisted, with one-minute and disqualification flags hoisted for additional penalties. If conditions are not suitable for racing, the postponement flag is shown.

Individual recall

General recall

Postponement

Preparatory ("P")

Disqualification ("Black flag")

One minute

READY TO RACE
The start is between the committee boat (far end) and outer distance mark shown by the orange flag. When the starting gun is fired, the race has started.

Small keelboats

Small keelboats range in length from around 6–9m (20–30ft). Unlike dinghies, they incorporate a ballasted keel that prevents them from capsizing. Unlike yachts, most keelboats do not have accommodation and are designed purely for "day-sailing".

STABLE SAILING

Most small keelboats have the advantage of increased stability due to the extra weight of the keel. However, despite their inherent stability, many keelboats are high-performance "sportsboats", with a very large sail area, that can certainly provide exciting sailing. The majority of small keelboats have open cockpits like big dinghies and are popular for racing with two or three crew, providing the challenges of competition without being quite so physically demanding as a

dinghy. Some small keelboats have a small cabin with enough space below deck for two or three people to get out of the wind and enjoy spartan overnight camping. This also makes it a great boat for days out for a family.

LIFT OUT

A lift system that sits inside the marina berth, and lifts the boat clear of the water at the press of a button, is popular among sailors who want to maintain a keelboat in perfect condition in a marina.

WET OR DRY

A small keelboat provides the owner with the choice of "wet" or "dry" sailing. Wet sailing boats stay in the water throughout the sailing season and by the end of the season have built up deposits on their bottoms and generally need periodic anti-fouling and scraping. Such boats have a tendency to put on a little weight with age. Dry sailing boats are kept out of the water most of the time and get wet only when they sail. Boats kept in this way don't require the same attention to bottom care and are much easier to keep in top condition.

If the keelboat has a lifting or retracting keel, it is fairly straightforward to launch or retrieve the boat on a trailer like a big dinghy. This provides the option of being able to "trailer-sail" the boat to different locations behind a car with sufficient pulling power, and also allows the owner to park the boat at home on its trailer, which can considerably reduce storage and maintenance costs. A small keelboat with a fixed keel can also be trailed, but will often require the use of a crane for lifting it in and out of the water. This can become an expensive and time-consuming way of dry sailing.

LIFTING KEELS

The SRD (Self-Righting Dinghy) pictured below is a novel design with a ballasted bulb on the end of a daggerboard-like keel. This is intended to ensure it cannot capsize, and still gives dinghy-style performance. This type of keel lifts vertically when the boat is out of water and is locked down for sailing.

TOP PERFORMER

Small keelboats can often provide a perfect compromise between dinghy-style performance and yacht-style demands on the crew. The J24 was designed by Rod Johnstone in 1977 and is now the world's most popular small keelboat.

KEELBOAT SAILING TECHNIQUES

The skills required to sail a keelboat combine dinghy- and yacht-sailing techniques. Much depends on the style of keelboat, which may range from a traditional classic keelboat, which sails to windward heeling at more than 30 degrees, to a modern sportsboat, which should be sailed as upright as possible just like a dinghy. All keelboats have to drive a heavy keel through the water, which hinders acceleration and increases loads on the rig compared with dinghy sailing. Deceleration is also slower, as the weight of the keel gives a keelboat more momentum than a dinghy has. For example, the Yngling (illustrated here) could keep moving for a considerable distance if it were suddenly deprived of sail power.

MIXED CREWS
Racing keelboats provide a variety of crewing options. The 6.35-m (20-ft) Yngling (pictured right) was designed in 1967 and later chosen as the women's Olympic keelboat class. It can be wraced by male, female, and mixed crews.

KEELBOAT RACING
Most keelboats do not plane due to the weight and water resistance of the keel combined with the narrow hull shape. This can make racing very close, with only seconds separating boats at the finish.

DISABLED SAILORS

A small keelboat can be an ideal craft for a disabled sailor. Keelboats are raced at the Paralympics, which are held every four years in conjunction with the Olympic Games. Three different classes were chosen for the 2008 Paralympics in China – the 2.4mR (8ft) single-person keelboat, the 5.8-m (19-ft) UD-18 two-person keelboat, and the 7-m (23-ft) Sonar three-person keelboat.

SINGLE-PERSON KEELBOAT
The 2.4mR was designed in 1983 as a miniature America's Cup yacht and chosen for the 2000 Paralympics in Sydney. It is raced by both able-bodied and disabled sailors.

FLOATS INSTEAD OF A KEEL

A trimaran uses floats as stabilizers instead of a keel. The 7.5-m (25-ft) trimaran shown here has similar length hull and day-sailing capability as a small keelboat, with floats that fold alongside the hull for easy launching and trailer-sailing. The principal advantage of this type of boat – the potential for high speeds – has to be offset by the considerably higher price of a triple-hulled boat.

"A MAN IS NEVER ALONE

WITH THE WIND – AND THE BOAT

MADE THREE."

Hilaire Belloc, Hills and the Sea

Mooring a dinghy

You need good timing and skilful boat handling to moor a dinghy.
The helmsman must bring the boat to a halt alongside a mooring buoy
and hold it there for long enough to give the crew time to grab hold
of the buoy and attach the mooring line.

APPROACHING A MOORING

The helmsman should approach at low
speed while maintaining full steerage
and control. Use whichever element
is strongest – wind or tide – to stop the
boat alongside the buoy, with sails fully
depowered. To assess the strength of
wind direction or tide, look at which way
other moored boats are lying. A pick-up
buoy will lie down-tide of the main buoy
– the stronger the tide, the more it will
be stretched out and pushed under water.
The crew will need to grab hold of the
buoy and attach the mooring line.

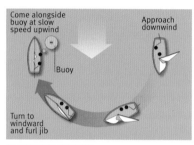

SAILING INTO THE WIND
If there is no tide, approach from downwind, roll the
jib, and bring the boat head to wind when the buoy
is on the windward side of the bow.

1 Approach the buoy slowly. The mooring line
should lead from the bow to a position by
the windward shroud, so the crew can get the
line on to the buoy quickly.

2 Come head to wind with the jib rolled.
The boat needs enough momentum to stop
when the buoy is next to the windward shroud.
If you are moving too fast, sail round again.

3 Once the crew has the
buoy, lift the centreboard.
Attach the line or bring the end
into the dinghy. Drop the
mainsail inside the cockpit.

ANCHORING A DINGHY

Always carry a small folding anchor, which can be stored easily and will not damage the boat. When approaching the anchorage, furl the jib and control speed with the mainsheet. Let the mainsail fly on a close reaching course, with the boat pointing into the tide or into the wind to stop the boat. Drop the anchor and let the boat fall back on the anchor against the wind or tide.

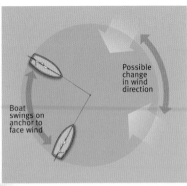

SWING ON THE WIND
Leave sufficient space around the anchor for the boat to swing on the wind. Be aware that the wind may change direction in the afternoon. Lift the centreboard and roll the mainsail inside the cockpit.

1 **Drop the anchor,** hand over hand, until it grips the bottom. Hold it well clear of the bow to prevent damage. Ensure the anchor is attached to the dinghy.

2 **Most dinghies have no mooring cleat** on the foredeck. The steel hoop at the mouth of the spinnaker chute may provide a good option for attaching the anchor.

WEIGHING ANCHOR

If the boat is pointing into wind, you can hoist the mainsail on the mooring. Lower the centreboard, pull up the anchor, then unfurl and back the jib to make the bow bear away on to a reach. If the boat is lying awkwardly to wind and tide, you may leave the mooring under jib, with only a small part of the mainsail raised to help provide steerage. Then turn head to wind to hoist the rest of the mainsail.

PULLING UP THE ANCHOR
Gradually pull in the anchor rope and chain. On a dinghy this should not require great effort.

Packing up a dinghy

If you sail in salt water, you will have to carry out rigorous cleaning before packing up your dinghy. When everything is clean and dry, the sails should be carefully folded and packed into sailbags for storage. Careful packing and storage will prolong the life of your equipment.

WASHING DOWN THE DINGHY

Hose down the boat every time you come ashore. If the water is not rinsed off the boat after use, salt can corrode unprotected metal and leave a trail of tiny abrasive crystals in the stitched seams of a sail. Leave everything to air dry before storing or you may return to a damp boat full of mildew. Don't forget to rinse out your wetsuit and other sailing clothing regularly as well.

1 Working from the top downwards, hose down the sails carefully with clean, fresh water.

2 Wash down the decks and cockpit. Be sure to rinse down all ropes and fittings. Drain any sand and grit out through the bung or self-bailer. Use a sponge to dry the cockpit thoroughly.

STORING WOVEN SAILCLOTH SAILS

Always make sure the sails are totally dry before storing. Mainsails, made out of woven polyester sailcloth, are traditionally "flaked" in a zig-zag series of folds as shown below, but avoid putting hard creases in the window. This job is often easier with two people – one on the leech and one on the luff. A jib of this material can be rolled from head to foot along the wire of the luff.

1 **Lay the dry sail out flat** and remove the battens. Start forming an evenly spaced series of folds in a concertina pattern. Keep the material free of creases.

2 **Make the final fold** with the head, ensuring the sail is laid out in a neat pile of folds. This is easiest to achieve in a wind-free zone.

3 **It can take practice** to make folds of the right size and shape to fit in your sailbag. If the sail looks messy after your first attempt at folding, take out the folds and start the process again.

4 **Roll the folded sail** from one end. Carefully slide the rolled and folded sail inside the sailbag. Store it in a dry place ready for use next time you need it.

STORING LAMINATE SAILS

Laminate sails, which are made from layers of material, often a combination of woven fabric and thin plastic film that are joined together under pressure, should always be rolled with no creases. Take off batten tension before rolling the sail. If the sail does not have full-length battens, two people may be required to keep the rolls even between the luff and the leech. The sail will tend to roll tightly along the luff and more loosely on the leech. Keep tightening the leech to ensure that no creases can form in the material. Always store the sail in its bag out of direct sunlight and away from any sources of heat.

1 **Start by rolling the laminate sail** from the head, using full-length battens as a guide.

2 **Slide the rolled sail** neatly into its sailbag. If it does not fit easily, try again, rolling it up into a slightly tighter roll.

Storing and transporting a dinghy

You can leave a dinghy on its trolley at the beach or in a boat park and transport it by road on a trailer. For peace of mind and for everyone's safety, the boat should be tied down as securely as possible, with top and bottom covers for maximum protection.

STORING A DINGHY

When leaving a dinghy unattended, you may need to remove sails, foils, and all loose fittings – dinghy gear is expensive to replace and theft does unfortunately happen. Pull halyards tight before you leave the boat – when it is windy, people do not want to hear the unpleasant noise of wires banging against aluminium masts. Leave the drain bung open to allow air to circulate inside the hull. It makes good sense to remove the bung or carry spares, in case a neighbouring boat owner decides to "borrow" it.

Always use a good-quality top cover to protect the dinghy from ultraviolet light and rain, and make sure it is securely attached to the boat – a "boom-up" design will help drain rainwater away from the dinghy. A bottom cover will provide further protection from damage and is always recommended when transporting a dinghy on a trailer.

Dinghies can get blown over by strong winds, so tie your boat down to ground anchors as an added precaution. Beware of neighbouring boats getting blown on to your dinghy in windy weather. It is well worth making sure that your insurance policy covers this kind of accident.

USING A BOAT COVER
Use a cover that will provide full protection from ultraviolet light and rain, with under-hull straps to ensure it is securely held in place.

TRAILING A DINGHY

You can transport a dinghy by loading it on to a purpose-made trailer, which you attach to your car. Modern combi-trailers allow the boat to stay on its trolley, which slides on and off the road base. Check the light board is properly attached and fully functional. The trolley must be locked to the road base and the trailer locked on to the tow ball with an additional security wire. Ensure the boat and mast are securely tied down. Any loose equipment, such as the boom, should be taped or tied in position for safety reasons. Put padding (carpet or thick rubber) under ropes, straps, and the mast base to prevent rubbing and abrasion. Always carry a spare trailer wheel and a set of tools in case of a puncture or bearing failure. Check the trailing regulations governing the weight, length, and width of the trailer.

READY TO ROLL
When transporting a dinghy, make sure that the mast will clear the roof of your car and there is no large overhang at the transom.

DINGHY PARK
Bow-down is the most stable angle in which to store your dinghy, but bow-up will allow rainwater to drain out through the transom or bung holes.

Dinghy maintenance

A sailing dinghy operates in a harsh environment that can combine corrosive salt water, abrasive sand, and extreme stress from wind and waves. A little care, repair, and occasional replacement are necessary to ensure you continue to enjoy good, trouble-free sailing.

BOAT CARE

To minimize the need for repairs to sails, fittings, and hull, be sure to take particular care when storing and transporting your boat (*see* pp.164–165 and pp.166–167). Regularly check the tightness of screws, bolts, and fittings, particularly at the transom, and inspect the rope and wires.

There are times when it is impossible to avoid impact damage to the hull and deck of a dinghy. Rotomoulded plastic should withstand hard knocks and only sustain minor scratches. More serious damage requires professional repair. Fibreglass construction is far more susceptible to minor damage to the gelcoat finish. Any damage must be repaired as soon as possible to prevent water seeping into the laminate. Dinghy specialists sell a wide range of repair materials, including gelcoat. The boat should be repaired in a warm, dry, and dust-free environment. Sand the damaged area so that it is dry and clean with no sharp edges and all loose flakes of gelcoat removed. Mix and apply the gelcoat and hardener according to the manufacturer's instructions. If the impact cut through the laminate, a professional repair is recommended.

SPINNAKER DAMAGE

Spinnakers can get small tears where the cloth catches on the chute. Patch this damage before a tiny hole turns into a large rip. Wash the spinnaker in fresh water and let it dry. Use self-adhesive spinnaker tape to cover each hole, flattening the tape to remove air bubbles and rounding off edges to prevent the tape catching. Use tape on both sides to patch larger holes.

TAPE IT UP

Split rings can work their way out of the pin, owing to movement of the boat. Always tape the split rings up, to protect the spinnaker or your wetsuit from tearing on the sharp metal.

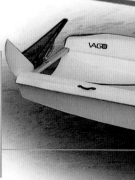

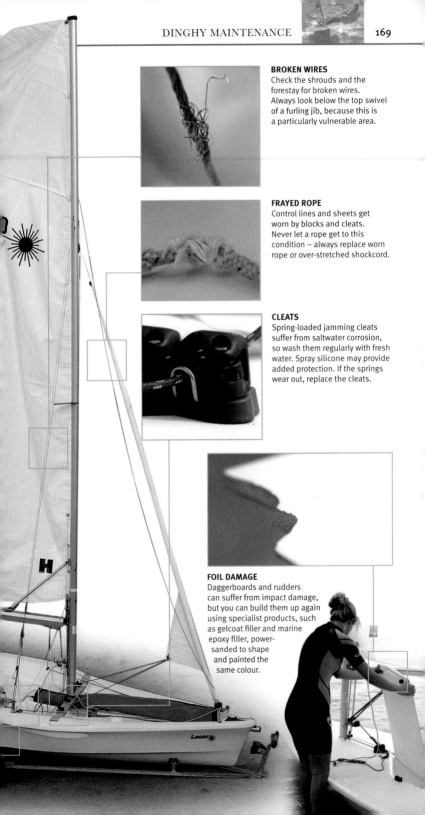

BROKEN WIRES
Check the shrouds and the forestay for broken wires. Always look below the top swivel of a furling jib, because this is a particularly vulnerable area.

FRAYED ROPE
Control lines and sheets get worn by blocks and cleats. Never let a rope get to this condition – always replace worn rope or over-stretched shockcord.

CLEATS
Spring-loaded jamming cleats suffer from saltwater corrosion, so wash them regularly with fresh water. Spray silicone may provide added protection. If the springs wear out, replace the cleats.

FOIL DAMAGE
Daggerboards and rudders can suffer from impact damage, but you can build them up again using specialist products, such as gelcoat filler and marine epoxy filler, power-sanded to shape and painted the same colour.

Sailing a yacht

Modern cruising yachts

The term "yacht" is a generic name for sailing boats with accommodation, ranging from basic and cramped to luxurious and grand. Modern equipment ensures that a small crew should be able to manage a cruising yacht of around 11m (36ft) with relative ease.

CRUISING YACHTS

Most yachts are fitted with a heavily ballasted keel, which prevents capsizing and helps stabilize the boat. Virtually all yachts are fitted with inboard or outboard auxiliary engines.

Most modern cruising yachts are made of glass-reinforced plastic (GRP) and have a relatively large internal volume to provide maximum living quarter space combined with reasonable performance under sail or motor. Most have a Bermudan sloop rig: a triangular mainsail and a single large headsail. Stability is provided by a fin keel with a separate rudder (see p.49).

Cruiser-racers are designed for both racing and cruising performance. Each design offers its own mix of speed, comfort, and easy handling. A light, sophisticated, expensive yacht designed primarily for racing requires a large, highly skilled crew but may also be practical for enjoyable family cruising. A heavier cruising yacht designed for both comfort and the best possible racing performance is very unlikely to challenge the performance of a pure racing yacht.

BERMUDAN SLOOP RIG
Like most modern cruising yachts, the Jeanneau Sunfast 37 has a high-aspect Bermudan sloop rig for high performance.

WINCHES
Most yachts have powerful, twin-speed winches. Primary winches on either side of the cockpit are used to wind in the foresail sheets, especially when tacking. Secondary winches on the coachroof (the top of the cabin) are used to raise halyards, pull down reefing lines, and control the kicking strap.

DOWN BELOW
The main cabin of a medium-sized cruising yacht usually combines a galley, navigation area, and saloon with a dining table and seating that can be turned into berths on both sides.

BIG OR SMALL?

On any yacht, the crew should first and foremost be able to handle the rig and its sails in all conditions. While a yacht in excess of 12m (39ft) or so in length generally has more space in both the cabin and cockpit and can sail or motor faster than a smaller yacht, it needs a bigger rig to drive it through the water. The rig will be heavier and more difficult for the crew to handle when hoisting and dropping sails or pulling in the sheets. Superior winches and roller furling can alleviate this problem to some extent, enabling a small crew to handle a big cruising yacht. Although bigger yachts are faster and more comfortable, this does not make them more enjoyable to sail for all people. Apart from being much less expensive, a yacht of only about 7–8m (23–26ft) is likely to feel much lighter on the helm and may have more rewarding sailing performance. Smaller yachts can also fit into smaller and shallower anchorages or tighter marina berths.

COACHROOF
The mast in most modern cruising yachts passes through the coachroof, which also contains hatches that provide ventilation for the living areas below.

HALYARDS AND CONTROL LINES
Halyards and control lines are routed through turning blocks on the coachroof, so they can be led back from the mast to the cockpit, where the crew can manage the sails.

Choosing a yacht

The choice of yachts is almost unlimited, with types of all ages available for every use, ranging from traditional wooden cruisers built many decades ago to the latest production yachts that are tailor-made for cruising. The first thing to decide is what you want a yacht for.

OWNERSHIP OPTIONS

Owning a yacht is a dream for many people. It is also likely to require a considerably larger commitment in terms of time and expense than owning a dinghy. Yachts cost anything between a few thousand to several million dollars. In general, the larger and more modern the yacht, the more expensive it will be to buy, own, and maintain. Part of the problem when owning a yacht is finding enough time to use it and to justify the cost of mooring, insurance, and regular upkeep.

STABILITY AFLOAT
This small trimaran has a centreboard rather than a keel, with a cabin in the main hull and floats providing stability.

If you can devote eight weeks or more a year to cruising, that's fine. If not, your yacht may spend a lot of time unused. A possible option may be to sign up for an ownership scheme, in which you buy a yacht on behalf of a charter company. The company pays all running costs and allows you to use the yacht (or a similar yacht in other locations) for several weeks each year, the amount of time being subject to the season. Alternatively, you could charter a yacht (with or without a skipper) and sail in delightful areas such as the Mediterranean or the Caribbean.

CATAMARAN CRUISER
A cruising cat can combine extremely spacious accommodation with shallow draught, plus it has the advantage of not heeling over. However, finding space in a marina may be tricky for a boat this wide.

WHAT IS A YACHT FOR?

When choosing a yacht, consider where you will sail and what the yacht is for. If you intend to cross the Atlantic or Pacific, you need a boat that is built and fitted out with ocean-going capability. If overnight coastal hops are as far as you want to go, a smaller, simpler yacht will almost certainly suffice. The advantages of a larger yacht are likely to include being able to sail or motor faster with less pitching or rolling, and enjoying more comfortable accommodation. The disadvantages may include higher marina fees and fewer mooring options.

The depth of a yacht's keel is an important consideration if you sail in a tidal area. Shoal draught keels will allow an anchorage or mooring closer to the shore than long fin keels; bilge keels or a centreboard will allow mooring in very shallow water and remove most of the difficulty from drying out at low tide.

Consider how many crew you want to sail with, or more realistically how many crew you can depend on. Smaller yachts

obviously need less crew than larger boats. Two crew with reasonable experience should be able to handle a yacht of up to about 8m (26ft), but for a yacht larger than this, the number of crew needed will depend on the sail-handling equipment on board.

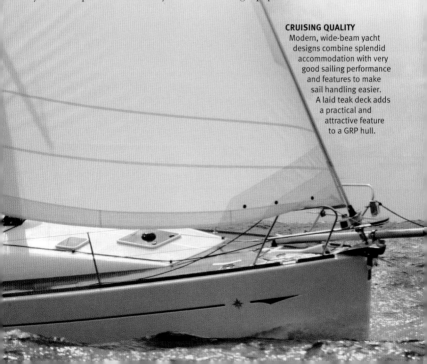

CRUISING QUALITY
Modern, wide-beam yacht designs combine splendid accommodation with very good sailing performance and features to make sail handling easier. A laid teak deck adds a practical and attractive feature to a GRP hull.

Crew roles

Sailing a yacht requires working as a team for the skipper and crew. This will ensure that all manoeuvres – such as leaving a mooring, hoisting sails, changing tacks, reefing, or entering a marina – can be completed with maximum enjoyment and minimum stress.

HOW MANY CREW?

Most modern cruising yachts are designed to be managed by a small number of crew, and a yacht of around 10–12m (30–40ft) may in theory be managed by a crew of two or even one. A crew of four should be able to handle such a yacht with ease. More hands are especially useful when carrying out demanding

manoeuvres, such as berthing in a tight space. When cruising, the maximum size of the crew tends to be governed by the size of the cockpit – you can't enjoy sailing in comfort if there is not enough space to sit down.

Smaller crews need considerable expertise and knowledge. Experience becomes a great asset during strong winds, big waves, and fast-flowing tides, when the yacht becomes more demanding to handle.

The skipper may allow other crew members to steer the yacht but must retain complete responsibility at all times

The crew on the port side on this yacht controls reefing lines, for reducing the size of the mainsail, and the kicking strap, which holds down the boom

THE SKIPPER

The skipper is responsible for the crew and boat at all times. The skipper should brief the crew on where they will be sailing and on specific features of the yacht, including its safety systems. He or she must also ensure the crew is properly equipped with protective clothing and has immediate access to lifejackets and harnesses that they know how to put on. In addition, it is the skipper's job to provide (or delegate a crew member to organize) sufficient nourishing, easily prepared food and drink. The crew will look to the skipper to allocate specific duties and organize a watch system if required. It is very important for the skipper to give clear instructions prior to every manoeuvre, so that each crew member understands what he or she will be doing. All skippers should be aware of the crew's limitations. Try not to expect too much from the crew and be aware that longer trips, particularly those involving an overnight passage, require more experience and expertise from the crew.

READY FOR MOORING
Coming alongside a pontoon or another yacht can be a taxing manoeuvre. A good skipper will have briefed the crew on what is going to happen and what they need to do.

WORKING ON DECK
On a modern cruising yacht, crew rarely need to go on deck, except when a spinnaker is to be hoisted.

HELMSMAN AND CREW
This medium-sized yacht comfortably accomodates a crew of four. Everyone has a role to play, and there will be bursts of activity whenever the skipper decides to make a manoeuvre.

The crew on the starboard side oversees various controls, including the main halyard and the starboard jib sheet

A crew member is responsible for adjusting the mainsheet in the centre of the cockpit

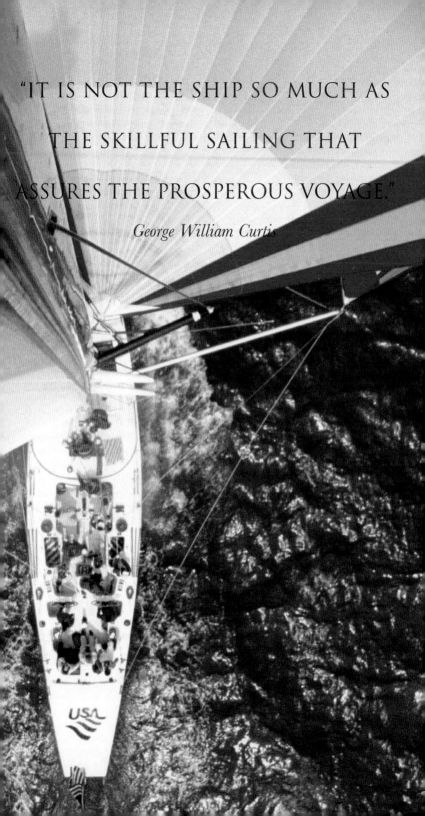

"IT IS NOT THE SHIP SO MUCH AS
THE SKILLFUL SAILING THAT
ASSURES THE PROSPEROUS VOYAGE."

George William Curtis

Hoisting the mainsail

It is important to leave plenty of time for hoisting the mainsail, which under normal circumstances may take around five minutes. As you hoist, the yacht will require a substantial amount of space around it for manoeuvring and must point directly into the wind.

Turn the boat head to wind before hoisting the mainsail

PREPARING TO HOIST

The yacht's engine should be running during the hoist. Hoisting the mainsail on a mooring and sailing away without using the engine requires considerable expertise. The skipper briefs the crew on where and when to hoist and decides if any reefs are required. Choose a sheltered area of flat water with plenty of room to motor slowly into the wind. Use alternate forward and neutral gears with low engine revs to keep the yacht's bow heading into the wind while the crew hoists the sail. More power may be needed in stronger winds, but motoring too fast may make the hoist difficult. During the hoist, the helmsman's view may be obscured by the mainsail and the crew should beware of the boom swaying from side to side.

1 **Having attached the main halyard** to the head of the sail, the foredeck crew pulls the halyard taut to prevent it from catching the spreaders and removes the sail ties.

2 **The main halyard** passes down the mast and through a clutch on the coachroof. For the hoist, the cockpit crew pulls back the clutch and takes three turns of the halyard round the drum of the winch.

3 **The quickest way to hoist** the mainsail is to pull the halyard at the mast by hand a metre or so at a time, while the cockpit crew pulls in slack on the winch.

4 **The mainsheet and kicker are eased** so that the mainsail can be hoisted with minimum effort. You may also need to ease reefing lines. Keep well clear of the boom during the hoist.

5 **The cockpit crew** then pulls the halyard on the winch to ensure the luff is taut. Finally, if one is fitted, the crew tightens the cunningham (*above*). if necessary.

6 **Finally undo the topping lift shackle** and secure it to the base of the mast. This allows the boom to be sheeted in tight. Alternatively, simply slacken it.

LOADING A WINCH

Always wind the length of rope clockwise round the drum. To prevent any chance of injury, do not put your fingers between the rope and the drum. Put on just enough turns to prevent the rope from slipping; too many turns may create a riding (overlapping) turn.

1 **Wind the rope clockwise** round the winch, keeping your thumb pointing away from the drum as shown to avoid the risk of your thumb or fingers becoming trapped.

2 **Three turns hold the rope** on this winch firmly in place; two turns may slip and more may result in the turns overlapping. Take a final turn round the self-tailing jaws.

3 **Put the handle** into the top of the winch with both hands, ensuring it is fully locked down before you start to wind. Beware of losing winch handles over the side!

Dropping the mainsail

Dropping is a reverse procedure of hoisting the mainsail. It is equally important to leave plenty of time and space on the water, with the yacht pointing directly into the wind and the engine running as the mainsail is lowered and stowed.

Wind

Keep the boat head to wind while dropping the mainsail.

MANAGING THE DROP

Drop the mainsail in plenty of time, before mooring or entering a marina. Choose an area with plenty of space and flat water if possible. The yacht should be pointing into the wind throughout the drop, moving ahead at slow speed with the engine running. The helmsman's view will be obscured during much of this

manoeuvre. It is important to keep well away from other yachts and to delay docking until the mainsail is fully stowed. The crew must keep clear of the boom, which may sway from side to side as the mainsail comes down.

PACKING THE SAIL

It is vital to get the mainsail packed as soon as it is down. The helmsman must prevent the yacht pitching and rolling during this operation. Two or three crew members are needed to flake the mainsail from side to side.

1 **The cockpit crew** puts the halyard back on to the winch and releases the clutch lever, while the foredeck crew prepares to pull down on the luff. The helmsman motors slowly into the wind with the mainsheet eased.

2 **Let the halyard off slowly,** the cockpit crew easing the turns round the drum with one hand and holding the end of the rope in the other.

3 **The foredeck crew** pulls down on the luff by hand to prevent the sail from bunching or jamming in the track.

4 **Having pulled in the mainsheet** and fastened the topping lift to prevent the boom from swaying, the crew flake the mainsail from side to side, which involves arranging it in neat folds on top of the boom.

5 **Secure the flaked sail** with sail ties, which are traditionally tied with reef knots. Beware of shockcord sail ties – under tension, one end may fly off and hit you in the face.

6 **When cruising it is advisable** to ensure the mainsail is always ready for a quick hoist in case of engine failure. Leave the halyard looped down around a cleat on the mast.

Managing the headsail

The roller-furler headsail makes cruising simple. It can be rolled out in seconds and rolled away again in a little more than a minute. This system also allows the skipper to reduce the size of the headsail for sailing in stronger winds.

A SAIL FOR ALL REASONS

The traditional headsail system relies on carrying a number of different sized sails for different wind strengths. However, this is not always ideal – it can be a tough job for the crew to change headsails. The roller-furling headsail, operated from the cockpit, is the top choice for cruising. The luff this type of headsail slides up a groove in a headfoil fitted to the forestay. The tack is attached to a roller-furling drum at the base of the foil, with a halyard swivel at the head of the sail. When the drum turns, the sail is rolled or unrolled, with the top swivel preventing the halyard from twisting.

1 **With the furling line clutch open,** the cockpit crew pulls on the leeward sheet to unfurl the headsail. Make sure the furling line can run free.

2 **As the headsail begins to unroll,** the wind will catch the sail. If you wish to sail under a partly furled headsail, release only a limited amount of furling line at a time.

3 **The headsail unrolls** in a matter of seconds. Rolling it up will take slightly longer, possibly a couple of minutes in stronger winds, when the load on the furling line is heavier.

UNFURLING

The furling line is led aft from the roller-furling drum along the side deck (usually port side). It passes through turning blocks to a clutch by the side of the cockpit coaming. Open the clutch, ensuring the furling line will run free. Let off both headsail sheets, then take two or three turns round the leeward winch and begin to pull the leeward sheet in hand over hand. The headsail will begin to unroll, rolling the furling line around the drum at the same time.

FURLING MECHANISM
The furling line is wound on to the drum as you unroll the headsail by pulling on the sheet, then wound off when you furl the sail.

KEEP IT UNDER CONTROL

In light winds, the headsail will unroll gently and slowly. In medium winds, it may unroll with a bang as soon as the wind fills the sail. It is vital to ensure that the furling line will not jam as it runs out through the clutch. In stronger winds, control the clutch so you release only a limited amount of furling line at a time. This makes it far easier to decide if you wish to sail with a partly furled headsail.

FURLING

Keep the furling line under tension, with the clutch closed at all times, except when unfurling the headsail. This will help to prevent the line falling off the roller-furling drum and jamming, which can happen with older designs. In light winds, you can normally furl the headsail by letting off the headsail sheets and pulling in the furling line hand over hand. As the headsail begins to roll up, keep light tension on one or both sheets. When the sheets start to roll around the sail, pull back on the sheets until really tight and cleat them both. In moderate or strong winds, there may be a heavy load on the furling line. Use a conveniently sited winch to steadily wind in the furling line.

WORKING TOGETHER
On this yacht, the primary headsail winch is mounted on the coachroof. One crew member winches from the companionway, while the other holds the tail of the sheet in a stable position braced against the bulkhead.

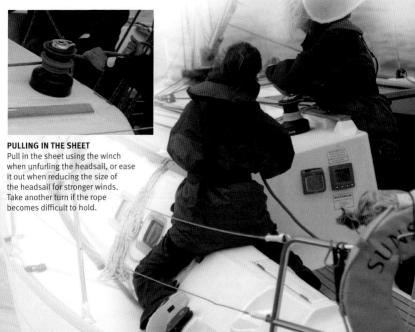

PULLING IN THE SHEET
Pull in the sheet using the winch when unfurling the headsail, or ease it out when reducing the size of the headsail for stronger winds. Take another turn if the rope becomes difficult to hold.

Reducing sail

If sailing in moderate to high winds, you will need to reduce the sail area – this is known as reefing. Roller-reefing systems for the headsail and slab reefing for the mainsail make this an easy task for two or three crew, particularly if all controls are operated from the cockpit.

Wind

Keep the boat head to wind while reefing the mainsail.

WHEN TO REEF

When you reduce sail, the boat will perform better and handle more comfortably in stronger winds. Sailing with the boat heeled too far is inefficient – it will slip sideways, go more slowly, and will be uncomfortable for the crew. If the side deck goes underwater, you almost certainly have too much sail.

It always pays to be cautious and reef sails sooner rather than later. Reefing is easy when the water is flat and the wind is not too strong. So, if you expect strong winds and waves, make a decision to put reefs in the mainsail while you hoist in a sheltered area, and only unfurl a small amount of headsail.

Later, when you are underway, if you find you have not got enough sail area for the conditions, it is relatively straightforward to take out a reef or to unfurl more headsail as and when you need to. However, if you have too much

1 **With both the mainsheet and kicker** eased, open the main halyard clutch while holding tension on the winch. Ease the halyard sufficiently for the crew to pull the reefing point in the luff down the mast to the boom.

2 **When the reefing point** in the luff is secure, wind the reefing point in the leech down and out along the boom until the foot of the sail is taut. Tension the main halyard, then pull in the mainsheet and tension the kicker.

3 **If the yacht has no lazy jacks** (a network of lines between the boom and mast to catch the sail) the excess sail will fall in a large fold under the boom. Roll up the flap and secure with sail ties along the boom.

4 **Each tie should be** wrapped round the sail, above the boom. Do not put them round the boom, because this would put the knots under so much stress that they may be impossible to get undone.

STAGES OF REEFING

In windy conditions, you need to reef the mainsail and headsail to keep the boat in balance. The extent depends on the wind strength. Remember to reduce headsail and mainsail in balance with each other; if there is excess weather helm, you have too much mainsail; if there is excess lee helm, you have too much headsail.

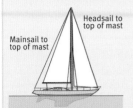

Mainsail to top of mast

Headsail to top of mast

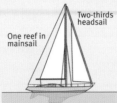

One reef in mainsail

Two-thirds headsail

Three reefs in mainsail

One-quarter headsail

FULL SAIL: LIGHT WINDS
Full mainsail and headsail are suitable for light to moderate winds up to around Force 4. In higher winds, you need to reef.

FIRST REEF: MODERATE WINDS
One reef in the mainsail with approximately two-thirds headsail makes the boat more comfortable in stronger winds.

FULLY REEFED: STRONG WINDS
Three reefs in the mainsail with one-quarter headsail for very strong winds slow the boat but make it more manageable.

sail for the conditions, it becomes progressively more challenging to reef sails in stronger winds and waves, since they become more difficult to control. If the wind is strong enough to require reefing, you may need to observe rough weather procedures (*see* pp.260–261).

HEADSAIL REEFING

In light winds, you can normally roll the headsail by hand simply by pulling on the furling line. Make sure the clutch that the furling line is led through on the side deck is closed. In stronger winds, it may be necessary to lead the furling line round a winch and wind it in with the working sheet eased. You may need to put some tension on both sheets to roll the jib tightly.

MAINSAIL REEFING

Most yachts have slab reefing, which pulls equal amounts of sail down at the luff and the leech. This system ensures that the remainder of the mainsail can set perfectly. The yacht shown on these pages has reefing lines for both the luff and the leech that lead back to the cockpit, so there is no need for the crew to leave the safety of the cockpit. On yachts without this facility, one crew has to go to the mast and pull a cringle (stainless steel ring) at the reef point down on to a hook on the boom.

COMFORT AND SPEED
Sailing with one reef in the mainsail and a partly rolled headsail keeps the boat upright for comfortable sailing at good speed.

Sunsail Sun Fast 37

Crew comfort and safety

Sailing is one of the world's safest sports, but the sea is always ready to catch sailors who are ill prepared or careless and therefore make too many mistakes. A few basic safety measures combined with common sense will help to guarantee comfortable and safe sailing.

READY FOR ACTION

All crew members must have access to functional clothing that will keep them dry and warm in all weathers. A yacht must have sufficient lifejackets and harnesses to fit all the crew (*see* pp.62–63). Children will need their own small sizes. It is the skipper's responsibility to show the crew where lifejackets and harnesses are stowed, how to don them securely, and when and how to operate them. It is good practice for all the crew to wear a lifejacket when on deck. Non-swimmers and those with poor swimming ability should wear a lifejacket at all times. Lifejackets and harnesses should be mandatory in the cockpit and on deck in poor weather conditions or at night. The skipper

SEASICKNESS

Many sailors experience and overcome seasickness. In extreme situations, however, it may become dangerous if the crew are too ill to handle the yacht. Medication works for some people and should be taken well before the trip. For more detailed advice, *see* First aid, p.265.

Seasickness pills

COCKPIT SAFETY

Modern lifejackets are unrestrictive and easy to wear around the boat. Do not hesitate to ask your crew to put them on.

should identify harness-attachment points for moving around the yacht. They should be close to the companion-way, so the crew can clip on before coming on deck, on either side of the cockpit and along the side decks.

Common sense dictates that if you need to wear a lifejacket you should also be wearing a harness and be ready to clip on. The most important safety requirement for anyone on board is not to fall over the side. Remember the old sailors' maxim – "One hand for yourself and one for the boat". Make sure that you tell the helmsman when you are moving forward and keep well clear of the boom, particularly if sailing downwind, in case of accidental gybes.

1 **Clip the harness line** (a strap with clips at both ends) to the ring on your harness.

2 **Clip on** to a convenient attachment point. The clip can be operated with one hand and in pitch dark

3 **When you need to change position** on the deck release the clip with your index finger.

WHERE TO BE ON DECK

The cockpit is the safest and most comfortable place for the crew while sailing. If the boat is heeling, try to sit on the windward side with your feet braced.It is also safest to move along the windward side deck away from the water. Identify handholds when moving around. Only go on the side decks or foredeck when necessary. Keep the harness line tether as short as possible and your weight low when moving around the boat. Always wear deck shoes or sailing boots, beware of slippery areas, and take care not to trip on blocks or cleats.

2 **When you are working** on the coachroof or foredeck be sure to clip on. With practice the harness line will not get in the way at all. Think of it as wearing a car seat belt.

1 **As you move about the deck,** keep low. Clip on to the webbing jackstays when moving forward along the side decks and hold on to the grab rails.

Using the engine

Most yachts have an inboard marine diesel engine situated under the cockpit, which drives the boat under power and charges its electrical systems. Basic, regular checks and maintenance will help ensure that the engine functions reliably in any situation.

FUEL SENSE

One of the main causes of engine failure is running out of fuel. Make sure that you carry enough fuel to motor for the entire journey, even if you are intending to sail. Check the manual to find out how many litres your engine will use at cruising speed in one hour, so that you can calculate how much fuel you need. Allow a reserve of at least 20 per cent of fuel tank capacity. Always have a full fuel can and funnel stowed in the cockpit locker for emergency use.

Diesel fuel must be as clean as possible because water, dirt, or bacteria (which feeds on condensation) may clog filters or destroy the injector pump. Filters should be regularly cleaned and changed. Keeping the fuel tank topped up will help reduce any

REFUELLING

When refuelling with diesel, take care that no fuel spills into the water and that no water gets into the fuel tank. Take particular care that the engine does not run out of fuel while motoring. To restart, you will need to bleed the injectors in order to remove any trapped air from the fuel supply.

Filling the tank

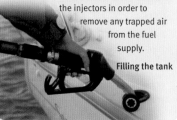

condensation. Adding antibacterial and water-absorbing additives to the fuel will also help to keep it clean.

PRE-JOURNEY CHECKS

Before starting the engine, there are several basic checks you should carry out besides ensuring you have enough fuel for the journey (*see above*). If the boat has a straight prop shaft with a stern-gland greaser, give the grease handle a turn. Top up the engine's freshwater

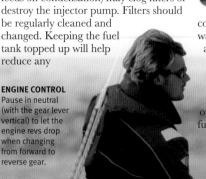

ENGINE CONTROL
Pause in neutral (with the gear lever vertical) to let the engine revs drop when changing from forward to reverse gear.

CONTROL PANEL
The engine control panel is usually located in the side of the cockpit. Most modern diesel engines are started with a simple turn of a key, which may be combined with a starter button.

cooling systems as needed, using water or antifreeze mixture, and clean the raw-water filter (*see below*). Also dispose of any accumulated water or dirt in the transparent fuel filter bowls. Check the engine and gearbox oil levels using the dipstick (*see below*); if you need to top up, note that the gearbox may require special oil.

Finally, make sure the engine battery switch is on before starting, and do not turn it off while the engine is running. As soon as the engine is running, check that cooling water is being pumped out of the exhaust pipe in the side of the hull.

As part of your regular maintenance of the boat, check that the engine's belts have not become loose or frayed, that hoses have not sustained cuts or splits, and that there is no evidence of oil or coolant leaks.

OUTBOARDS

Use the correct oil-and-petrol mixture for two-stroke engines, and be aware that it may deteriorate if stored for long periods, causing reliability problems. When refilling, be careful not to spill fuel or allow water to get into in the tank. Close fuel taps when the engine is off. If the cooling water stream is not flowing when the engine has started, shut the engine down before it overheats.

OIL CHECK
Check the oil level is between maximum and minimum. For an accurate reading, it may be necessary to check immediately after the engine has been running.

Exhaust and cooling-water outlet hose

Filtered raw-water hose

Raw-water filter

INSPECTING THE ENGINE
Make sure you are familiar with the location and layout of the engine. On midsize yachts, primary access is generally behind the companionway steps. After you have checked the engine, make sure hatches and steps are securely fastened.

RAW-WATER FILTER
Shut off the cooling-water sea cock, then remove any seaweed or other debris that may be sucked into the engine from the filter.

Manoeuvring under power

A yacht does not steer in the same way as a car. When you push the tiller or turn the wheel, the yacht pivots around its centre of lateral resistance, which is determined by the position and size of the keel. Factors such as windage and prop walk also influence a boat's handling.

STEERAGE

Maintaining steerage requires sufficient speed through the water to reduce the effects of prop walk and windage, or wind drag. If you enter a marina or crowded mooring too fast, you risk a crash if something goes wrong.

PROP WALK AND WINDAGE

All yachts suffer from prop walk – a paddlewheel effect from the propeller that pushes the stern sideways. Having a good feel for the strength of prop walk in different situations is the key to handling your yacht well under power at low speed. You can assess the degree of prop walk by putting the engine in reverse when moored. The stern will turn away from the direction of turbulence being thrown out by the propeller. You could

also perform a tight "power turn" by alternating between forward and reverse gears with the rudder hard over to maximize the degree of prop walk – turn to port if the propeller rotates clockwise.

Prop walk causes most problems when going astern and will need to be taken account of when determining your course. When aiming for a space astern, for example, reversing in an arc may allow for prop walk to push the stern until the boat has sufficient speed and steerage to travel in a straight line.

The more surface area a yacht exposes to the wind, the greater the effects of windage at low speed. Wind from the side tends to blow the bow downwind, either countering or strengthening the effect of prop walk.

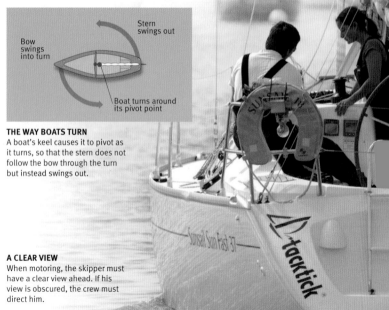

THE WAY BOATS TURN
A boat's keel causes it to pivot as it turns, so that the stern does not follow the bow through the turn but instead swings out.

A CLEAR VIEW
When motoring, the skipper must have a clear view ahead. If his view is obscured, the crew must direct him.

DECK DRILL
Make sure everything is correctly stowed and ship-shape before entering a harbour or marina, where you may need to manoeuvre the yacht in a confined space. Once the sails are packed or rolled away, the next step is to prepare warps and fenders for mooring.

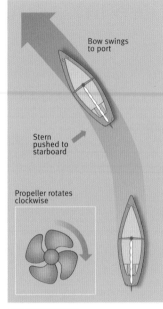

Bow swings to port

Stern pushed to starboard

Propeller rotates clockwise

PROP WALK AHEAD
A conventional propeller rotates clockwise when running ahead, causing the stern to move slightly to starboard as you move off.

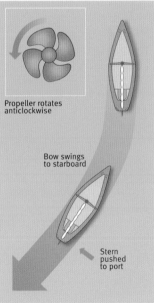

Propeller rotates anticlockwise

Bow swings to starboard

Stern pushed to port

PROP WALK ASTERN
When running astern, a conventional propeller rotates anticlockwise, causing the stern to move slightly to port.

Steering a course

Keeping a yacht and its sails in balance is the solution to steering a course well. You must have the correct amount of sail area for the prevailing conditions, and the crew must trim the sails in accordance with the course being followed by the helmsman.

NEUTRAL HELM

A perfectly balanced yacht with correctly set sails (*see* pp.78–79) has neutral helm and will continue sailing in a straight line if you let go of the wheel. If the yacht turns into the wind, it has weather helm, a small amount of which may be desirable. If the wheel becomes heavy and difficult to turn, weather helm is excessive. If the yacht turns away from the wind, it has lee helm, which is undesirable and could lead to loss of control in stronger winds.

STEERING USING THE SAILS

In all but the lightest winds, a yacht under sail will heel, which affects steering and increases weather helm. If heeling is extreme, you must reduce sail area and keep mainsail and headsail balanced.

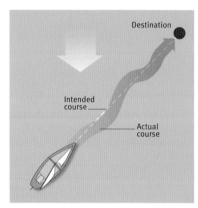

Destination

Intended course

Actual course

A "STRAIGHT" COURSE
The effects of wind and waves mean it is hard to sail a straight course unless the yacht is motoring over a flat sea. Constant correction is usually needed.

OBSERVING SAIL TRIM
Watching sail trim and wind direction helps the helmsman to steer a downwind course, with sheets eased and the yacht level to ensure the wheel feels light.

Too much headsail adds to lee helm; too much mainsail increases weather helm.

Sail trim should be used to keep the boat on course and to change direction, while the helmsman provides fine tuning. If the helmsman is following a straight course, mainsail and headsail sheets should be trimmed so that steering feels almost neutral. If the helmsman wants to change direction towards the wind, sheeting in will help the yacht turn upwind. If the helmsman wants to steer away from the wind, sheeting out will help to keep the yacht upright and allow it to turn downwind – if you do not let the mainsheet out far enough, the yacht may not be able to bear away at all.

WIND INDICATORS
Mounted on the mast, the wind indicator (*above, left*) gives a physical display of wind direction. The anemometer (*right*) records wind speed electronically.

AIMING FOR LANDMARKS
Keep a clear lookout ahead, especially on the leeward side, where the headsail obscures the helmsman's view. Check the chart for hazards beneath the water.

COMPASS
The binnacle compass is located directly in front of the wheel and provides helmsman and crew with a clear view of the course being steered.

WIND DIRECTION AND SIGHT

The helmsman should always steer by a compass course, unless the crew are familiar with the sailing area and know exactly which way to go. The yacht's course is governed by wind direction, with helmsman and crew using data provided by instruments, flags, and wind indicator, plus feedback from the wheel and sails. Landmarks, objects at sea such as lighthouses and buoys, and transits (*see right*) at the entrance to a harbour or in a channel, help provide a visual guide for steering.

Steer boat straight ahead

Turn boat to port

Turn boat to starboard

USING TRANSITS
Two objects are in transit when they are in line. Transit marks are used in harbours and channels to indicate the correct course. Posts in the water are used as transit markers, as are conspicuous objects on land shown in the pilot book or chart.

Sailing to windward and tacking

A yacht is sailing towards the wind or "to windward" when the wind is blowing from forward of the beam. It is while sailing to windward that the yacht is most likely to heel, with sails sheeted in tight if the helmsman wishes to sail as close to the wind as possible.

BEATING

When sailing on a close reach, the helmsman will choose a course at around 50 degrees to the wind and the crew should adjust sail trim accordingly. To alter course from close reach to close hauled, or "beating" (*see* Points of sailing, pp.72–73.), the helmsman steers the yacht about 20 degrees further into the wind while the crew wind in the mainsail and headsail sheets.

In a moderate or strong wind, the mainsheet should be pulled in as tight as possible, and the headsail should be sheeted in until the leech almost touches the spreaders. In lighter winds, both sails should be eased to take a fuller shape.

CLOSE HAULED

Sailing to windward on starboard tack, the mainsail is sheeted tight to the centreline, with the headsail sheeted in until it almost touches the spreaders.

TACKING

Tacking involves turning the boat "through" the wind. The helmsman should steer the yacht smoothly through the tack.

TACKING IN A YACHT

Although a yacht tacks more slowly than a dinghy and may have more crew, high sheet loads on the headsail require careful timing. The old sheet must be let off and the new one pulled in as the helmsman steers carefully through the tack.

1 **On the instruction** "Prepare to tack", one crew member prepares to let off the working sheet on the leeward side while another prepares to pull in the new working sheet on the windward side.

2 **The helmsman says** "Ready to tack?" and, once prepared, the crew reply "Ready". Calling "Lee-ho", the helmsman turns the yacht steadily and slowly through the eye of the wind.

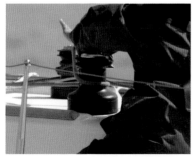

3 **As the yacht** begins to bear off on the new tack, one crew takes the old working sheet off its winch; another puts two turns on the leeward winch and pulls in the new working sheet.

4 **The crew pulls in** as much sheet as possible, adds two more turns, and winds the headsail in tight. If winding is too hard, the helmsman luffs to windward to depower the headsail.

Sailing downwind

When a yacht is sailing with the wind aft of the beam, it is said to be downwind, or offwind. This type of course could be a broad reach, which is the fastest point of sailing (*see* pp.72–73), or a "dead run" straight downwind, when the most important skill is to control gybes.

REACHING AND RUNNING

A broad reach with the wind aft of the beam is often the most enjoyable sailing course. With correct trim, the yacht should be at its most stable with the wind coming from this direction. It will be sailing at maximum speed without heeling too much and should be easy to steer.

If bearing away from a broad reach on to a dead downwind course, the helmsman and crew must always be aware of the risk of an unplanned gybe. If there are waves, the yacht will tend to roll from side to side, making steering difficult. The helmsman needs to anticipate how the waves will push the stern from side to side, altering course just before the boat changes direction. If the

motion becomes too difficult, head up on to a reach to stabilize the yacht. You can also "tack downwind" with a series of gybes, which takex longer but may be easier and more comfortable for the crew.

BROAD REACHING
A broad reach can be the fastest yet most comfortable point of sailing. This course avoids the risk of an accidental gybe.

GOOSEWINGING
Sailing on a run, you can get maximum sail power by "goosewinging" the headsail on the windward side.

Rope attached to end of boom is led through bow fairlead and secured to a cleat

GYBE PREVENTER
A rope attached to the end of the boom helps prevent an unexpected gybe while the helmsman steers downwind with the mainsail to port and the headsail "goosewinged" across to starboard.

GYBING HAZARDS

The heavy boom of a yacht must be controlled as it swings from side to side. The helmsman should steer carefully and slowly into the gybe, waiting until the mainsheet is fully sheeted before turning the stern through the eye of the wind until the wind hits the mainsail on the other side and pushes the boom over. The yacht should still be sailing nearly dead downwind as the mainsail gybes on to the new side. The helmsman must be ready to correct course to prevent the yacht from bearing up on to a beam reach, which in windy conditions could make it heel right over as it turns into the wind.

An uncontrolled gybe is extremely dangerous – sailors have been killed by the boom in this situation.

GYBING
The helmsman must time the gybe carefully as the crew sheet in the mainsail first, then let the mainsheet out on the new course.

GYBING SAFELY

When preparing for a gybe, best practice is to sheet the mainsail to the centreline so that the boom can swing through only a very small arc. Watch the boom, keep your head low, and do not go on the sidedeck if the yacht is or may be about to gybe. Always sheet in for the gybe. Never let the boom crash the full distance from one side to the other.

1 **On the instruction** "Prepare to gybe!" from the helmsman, the crew starts to pull in the mainsheet until the boom is close to the centreline. The sheet is then cleated.

2 **When the helmsman cries** "Ready to gybe?", the crew reply "Ready" when prepared. The helmsman then steers carefully to leeward until the wind catches the mainsail on the other side.

3 **While one crew** eases out the mainsheet on the new gybe, two other crew let off the old working headsail sheet and pull in the new working sheet on the other side of the boat.

4 **The helmsman may need** to correct the yacht's natural tendency to turn up into the wind on the new gybe by making regular adjustments with the wheel.

Hoisting the spinnaker

A traditional symmetrical spinnaker gives a huge boost in performance for downwind sailing. It also provides excitement and a challenge – particularly in stronger winds – which calls for expertise from the crew. But once you master a spinnaker, you will want to fly it all the time.

PREPARING TO HOIST

Spinnakers look beautiful, but can be troublesome if you handle them wrongly. The most important trick with these downwind sails is to keep both clew and tack level, while ensuring that the main power area of the spinnaker does not fly too high. The helmsman needs at least three experienced crew to fly the spinnaker – one working on the foredeck and two in the cockpit. A day with a light wind, as shown in the photos on these pages, is perfect for getting accustomed to spinnaker handling. Until you feel confident, do not attempt to fly a spinnaker in winds stronger than a Force 2. If the wind picks up while you are sailing, get the spinnaker down unless you are sailing with an expert crew.

1 **The spinnaker pole** is attached to the mast and is raised to about head height on a track by the cockpit crew. The angle of the pole is controlled by an uphaul line to the cockpit.

2 **The foredeck crew** brings the spinnaker on deck in its bag and secures it at both ends to the guard rail to prevent it from lifting up and going over the side.

3 **Having opened the flaps of the bag,** the foredeck crew locates the three corners of the spinnaker – the head and the port and starboard tacks.

4 **He attaches both sheets** and the halyard, making sure it is on the windward side of the forestay. The free end of the spinnaker pole is attached to the windward sheet, or guy.

5 **The cockpit crew** pull up the spinnaker halyard as quickly as possible, hand over hand, while the helmsman steers downwind to blanket the spinnaker.

PERFECT SPINNAKER SET
The crew keeps the spinnaker level and symmetrical, ensuring that its power provides forward motion rather than rolling the yacht from side to side.

6 **During the hoist,** the spinnaker pole is by the forestay. When the spinnaker is fully hoisted, the crew pull on the leeward side working sheet and windward side guy, allowing the spinnaker to inflate.

Gybing and stowing a spinnaker

Correctly gybing a symmetrical spinnaker relies on the skill of the foredeck crew, who is backed up by the crew in the cockpit. Taking the spinnaker down is an equally important task that ensures the spinnaker is stowed below deck neatly and is ready for the next hoist.

GYBING A SPINNAKER

Gybing with a spinnaker involves two linked operations during which the mainsail boom and the spinnaker pole each change to their opposite sides. The mainsail is gybed by the helmsman following standard procedure (*see* Sailing downwind, pp.198–199). In addition he or she will concentrate on timing the gybe to match that of the foredeck crew handling the spinnaker. The most difficult part is attaching the pole to the new side of the spinnaker. Techniques

for doing this include: dipping the pole so its end can pass inside the forestay; using two poles, which are briefly attached to the spinnaker at the same time; and, most popularly, the "end-for-end" method shown here. This technique requires careful cooperation between foredeck and cockpit crew, who must loosen the guy at the correct moment to provide enough slack to unclip the boom from the mast, clip it to the new guy, and clip the other end of the pole to the mast.

1 **With the yacht** sailing dead downwind, the foredeck crew unclips the inner end of the spinnaker pole from the mast. This end of the pole will be the outer end once the spinnaker is gybed.

2 **The foredeck crew takes the leeward sheet**, clips on the free end of the pole, and pushes the pole out to the new side. He then unclips the other end of the pole from the windward guy.

3 **The helmsman bears away** to gybe the mainsail, as the crew pulls the new inner end of the pole towards the mast, with the cockpit crew providing sufficient slack in the new guy.

4 **The pole is clipped on to the mast** while the spinnaker remains blanketed by the mainsail and not fully powered. The cockpit crew adjust the sheet and guy to set the spinnaker on the new tack.

DROPPING THE SPINNAKER

Be careful that none of the spinnaker spills over the side while it is being lowered. If it does, the spinnaker will drag in the water and the foredeck crew will find it very difficult to get it back on board. Keeping the spinnaker under control relies on the cockpit crew lowering the halyard at the correct speed for the foredeck crew, who will be gathering the sail and bundling it down the forehatch. During this manoeuvre, the helmsman should make sure that the spinnaker remains blanketed by the mainsail in order to prevent the wind from wresting the sail from the foredeck crew's control. In stronger winds, extra hands will be needed to gather the sail and get it safely inside the boat.

1 **With the spinnaker** depowered by the mainsail, the foredeck crew grabs the leeward sheet close to the clew and opens the forehatch. The cockpit crew makes sure the spinnaker is kept blanketed by the mainsail.

2 **The foredeck crew** sits in the forehatch, gathering in the spinnaker and feeding it down below into the forepeak, where another pair of hands may be useful.

3 **The cockpit crew** steadily eases the windward guy and progressively the spinnaker halyard, enabling the foredeck crew to gather in the sail in an orderly way.

4 **The foredeck crew** unclips the guy and sheet, clips them together, and unclips the halyard. He ensures that the three corners of the spinnaker are secured together at the forehatch.

5 **With the pole uphaul eased**, the foredeck crew drops the spinnaker pole down the mast. On many yachts it will be secured on the sidedeck. Spinnaker sheets can be attached to the pulpit.

"THE QUALITY OF WATER AND LIFE IN ALL ITS FORMS ARE A CRITICAL PART OF THE HEALTH OF THIS PLANET."

Sir Peter Blake

Mooring techniques

Mooring a yacht at a dock or a marina requires careful preparation and a well-briefed crew. Different situations may include mooring alongside a pontoon, bows-on or stern-to on a harbour wall, and rafting alongside other yachts.

APPROACHING A BERTH

Hundreds of yachts may be berthed close together in a marina, and room to manoeuvre may be limited. Good boat-handling and a cautious approach is essential. As you near the berth, the skipper needs to make a decision on what kind of approach is best in the conditions, and then give instructions to the crew to prepare the yacht with fenders in position and mooring lines ready; they should be attached to cleats at the bow and stern, led through fairleads, and coiled for passing on to the pontoon. The crew should then take up positions on deck, ready to step ashore or throw a line to someone ashore.

WELL PREPARED
As the skipper reverses the boat into a berth, everything has been prepared. The crew have fixed fenders in position and are ready to step ashore.

TYING ON FENDERS

A yacht of 10–12m (33–39ft) should have at least eight fenders of a suitable size. When approaching a berth, the skipper must decide if fenders are required on one or both sides. One or more fenders may also be required on the transom when berthing stern-to and one on the bow if berthing bow-on. Always remove fenders after leaving a berth.

1 **Protect the widest part** of the yacht with a fender at the correct height. It can be useful to have at least one crew standing by with a "roving fender" for instant use.

2 **You can tie the fenders to** the guard rails. Use a quick-release clove hitch (see p.89), in which you pass a loop rather than the working end under the standing part.

3 **Pull the loop tight** so that the fender is secured at the correct height. To remove the fender, undo the knot by pulling on the free end of the rope.

CLEATING A WARP

"Warp" is the term for any ropes that secure or are used to move a vessel. Warps are secured to cleats onboard and led through fairleads (openings) to fixing points on shore. The warp at the bow is also known as the bow line and that at the stern is known as the stern line.

1 **Always take at least one turn** round a horn cleat when "holding" the yacht on a warp.

2 **When the skipper** instructs you to tie off bow and stern lines, start by taking a second turn round the cleat.

3 **Take the warp** diagonally over the top of the cleat and under the horn, above the other end of the warp.

4 **Complete a figure-of-eight turn,** bringing the warp under the other horn of the cleat as shown.

5 **Prevent the warp from slipping** by taking two turns around the base of the cleat.

SPRINGS AND BREAST ROPES

"Spring" is the term used for ropes that are used to prevent the yacht moving ahead or astern when moored alongside. A breast rope is a rope that is led from the boat approximately at right angles to the pontoon or jetty. These are used to keep the boat close alongside to facilitate loading. They may be removed later.

MOORING ROPES
Ropes used for mooring are known by different terms according to their position and role in securing the boat. There is no difference in their appearance.

BOW SPRING IN PLACE
This boat is secured alongside with a stern spring and a fore breast rope. Both are lead on to the yacht via a fairlead (rope guide). Fenders are in place.

SUNSAIL 18

JEANNEAU

Mooring alongside: stern first

When mooring alongside, it might appear easiest to approach and leave the pontoon with the yacht moving forwards. However, some situations – for example, a crowded marina, strong wind, or fast tide – may make it preferable to enter or leave stern first.

MOORING ALONGSIDE

Whether approaching stern or bow first, keep your approach slow, but with enough speed to maintain effective steerage. When possible, it is best to arrive and leave with the yacht pointing into the wind or tide, whichever is having the strongest influence at the time. This will help stop the yacht alongside the berth so the crew can get ashore with mooring lines more easily. In many situations you will be able to use the effect of prop walk (*see* Manoeuvring under power, pp.192–193) to help you position the boat accurately.

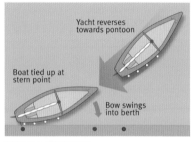

ARRIVING STERN FIRST
When arriving stern first, reverse the yacht into the wind or tide, to help stop the boat and swing the bow towards the pontoon. The crew should secure the stern line first, then the bow line.

1 **The helmsman reverses the boat** slowly towards the pontoon, taking into account the effects of prop walk to help position the boat as desired.

2 **The helmsman brings** the stern close enough so that one crew can step (not jump) on to the pontoon with the coiled stern line, which is secured to a cleat on deck.

3 **The crew secures the stern line** (passing through the fairlead) to hold the stern in place. This rope is also long enough to be used as a spring, led to the midpoint of the yacht.

4 **Making sure the line** is passed under the guard rails and through the fairlead, the crew on board throws the bow line to the crew ashore, who secures it to a cleat or bollard.

LEAVING FROM ALONGSIDE

The helmsman cannot steer a yacht away from close alongside a pontoon unless the bow or stern has been pushed out. On a small yacht, it may be possible to push off with a boat hook. If there is a strong wind or tide in the opposite direction, let off the stern line and depart stern first. If there is a strong wind or tide against the bow, let off the bow line first then leave bow first (*see* pp.210–211). When leaving a tight berth, springs can be very effective. Motor ahead against a bow spring to push out the stern; motor astern against a stern spring to push out the bow.

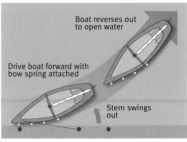

LEAVING A TIGHT BERTH STERN FIRST
When leaving a pontoon stern first, cast off the stern line, then the bow line. Motor forward with the bow spring attached so that the stern swings out. Release the spring, then reverse the boat away from the pontoon into open water.

1 **The crew attaches a fender** at the bow of the boat to protect it as the stern will later swing out, pushing the bow against the pontoon.

2 **Having stepped ashore** the crew releases the stern line and stern spring, throwing the warps back on board. These are coiled by crew on board.

3 **The crew releases the bow line** and then gives a signal that the helmsman can motor slowly forwards against the bow spring.

4 **The yacht pivots** on the taut bow spring, pushing the stern out with the bow hard against the pontoon. The fenders protect the bow from damage.

5 **When the stern** has swung out far enough, the crew climbs aboard carrying the bow spring. The helmsman then reverses the boat out to the open water.

Mooring alongside: bow first

A bow-first approach to an alongside berth should be done at a slow speed, preferably with the boat facing into the wind andor tide. As with stern-first approaches, careful forethought by the skipper and preparation by the crew are essential.

DEALING WITH WIND

Be prepared to slow the boat with a brief burst of reverse gear. If the wind is blowing straight on to the dock, stop the yacht about 1m (3ft) away from where you want to end up and let the wind blow the boat alongside. If the wind is blowing off the dock, make your approach at a more acute angle and use the wind to blow the bow parallel as you reach the dock. Prop walk (see Manoeuvring under power, pp.192–193) can often be used for fine adjustments of the boat's position in relation to the pontoon.

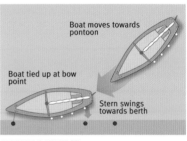

Boat moves towards pontoon

Boat tied up at bow point

Stern swings towards berth

ARRIVING BOW FIRST
Approach the berth at an angle. As the boat nears the pontoon, the crew secures the bow line ashore. The stern swings towards the pontoon.

1 **Approach the dock** slowly against the direction of the wind or tide (whichever is stronger) to slow the boat.

2 **When close to shore,** one crew steps on to land with the bow line. Beware of the gap between boat and land.

3 **The crew secures** the bow line around a cleat or bollard to prevent the yacht drifting back on the wind or tide.

5 **There should be enough spare rope** to rig a bow spring, taking the rope from the cleat on the dock to the bow of the yacht.

4 **The crew on board** passes the stern line to the crew on shore, who secures it around a cleat.

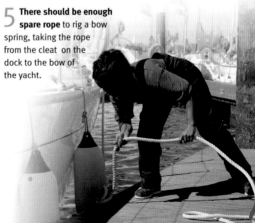

LEAVING BOW FIRST

In order to leave bow first, the bow must be pushed away from the pontoon at an angle to allow for the tendency of the stern to pivot against the dock as you steer away. If the tide or a strong wind is on the bow it will help push the bow out. Alternatively, you can reverse on to a short stern line or a stern spring for the same effect. Before starting the manoeuvre, the skipper should be sure to protect the boat from direct contact with the pontoon by instructing the crew to position additional fenders at the stern.

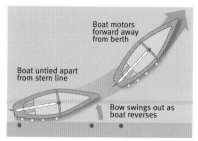

LEAVING BOW FIRST
All lines are released except at the stern. As the boat reverses against the stern line, the bow swings out. The stern line is released. The boat moves forward.

1 **The crew positions** an extra fender at the stern of the boat to protect it from contact with the pontoon.

2 **The crew releases the bow line** and passes it back onboard. The bow is now free to drift away from the pontoon.

3 **A bowline is tied** (*see* p.88) in the stern line to make the bow move out further when the boat reverses

4 **The helmsman reverses** against the stern line to pivot the bow out. The crew is ready to release the line when instructed to do so.

5 **When the bow** is sufficiently far out, the crew steps onboard at the stern, and brings the stern line onboard.

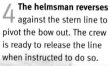

Berthing stern-to or bow-on

Lying stern-to or bow-on to a dock is standard practice when cruising in areas such as the Mediterranean. There are advantages and disadvantages to each method but both allow yachts to pack more tightly into harbours and marinas than mooring alongside.

BERTHING STERN-TO

There are various advantages to berthing with the stern up against the pontoon or jetty. It gives the crew easy access to the dock for getting ashore or taking on supplies and it is ideal for plugging into shore power. It is also relatively straightforward to leave the berth, since the boat is already pointing towards open water. But, there is less privacy and you need to be sure that the water is deep enough for the rudder and propeller.

1 The crew drops the anchor when the boat is correctly positioned some distance out from the pontoon before the helmsman reverses stern first into the berth.

2 Steer the boat slowly, in reverse gear, towards the berth. Only use small movements with the rudder. As you move towards the jetty, the foredeck crew pays out the anchor chain.

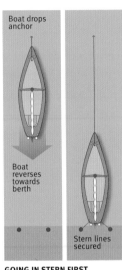

Boat drops anchor

Boat reverses towards berth

Stern lines secured

GOING IN STERN FIRST
The anchor is dropped to hold the bow. The boat is then reversed into the berth, where it is secured at the stern.

Sunsail Sun Fast 37

Macktick

SUNSAIL 18

3 **The crew step ashore** with warps on the port and starboard side. The helmsman may need to give a short burst of forward gear to prevent the boat hitting the pontoon.

4 **The crew secure the stern lines** ashore. Make final adjustments to the amount of anchor chain either by taking up slack or letting it out a little more.

BERTHING BOW-ON

Berthing bow-on has three main advantages. It is much easier to motor ahead into a berth, you get privacy in the cockpit, and it avoids any danger of the rudder hitting an outcrop under the dock. A disadvantage is that it can be difficult getting on or off the boat via the bow. Some marinas have lazy lines for mooring (either stern- or bow-to). These are permanent lines fixed both to the pontoon or jetty and to a mooring under the water a short distance from the berth. You simply pick up the line with a boat hook and secure it to a deck cleat (*see below*) furthest from the pontoon. If lazy lines are not provided you will have to secure the boat at the stern with the auxiliary anchor and chain. When mooring bow-on always protect the bow of the boat with a fender suspended from the pulpit.

USING A LAZY LINE
A lazy line along the starboard side makes it easy to pick up a permanent mooring line attached to a concrete block on the bottom. Here a bow fender has been rigged to prevent damage in case the boat moves forward and touches the jetty.

Boat drops anchor

Boat motors forward towards jetty

Bow lines secured

GOING IN BOW FIRST
The anchor is dropped from the stern. The boat then motors forward and is secured by bow

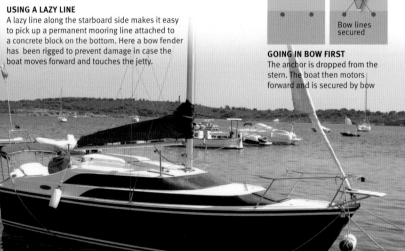

Choosing an anchorage

An anchorage must be well protected from strong wind, unpleasant swell, and dangerous currents. A high-sided bay with prevailing offshore winds, combined with good holding and suitable depth of water for the anchor, should provide ideal conditions.

GOOD HOLDING

The seabed must enable the anchor to gain good holding, and the most reliable substrates for this are mud and sand. Good holding also relies on the anchor chain or rope having a sufficient "scope" (the ratio of its length to the depth to the seabed) to be stretched out along the seabed. To estimate how much is needed, multiply the depth by four for chain and by six for warp. Take care in tidal areas, where the depth of an anchorage will vary according to the state of the tide. At low water, the anchorage may even dry out.

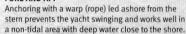

FORE AND AFT
Anchoring with a warp (rope) led ashore from the stern prevents the yacht swinging and works well in a non-tidal area with deep water close to the shore.

SPACE TO SWING
A bay surrounded by high hills usually gives excellent protection, allowing plenty of room for yachts and motorboats at anchor to swing with the wind.

ANCHORING OVERNIGHT

Sailors looking to enjoy a stay in an overnight anchorage need to look for three qualities: good holding, reliably flat water, and safe access to the shore. Rock and shingle provide poor holding and should be avoided. Coral should never be anchored as it will inevitably sustain irreparable damage. Avoid bays that experience prevailing onshore winds. Beware also of late afternoon swells, which may wrap around the entrance to your anchorage and roll in as night falls.

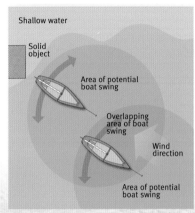

SHIFTING WIND
Allow enough space for your yacht to swing as the wind or tide changes without getting too close to solid, fixed objects or shallow water. Check the weather forecast for likely changes in wind direction.

SWINGING TOGETHER
Yachts tend to swing in unison, which makes it possible to anchor them relatively close together. Motorboats, which do not have rigs or deep keels, tend to have different swing characteristics.

Anchoring techniques

Dropping an anchor by hand relies on communication between the skipper and foredeck crew, who control the combined weight of anchor and chain. A power windlass removes much of the physical effort, with engine revs providing the power.

DROPPING THE ANCHOR

The anchor and chain are heavy and potentially dangerous, so beware of feet and hands when dealing with the anchor. Do not allow young children on the foredeck during this operation, and never let the chain or warp run out of control. The skipper should wait until the yacht has stopped or started moving backwards before telling the foredeck crew to let go of the anchor. When sufficient chain or warp has been dropped for the depth of water (chain 4 x depth; warp 6 x depth), reverse the engine to set the anchor. Watch other boats or points on shore to check if the anchor continues to drag.

1 **Secure the anchor locker lid** to the guard rail. Carefully lift the anchor out through the pulpit on to the bow roller.

2 **One crew member** holds the anchor in the bow roller, pulling the retaining line tight, while a second crew lifts a length of chain out of the locker. It is very important to ensure that the anchor does not fall over the bow at the wrong moment.

3 **Take a turn round the foredeck cleat** with the chain to ensure you can keep the anchor under complete control. The chain and anchor are extremely heavy and caution is required at all times.

4 **Carefully lift the back of the anchor** and slide it forward in the bow roller. Throughout this process, the other crew member should continue to keep tension on the retaining line.

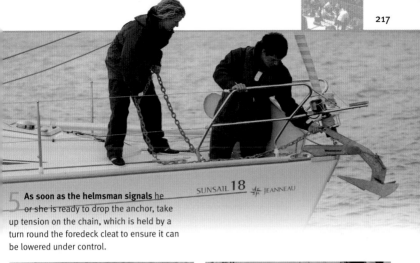

5 **As soon as the helmsman signals** he or she is ready to drop the anchor, take up tension on the chain, which is held by a turn round the foredeck cleat to ensure it can be lowered under control.

6 **Pay out the anchor chain** in even lengths hand over hand. This will allow you to estimate how many metres of chain and/or warp have been let out to match the depth of the water.

7 **Having paid out all the anchor chain** and sufficient warp for the depth of water, make the warp fast around a cleat on the foredeck. As the boat drifts back, the anchor digs into the seabed.

PULLING UP THE ANCHOR

It is possible to pull up warp hand over hand, but anchor chain should be pulled up almost completely vertically, rather than at an angle. The helmsman motors slowly ahead so the yacht is over the anchor, with the crew indicating the approximate position. The crew should tell the skipper as soon as the anchor breaks out from the bottom.

1 **The crew indicates** the position of the anchor to the helmsman, who cautiously motors ahead. Pulling with the anchor chain under tension at 45 degrees can be dangerous.

2 **Wait until the chain** has gone slack. With no pull from the yacht, two crew can easily lift the weight of the chain. Take a turn round the cleat if you need to.

3 **Tell the helmsman** when the anchor is lifted – the bow will start to blow away from the wind. Remove weeds and mud from the anchor before getting it on deck.

Tenders

The inflatable dinghy is the most popular type of tender for yachts. It is compact enough to be stowed on deck or towed behind the yacht, can be rowed or powered by an outboard motor, is quick to inflate or deflate, and can be stored in a cockpit locker when not in use.

OUTBOARD MOTORS AND OARS

Most tenders rely on an outboard motor to travel any distance, but make sure you always take oars or paddles with you in case of engine failure. Be aware that some tenders do not row at all well, particularly when heavily laden or blown around by the wind. Familiarize yourself with how the oars attach to the rowlocks – some systems can be fiddly. Make sure all the tubes are fully inflated every time you go afloat.

OUTBOARD SAFETY
Always attach the "kill cord", which cuts out the engine, to your leg. If you fall over the side without a kill cord, the engine will continue to run and the tender will go round in circles, possibly running you down with the propeller.

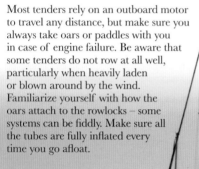

USING THE OUTBOARD MOTOR
When using an outboard motor, do not exceed the maximum power rating for a tender. Ensure the petrol tank is sufficiently full every time you go ashore.

TOWING BEHIND
The tender is frequently towed from the stern of the yacht. A short painter is normally best as it lifts the bow. However, for optimum sailing performance it is advisable to bring the tender on board.

TOWING ALONGSIDE
It is possible to motor at slow speed with the tender alongside. This is useful when the tender needs to be moved from the stern to the bow – for example, when manoeuvring in a marina.

LOADING AND USING A TENDER

Always wear a lifejacket on a tender and never exceed the maximum number of passengers for which a tender is designed. Instead, make extra journeys to or from the shore. If you are leaving the yacht in the dark, carry a hand-held light to alert other boats, make sure you turn on the anchor light before you go, and look for possible landmarks around. When approaching a beach using an outboard motor, slow right down. Never drag a tender up and down the beach – lift it to avoid damage to the tubes.

1 **With the painter secured** on board the yacht, the first person steps backwards gently into the bottom of the tender, not on the tubes. Keeping low, she moves carefully back, to make room for other passengers to load.

2 **The first person is sitting** towards the back, the second person – the rower – climbs into the tender, with one hand on the tender's tube and the other holding the yacht's pushpit, and avoiding standing on the tubes.

3 **The rower takes** up position facing astern and releases the oars from their stowing clips, inserts them in the rowlocks and swivels them through 90 degrees, ready to row ashore.

4 **Releasing the painter** from the yacht, the third person gets in ready to sit in the bow to balance the tender. The rower rows away from the yacht.

GETTING OUT OF A TENDER

To disembark from a tender is the reverse of the procedure for getting in. It is important to keep the boat balanced; as each person gets out, those remaining should adjust their positions to compensate. When everyone has disembarked, the tender should be secured by its painter or brought on board. If using oars, these should always be stowed securely, preferably brought on board the yacht if you are going to be towing. Always remove the outboard from a tender that is to be towed.

SECURING THE TENDER
The person in the bow gets out with the painter first and secures the boat to the yacht or pontoon.

"...LIFE AT SEA

IS BETTER."

Sir Francis Drake

Living aboard

A modern cruising yacht must function well in all conditions, at sea or in the marina. Good sailing performance and the ability to withstand rough conditions should be combined with comfortable, spacious accommodation that can provide a complete floating home.

SPACE MASTERS

Modern yachts, designed with a wide beam and high freeboard, provide a large living space inside the boat without too great a compromise on sailing performance. A cruising yacht of around 12m (39ft) is typically fitted with three self-contained double cabins, two heads, a spacious galley and navigation areas, plus a large saloon with dining table and seating for up to eight people. They can also accommodate plenty of stowage space for provisions, clothing, and safety gear.

When a full complement of crew is living on a yacht, tidiness becomes a priority. Crew members should bring a minimum of possessions which should be packed in soft sailing bags – there is no room aboard for conventional suitcases. Each crew should be assigned cabin space with their own lockers for clothing.

LIVING OUTSIDE
A large cockpit with sunshade (bimini) and transom that doubles as a swimming platform offer the crew a comfortable, safe place to enjoy outdoor living.

Empty bags can be stowed under berths or in cockpit lockers. Hygiene is very important on a boat. Keep the interior as clean as possible.

Make sure everyone knows exactly how to operate the onboard lavatory, known as the "heads", so there is no

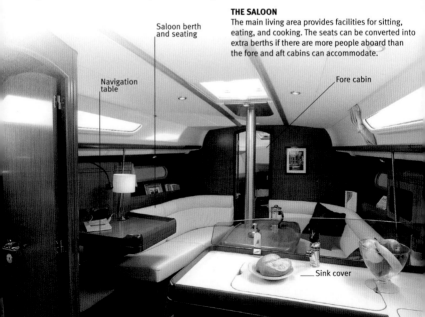

THE SALOON
The main living area provides facilities for sitting, eating, and cooking. The seats can be converted into extra berths if there are more people aboard than the fore and aft cabins can accommodate.

Saloon berth and seating

Navigation table

Fore cabin

Sink cover

chance of a blockage. Pressurized hot and cold water in the shower is convenient, but make sure the crew understand that you may have only 300 litres in the tank. Cabins inevitably become damp, so open the hatches and companionway to air the interior whenever possible. When storing food in the galley, make sure it is packed in airtight, damp-proof containers and is easy to find; never store food in cardboard boxes. Remember to clean and drain the fridge regularly in order to avoid smells, etc.

THE HEADS
Waste from the heads (so called because the lavatory was traditionally at the front of the boat) is pumped out through a sea cock in the side of the hull, with sea water pumped in to flush the bowl.

SAFETY GEAR
All the crew should know where their harnesses and lifejackets are stored, ready to be donned with no delay whenever necessary. Make sure they are accessible and easy to retrieve.

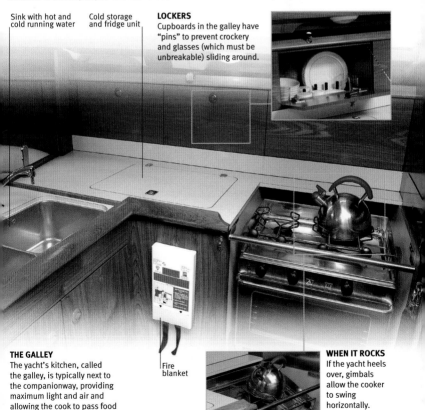

Sink with hot and cold running water

Cold storage and fridge unit

LOCKERS
Cupboards in the galley have "pins" to prevent crockery and glasses (which must be unbreakable) sliding around.

THE GALLEY
The yacht's kitchen, called the galley, is typically next to the companionway, providing maximum light and air and allowing the cook to pass food and drink to crew in the cockpit. The L-shape design gives the cook holding points for when the yacht is heeling or rolling.

Fire blanket

WHEN IT ROCKS
If the yacht heels over, gimbals allow the cooker to swing horizontally. Fiddles lock the kettle or pots securely on top of the gas rings.

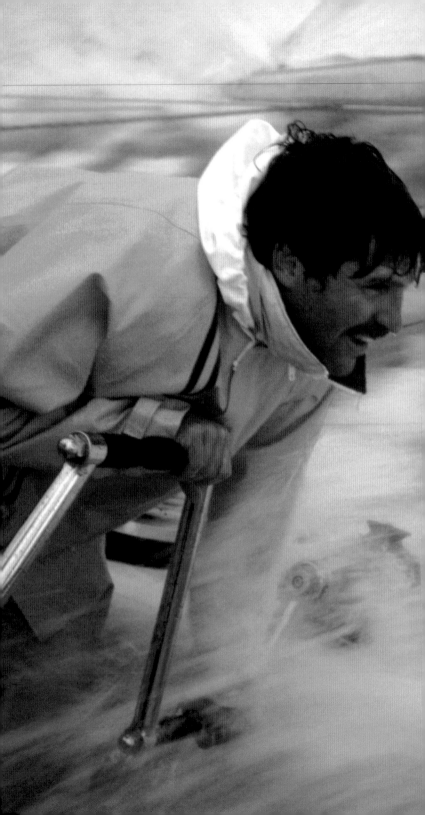

Weather

Importance of weather

For most people, a perfect sailing day has warm sun, blue sky, and a Force 3–4 breeze. Unfortunately, the weather cannot be booked to order, which is why sailors need forecasts and some basic knowledge to assess if the wind will be too light, too strong, or just right.

WORLD WEATHER

Weather is driven by the sun heating the Earth. As hot air rises, it is replaced by heavier, denser, cold air that holds less moisture. Air is drawn from high- to low-pressure areas and ocean currents also move hot and cold air to different parts of the globe. Large temperature differences between the poles and the equator, combined with the Earth spinning, create bands of low pressure at the equator and mid-latitudes, with bands of higher pressure at the poles and subtropics. These pressure bands produce stable wind systems over the oceans, which are disrupted by temperature changes over land. The spinning Earth makes northern hemisphere winds incline to the right and southern hemisphere winds incline to the left.

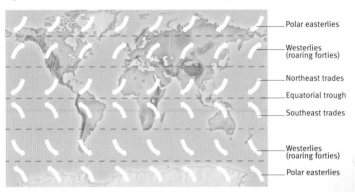

Polar easterlies

Westerlies (roaring forties)

Northeast trades

Equatorial trough

Southeast trades

Westerlies (roaring forties)

Polar easterlies

PREVAILING WINDS
Pressure bands and the spin of the Earth create the high-pressure polar easterly winds. In between are the low-pressure westerlies, the high-pressure northeast and southeast trade winds, and the low-pressure equatorial trough.

OCEAN WEATHER SYSTEMS
Between polar and tropical regions, mid-latitude depressions (areas of low pressure) tend to travel from east to west in both hemispheres before turning more towards the nearest pole.

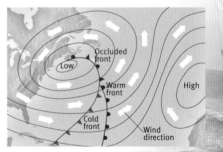

Occluded front

Low

Warm front

High

Cold front

Wind direction

LOCAL WINDS

Pilot books and yachtsmen's coastal guides give data on strong winds in specific areas. In the Mediterranean, the most famous such wind is the *mistral*, which blows down the Rhône Valley and can produce gale-force conditions between France and Corsica for several days. Further east, the *meltemi* provides a strong thermal wind that blows across Greek and Turkish waters for a few hours each summer afternoon. Down in the Indian Ocean, the "Fremantle Doctor" makes the seas choppy off Western Australia from around noon each day in summer, bringing relief from the intense heat.

CLEAR SKIES

High pressure can bring light winds and clear skies. The effect of sun warming up the land will frequently reward the sailor with fresh afternoon sea breezes.

WEATHER DANGERS

Gusty conditions, in which the wind suddenly increases and changes direction, followed by a lull, can be a challenge to sailors (*see* Beaufort wind scale, p.233). Huge, vertical cumulus clouds can provide a warning. Squalls are violent gusts that last for more than a minute, generally accompanied by dark clouds with heavy rain. Thunderstorms can bring strong gusts of wind followed by heavy rain, and are signalled by towering cumulus clouds. Sea fog (advection fog) is created by warm, damp air over cold sea and may persist until there is a fresh breeze. Radiation fog is a land fog that will frequently affect nearby coastal waters.

FORECAST FACTORS

Any wind over Force 5 can be dangerous. Force 6 is very windy in a dinghy or a yacht – best advice is seek shelter or stay on shore. The effect of a moderately strong wind can be made worse by factors such as wind blowing against the tide, strong gusts off headlands, a disturbed sea state, bad visibility, or cold weather impairing the ability of the crew.

STORMY WEATHER

Beating to windward in a moderate breeze becomes considerably more uncomfortable for the crew if there is a confused sea. Waves are created by the strength and duration of the wind, plus how far it blows over clear water. Foul tide and shallow water will push waves together, making them steeper and more difficult to sail through.

Weather charts

A weather chart, also known as a synoptic chart, displays existing or forecast weather systems on a large-scale map of land and sea. Contour lines, in the form of isobars, indicate the likely strength and direction of the wind as it blows over a particular area.

WEATHER FRONTS

A front is the forward edge of an advancing mass of air. When warm air from a subtropical high meets cold air from a cold polar front, the warm air is driven above the cold air. This creates unstable conditions, which lead to frontal depressions with unsettled, stormy weather. Frontal depressions tend to move from west to east. They are usually forecast ahead of time, but their speed and direction may be unpredictable. A trough, which is shown by a thick coloured line on the weather chart, is a small front, and is likely to bring a short period of poor weather. Pressure is shown on weather maps by isobars, which join areas of equal pressure. Closely spaced isobars indicate a steep pressure gradient with strong winds; widely spaced isobars indicate a shallow pressure gradient with light winds.

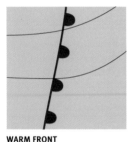

WARM FRONT
A warm front is the leading edge of a mass of warm air pushing over cooler air. It may create heavy rain and poor visibility.

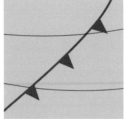

COLD FRONT
A cold front is the leading edge of a mass of cold air pushing under warmer air. It may be followed by showers and possibly storms.

OCCLUDED FRONT
In an occluded front, a fast-moving cold front ploughs under the warm front ahead. Its effect depends on the temperature of the air ahead.

HIGHS AND LOWS

Areas of high pressure with cold air sinking are called anticyclones. They can move slowly over large areas, and are illustrated by widely spaced isobars on a weather map. For sailors, this is a sign of fine weather, with light to moderate winds tempered by sea breezes. Areas of low pressure with warm air rising are called depressions. They vary in size, speed, and intensity and are shown by closely spaced isobars on a weather map. Depressions often create unsettled sailing weather, combining strong winds and heavy rain. Wind blows clockwise round anticyclones and anticlockwise round depressions in the northern hemisphere; in the southern hemisphere, the directions are reversed.

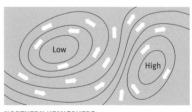

NORTHERN HEMISPHERE

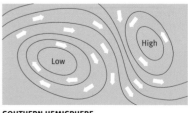

SOUTHERN HEMISPHERE

WEATHER FORECASTS

While a quick rise and fall on the barometer indicates that a gale may be approaching, there are many more sources of specialized forecasting data available to sailors. The radio broadcasts regular shipping forecasts and gale warnings for specific areas, as well as inshore and coastal waters forecasts for up to five days. The internet is also a good source of information and includes services that specialize in, for example, wind forecasts. Online marine services providers also supply a range of weather-related data including surface pressure charts, inshore forecasts and outlooks, two- to five-day planning, satellite pictures, shipping forecasts, gale warnings, coastal reports, five-day forecasts for specific regions, and general weather reports. The regional coastguard broadcasts forecasts and storm warnings on VHF radio. Dial-up telephone forecasts in which you talk directly to a forecaster and obtain a precise "time and place" forecast are also available. Forecasts and warnings for coastal waters are provided onscreen as part of the Global Maritime Distress and Safety System.

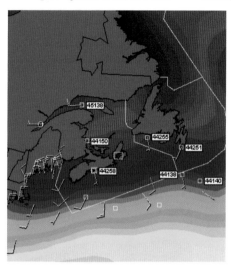

INTERNET FORECASTS
This online map from a forecasting services provider shows wind strength and direction and – using coloured-coded contours – sea-water temperature.

CHECKING THE FORECAST
Printed weather forecasts are often posted on marina and sailing club notice boards and are usually updated at least daily.

WEATHER FORECAST TERMS

TERM	MEANING
Gale warnings	Imminent (within 6 hours); Soon (within 6–12 hours); Later (more than 12 hours after forecast)
Strong winds	Average wind above Force 6 to 7 expected
Fair	No precipitation expected
Backing	Wind direction expected to change in anticlockwise direction
Veering	Wind direction expected to change in clockwise direction
Visibility good	Greater than 9km (5nm)
Visibility moderate	Between 4–9km (2–5nm)
Visibility poor	Less than 4km (2nm)
Sea moderate	Wave height 1.25–2.5m (4–8ft)
Sea rough	Wave height 2.5–4m (8–13ft)
Sea very rough	Wave height 4–6m (13–20ft)

Weather indicators

In addition to checking forecasts, we can use our own eyes and expertise to get an indication of which way the weather may turn. The effect of sun warming the land, coastal topography, prevailing winds, and cloud formation all provide a picture of how the wind will blow.

EFFECTS OF THE LAND

Most sailors sail close to shore during the warmest months, when the weather is mainly settled, producing a regular daily cycle of local onshore (towards the land) and offshore (away from the land) breezes. The strength of a sea breeze (a daytime onshore breeze) or a land breeze (a night-time offshore breeze) is affected by the heat of the sun and by other winds created by other pressure systems (gradient wind). An offshore gradient wind might cancel out a developing sea breeze, while an onshore wind would add to it. A land breeze is likely to be strongest when the sea is warmest, during autumn. Its effect may be felt several miles offshore, with the breeze continuing to blow through the early morning until the cycle begins again.

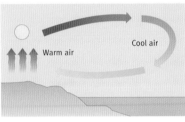

SEA BREEZES
As the land heats up each morning, warm air begins to rise, forming a low-pressure area into which colder air from over the sea is drawn. The onshore breeze typically starts around midday.

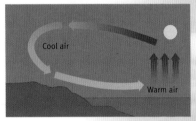

LAND BREEZES
The sea breeze fades as the land cools and air above it starts to sink. Warm air above the sea now starts to rise, creating a lighter, offshore breeze that may blow through the night.

GUSTY BREEZES

Beware of wind bending round headlands with possible unexpected gusts. Steep-sided valleys will accelerate the wind and create stronger gusts that blow for some distance offshore. Similar effects may be felt when wind blows round the sides of a mountain, with higher pressure on the windward side accelerating air flow.

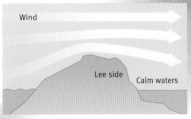

SHELTERED LEE SIDE
The lee side of a land mass is calm, but beware of waves that may wrap around it. Take care also at overnight anchorages below steep cliffs in mountainous areas; sinking cold air flows down the slope at night, creating violent gusts if combined with a land breeze.

WIND SHADOW
Sailing in the lee of a headland, the wind may seem light close inshore. It is easy to assume the wind will stay light around the corner, but a sea breeze may be building to Force 6 on the other side.

CLOUD FORMATIONS

Air contains water that has evaporated from the surface of the Earth. Warm air carries large amounts of water vapour, which will condense into droplets if the air cools down to a temperature known as the dew point. If warm air rises and then cools to its dew point, clouds are formed. Clouds indicate the stability of the atmosphere, providing a picture of the dominant weather system and any likely change to come. Large amounts of cloud cover are to be expected with depressions and ahead of warm fronts, when a mass of warm, moist air lifts over cold air to produce a threatening cloud. Large, tall, cumulonimbus clouds are most likely to produce water vapour droplets falling as heavy rain. Droplets that freeze at higher altitude create snow or hailstones, which will reach sea level if the temperature is sufficiently low.

CUMULONIMBUS CLOUDS
These dark, menacing clouds have great height. They tower over the landscape and may bring torrential rain or snow, thunderstorms, hailstorms, or tornadoes.

CIRRUS CLOUDS
High cirrus clouds above 5,000m (16,000ft) are a mass of ice crystals that may indicate that a depression is fast approaching, particularly if the barometer starts to plummet.

CUMULUS CLOUDS
Lower-layer cumulus are created when warm, moist air rises and cools in a continuous cycle to form fluffy white clouds that may produce gusty winds and showers.

ALTOSTRATUS CLOUDS
A thin layer of clouds at around 2,000–5,000m (6,500–16,500ft) indicates an approaching warm front, with increasing wind and reduced visibility.

Planning for weather

Plan your passage carefully from departure to destination, taking into account navigation, the tides, and pilotage. Wind and weather forecasts should be used to ensure conditions remain favourable throughout the trip, with contingency plans if the weather changes.

WIND OVER WATER

The perfect passage is with wind aft of the beam, sailing mostly on a beam or broad reach, which is more stable and faster than a downwind run. If necessary, delay your passage to avoid long periods of beating to windward against contrary winds. Be aware of recent weather. If there have been gale-force winds across open water, leave time for the waves to subside. Always combine input from the weather forecast with movement of the tides, so that you never end up beating into a gale against a foul (adverse) tide.

A FAST PASSAGE
A broad reach with wind aft and a fair tide should provide the fastest and most stable passage.

A SLOW PASSAGE
Wind against tide produces steep waves. Beating into wind against tide provides a long passage.

AN UNCOMFORTABLE PASSAGE
The boat may roll on a dead downwind course, sailing slowly and in confused motion.

CHANGES IN WEATHER

Both the skipper and navigator must be prepared for certain changes in weather. If the wind dies, the yacht must have enough fuel to motor the remaining distance. If it increases, the skipper must be confident that the yacht and crew will be able to withstand a rough-water passage – if not, the skipper should be ready to change course and head for a nearer anchorage. A change in wind direction from downwind to upwind sailing will slow the yacht right down, substantially altering the estimated time of arrival (ETA).

Fog can envelop a sea area quickly and it can be stressful to navigate a yacht in such conditions. The Global Positioning System (GPS) will fix your position and its data can be combined with that of the depth sounder to enable you to follow the contour line of a chart into a safe anchorage. Radar is the most reliable tool for collision avoidance.

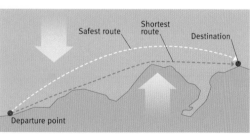

PLANNING FOR ONSHORE AND OFFSHORE WINDS
Courses farther from the shore are often likely to be safer than shorter, inshore routes. An offshore wind is likely to be steadier and stronger farther offshore. An onshore wind is potentially dangerous nearer shore, where it might push up breaking waves in shallow water.

BEAUFORT SCALE

WIND FORCE	WIND SPEED	DESCRIPTION
0	0–1 knots	Calm; mirror-like water; paddle a dinghy or use the engine.
1	1–3 knots	Light air; wind direction shown by smoke drift.
2	4–6 knots	Light breeze; wind felt on face; sail with minimal heeling.
3	7–10 knots	Gentle breeze; wind extends light flag; a good sailing wind.
4	11–16 knots	Moderate breeze; perfect for fairly experienced sailors.
5	17–21 knots	Fresh breeze; crested wavelets form; challenging conditions.
6	22–27 knots	Strong breeze; a dinghy sailor's gale reserved for the best.
7	28–33 knots	Near gale; no dinghy sailing; yachts should seek shelter.
8	34–40 knots	Gale; yachts must be reefed right down.
9	41–47 knots	Severe gale; dangerous conditions, depending on sea state.
10–12	48+ knots	Storm to hurricane; potential fatalities.

HOW WINDY?

The Beaufort Scale was created by Admiral Sir Francis Beaufort in 1805 to help sailors estimate wind strength on the open sea, where conditions tend to be more extreme than in inshore waters. To get a true idea of the wind speed, check an anemometer for strength and direction. Anemometers are usually fitted at yacht clubs or marinas, with instant readings available from weather stations on the internet. Handheld anemometers are inexpensive and reliable for personal use

ALMOST BECALMED
Force 1 is enough to start sailing a dinghy or yacht slowly ahead. Concentrate on keeping the boat moving and the sails filled.

– just be sure to get a wind reading in a clear area away from buildings and other obstructions.

The Beaufort Scale must be related to the prevailing situation. For example, running for shelter may not be the safest option in very strong winds, when clearing a harbour entrance could be more dangerous than heaving-to with a yacht well offshore and waiting for the storm to subside.

CAUGHT UNAWARES
Even when not sailing, a skipper should always take account of the weather. This vessel has probably been dislodged from its mooring by rough seas.

Navigation

What is navigation?

Navigation and passage planning are fundamental skills needed to safely manage a yacht. Conventional, or classic, navigation relies on a compass, manual plotter, and paper chart, and should always be used in tandem with electronic navigation, led by systems that use satellite signals.

MODERN NAVIGATION

The ability to fix position and carry out other navigational tasks using satellite signals has transformed navigation on both sea and land. The most widely used system is the GPS (Global Positioning System), which, in combination with an electronic chart plotter, will chart your progress across the sea with navigational marks, coastline, and dangers all clearly marked on an onscreen map.

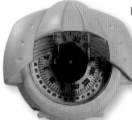

HAND-BEARING COMPASS
This lightweight compass fits in the palm of your hand. Hold it up to your eye, point it in a specific direction, and read a bearing.

basics of classic navigation. You need to be able to read a paper chart, know how to plot your course or position with a plotter or parallel rules, and use dividers to measure distance and a compass to gain magnetic bearings. Novice sailors may find that attending a course in seamanship is the easiest and best way to gain effective training.

However, navigators should not rely solely on the GPS. Electronic systems can suffer power failure or drive malfunction, and GPS data is occasionally very inaccurate. Always complete a thorough passage plan before you set off, and use the GPS en route alongside other, more traditional methods.

CONVENTIONAL METHODS

Anyone intending to sail should be well-acquainted with the

STEERING COMPASS
The main compass is fixed in a position easily visible to the helmsman and well away from the engine, to minimize the effect of magnetic deviation.

STUDYING NAVIGATION
A mastery of conventional navigation takes commitment in time and effort. Attendance at a seamanship course is the best way of acquiring the skills you need to go offshore sailing.

COCKPIT INDICATORS

Cockpit indicators, or display heads, provide navigator and cockpit crew with feedback from various instruments around the boat. Under the hull, a transducer takes depth soundings that can be matched against soundings on the chart; another transducer tracks boat speed and distance travelled, helping monitor performance and position; and true and apparent wind speed and direction, gauged by mast indicators, helps with sail trim.

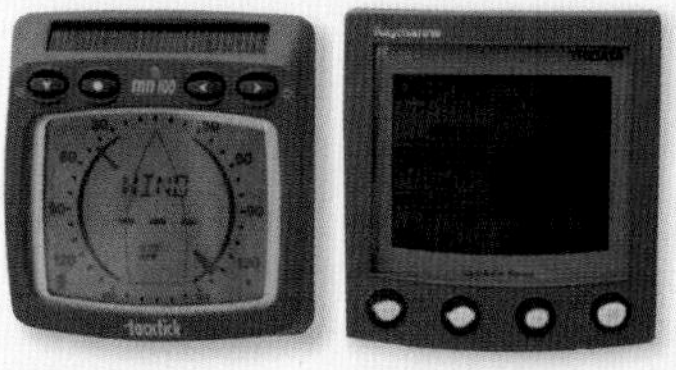

Wind display head

Depth and speed display head

NAVIGATOR'S TABLE

The table should have space for a full size chart folded in half and a storage area for instruments and charts beneath. Clock, barometer, main GPS unit, and VHF radio with DSC (Digital Selective Calling) should all be within easy reach.

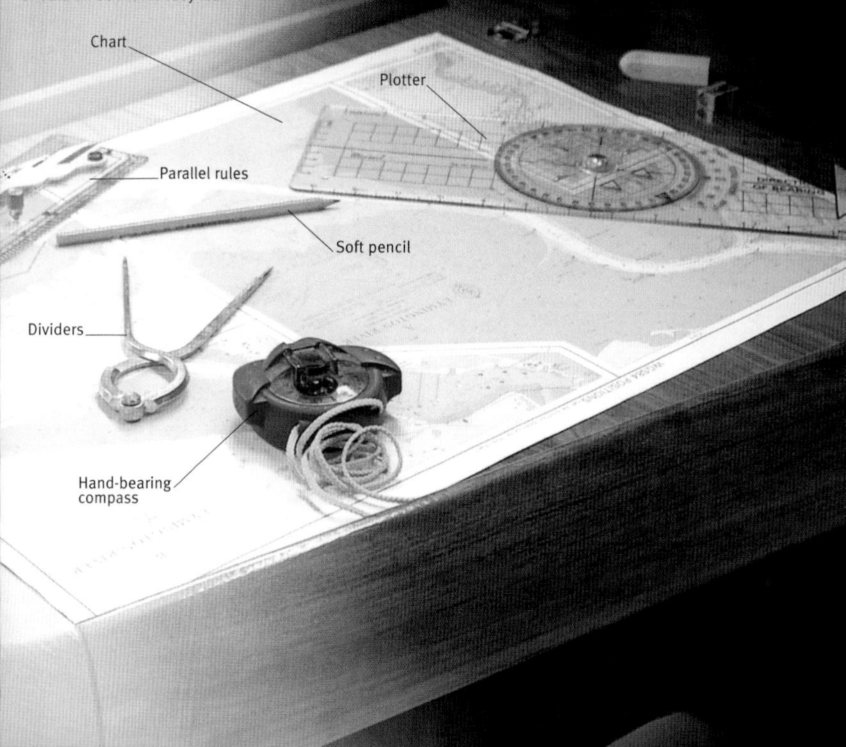

Chart

Plotter

Parallel rules

Soft pencil

Dividers

Hand-bearing compass

Understanding charts

Charts are vital to navigating at sea, conveying key data using symbols, colours, and contour lines. They record potential dangers, locate navigation lights, buoys, and features on shore, and give depths and lines of longitude and latitude to help fix position and measure distance.

THE LANGUAGE OF CHARTS

There are thousands of charts available that cover all corners of the world in as much or as little detail as you need. They range from large-scale maps that cover a small area in great detail, to small-scale maps that cover an entire sea. Most charts use a Mercator projection to represent the curved surface of the Earth, with parallels of latitude represented as straight horizontal lines spaced farther apart towards the poles, and meridians of longitude represented as parallel, but equidistant, straight vertical lines. Depths may be shown in metric or imperial units but distance is measured in nautical miles on the latitude scale up the side of the chart. Charts are updated regularly as critical features change. Anyone in charge of navigation on a yacht will need to familiarize themselves with the full range of standard chart symbols. A small selection of symbols are described here.

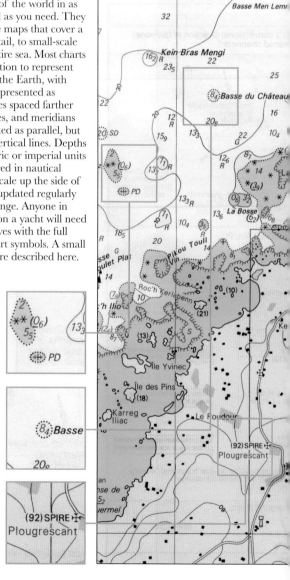

ROCKS AND WRECKS
The upper symbol indicates that rocks are awash above water at chart datum. The lower one warns of a dangerous wreck nearby, of which the masts may be visible.

SHOAL
The figure in the circle shows the depth to which a shoal (area of shallow water) dries at chart datum – in this case 8.4m (27½ft). Shoals may cause rough water in strong winds.

LANDMARKS
Certain landmarks are ideal for fixing position at sea. The church spire shown here is 92m (302ft) above Mean High Water Springs, the height of an average spring tide's high waters.

CHART DATUM

A chart is covered in numbers that record spot depths, or soundings, which record the lowest level to which a tide is likely to fall, known as "chart datum". Different standards for chart datum are used by national charting agencies around the world, and so different charts may show different soundings for the same area. Contour lines join points of equal depth on the chart.

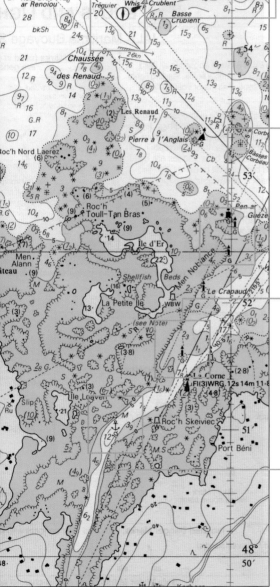

SHIP'S PILOT
The circular purple symbol shown here marks a boarding place for a ship's pilot to guide the boat into harbour. A light buoy with a fog whistle is located nearby.

BUOYAGE
Charts show the position and type of buoys. The beacon tower (top) shown here and two floating beacons below are accompanied by the letter G, indicating they are green.

LOW-WATER DEPTHS
In this map, low-water depths are colour-coded: areas that dry are shown in green; 0–5m (0–16ft) depths in blue; 5–10m (15–33ft) depths in pale blue; and deeper areas in white.

ANCHORAGE
The anchor symbol shown here is accompanied by the figure 12, indicating that the water has a minimum depth of 12m (39ft). The letter M indicates a muddy bottom.

Electronic navigation

The modern navigator has a wide range of interlinked electronic tools at his disposal. These revolve around the Global Positioning System (GPS), which can interface with electronic charts running on a dedicated chart plotter or a personal computer, a depth sounder, log, and radar.

SATELLITE NAVIGATION

The Global Positioning System uses a constellation of 24 satellites in orbit around the Earth, of which at least four are visible from anywhere on Earth at a given time. A GPS unit can calculate its own position to within 15m (50ft) by receiving radio signals from at least three satellites. A feature known as Horizontal Dilution of Precision indicates when satellites may be too closely spaced for such an accurate fix. The GPS aerial should have a clear view of the sky, ideally sited away from the rig, low down at the back of the yacht. When turned on, the GPS will lock on to satellites with the greatest signal strength. A marine GPS should be set in nautical miles with chart datum to match that of your charts (*see* p.239).

HANDHELD GPS

A handheld GPS provides backup for the main unit and is invaluable in the cockpit or in a tender at night.

The navigator can store a series of waypoints (*see* p.247) in the GPS that mark out an intended course. Various pages on the GPS screen provide a wide range of data, including: current position in latitude and longitude; speed and course over the ground; bearing, distance, and estimated time to the next waypoint; velocity made good (VMG) to next waypoint; and cross track error (XTE), which is the lateral distance from the direct course (known as the "rhumb line") between two waypoints.

CONVENTIONAL BACKUP

GPS data should be checked using classic navigation methods in case of any human error in inputting or interpreting data, power failure, or bad signal.

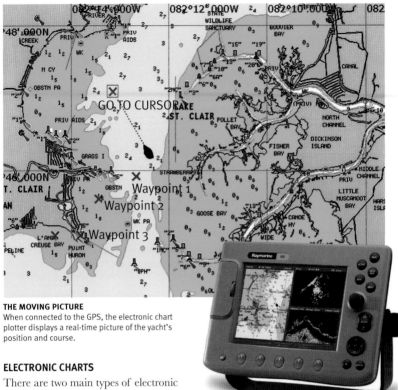

THE MOVING PICTURE
When connected to the GPS, the electronic chart plotter displays a real-time picture of the yacht's position and course.

ELECTRONIC CHARTS

There are two main types of electronic charts: raster and vector. Raster charts, made by scanning paper charts, are guaranteed to be accurate, but have large file sizes and may be slow to load. Vector charts, made by tracing originals, are theoretically more prone to inaccuracies. However, they show different types of data, such as depth and buoyage, on different layers that can be turned on and off, so that you can tailor the chart to your needs.

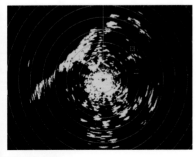

SAILING BLIND
Radar provides vital data in poor visibility or when crossing shipping areas. Some skill is needed to interpret the image, and a short course will help you.

MULTIFUNCTION NAVIGATION
A split-screen facility can be used to display the chart plotter at different scales and with simultaneous radar and sonar to give a complete picture of your position.

Both types of chart can be used with plotting software on a dedicated chart plotter or a personal computer (PC), but beware of using a PC in a damp, unstable boat. The GPS and chart plotter or PC can be interfaced to provide real-time data as your boat moves across the screen.

DEPTH, DISTANCE, COLLISION

A depth sounder reflects ultrasonic signals off the seabed to measure depth, and this data may help you to fix your position on a chart. A log uses a small impeller under the hull to record speed through the water and distance travelled, and is a useful backup to GPS. Radar transmits signals that are reflected by objects such as land and other vessels, providing data on range and bearing that can be used for collision avoidance and general navigation.

Tides

If you sail in a tidal area, navigation provides a great challenge. Tidal height will determine the depth of water under your keel at any given time, while tidal flow will influence whether your yacht is pushed forwards, backwards, or sideways.

HOW TIDES WORK

Tides are the vertical rise and fall of the sea caused by the gravitational pull of the moon and, to a lesser extent, the sun. At full moon and new moon, when the sun, moon, and Earth are aligned, the gravitational pull is largest. This results in spring tides, which have the largest range between high and low water. When the three bodies are opposed (at right angles), neap tides result, with the smallest range between high and low water.

Most tidal areas have twice-daily tides created by the Earth's rotation. The time between high water and low water is approximately six hours, with two high waters and two low waters every day. In the tropics, there is one high and one low water each day with a small tidal range.

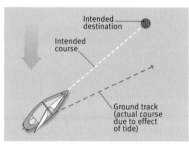

PUSHED OFF COURSE
If no allowance is made, the tidal stream will push this boat away from its objective. The tide's strength and direction determine how far off course it will be.

DRYING OUT
If your boat is likely to dry out at low tide, you should know how many hours either side of high water are available for sailing.

TIDAL CURVES

Annual tide tables give times and heights of high and low water at larger ports round the coastline, known as standard ports, for every day of the year. They are published in nautical almanacs, which include tidal curve graphs. Tidal curves illustrate a cycle of spring or neap tides and can be used to calculate the depth between high and low water at any specific time. This can also be done using an electronic tidal calculator or a web-based service.

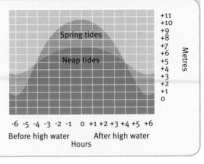

Charts show the lowest predictable tide, or chart datum (*see* p.239), whereas nautical almanacs show the average heights for high and low water.

The tidal stream is a horizontal flow of water created by rising and falling tides. The stream flows much faster during spring tides than during neap tides. Its direction is known as the tidal set and its strength is called the tidal drift; both of these values will change throughout the tidal cycle. Information on tidal behaviour for specific areas related to a standard port can be provided by charts, tide tables, tidal atlases, nautical almanacs, and electronic chart systems.

Areas with a large tidal range may have tidal gates – regions where the tidal stream intensifies, typically due to the stream accelerating round a headland or passing through a narrow passage – that "close" at certain states of the tide. In extreme situations, a 10-m (33-ft) yacht motoring flat out at 8 knots may be brought to a standstill or even driven backwards by the stream. It always makes sense to time your passage with the tide.

TIDAL STREAM ATLAS
Arrows indicate the direction and strength of spring or neap tides for each hour before or after high water (HW) at a standard port.

ONE WAY TO GO
Beacons or buoys may give a good visual indication of the strength of the tide. Here, there is clearly a strong tidal flow from right to left.

Distance and direction

The prime requirement of navigation is to know exactly where you are on a chart and be able to relate it to the surrounding water and nearby land. Your position can be plotted on GPS and electronic or paper chart using lines of latitude and longitude as coordinates.

DISTANCE AND POSITION

Distances at sea are measured in nautical miles. A nautical mile is defined as 1 minute (1′) of latitude (a minute is one-sixtieth of 1 degree of latitude). This distance is slightly greater at the poles than at the equator, due to the Earth being an imperfect sphere, but a standard nautical mile is internationally accepted as 1,852m (6,076ft). A cable is one-tenth of a nautical mile. Speed at sea is measured in knots (nautical miles per hour).

A position at sea is measured in degrees of latitude north or south of the equator and degrees of longitude east or west of the prime (or Greenwich) meridian. It is plotted by marking latitude on the side and longitude on the bottom of a chart. Horizontal and vertical lines drawn from these points will intersect at your position. For example, the position of Cape Cod Lighthouse, Massachusetts, United States, is expressed (in degrees and minutes) as N 42° 02.3′, W 70° 03.7′.

VARIATION AND DEVIATION

A compass always points to the magnetic north pole, which steadily moves in a predictable manner and is known as "magnetic north". It may lie to the east or west of true (geographic) north, depending on your location. The difference between magnetic and true north is called magnetic variation. The direction of magnetic north and its annual rate of change is shown on the compass rose of a chart.

When using a chart and compass, you need to be able to convert between true and magnetic bearings. To convert from true to magnetic, add the westerly or subtract the easterly variation. To convert from magnetic to true, add the easterly or subtract the westerly variation.

Onboard magnetic and electromagnetic fields may cause the compass to deviate from magnetic north. Temporary deviation can be avoided by keeping everyday objects, such as drink cans and MP3 players, well away from the compass. Permanent compass deviation is usually minor unless your yacht is steel-hulled,

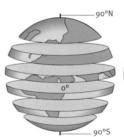

LINES OF LATITUDE
Lines of latitude divide the Earth into parallel horizontal slices that run from 0° at the equator to 90° north and south at the poles.

MERIDIANS OF LONGITUDE
Lines of longitude divide the Earth into vertical slices that meet at the poles. They range from 0° at the prime meridian to 180° east or west.

USING A PLOTTER
The plotter arrow must point in the direction of travel, with the rotating grid aligned with conveniently positioned lines of latitude or longitude on the chart.

USING DIVIDERS
Use brass, steel-tipped dividers to span the distance on the chart you want to measure. Use the latitude scale up the side of the chart to read off the nautical miles.

but it must be taken into account. This requires that a series of measurements ("swinging the compass") is taken to assess the deviation on different courses. The data is used to create a deviation card that can be used to add or subtract from the compass bearing to produce a true bearing. If there is any doubt, use a hand bearing compass to check bearings from a position right at the back of the boat.

DIRECTION

Parallel rules are a traditional navigator's tool for plotting direction. The two rules are hinged so they can be "walked" to or from a compass rose across a paper chart to transfer a direction from the rose to the relevant area of the chart. Parallel rules can be difficult to keep steady in a rolling boat. A plotter does the same job but remains positioned over the chart area on which the navigator is working. All designs of plotter have the facility to read a true bearing without moving to the compass rose. When using a plotter, it must point in the direction of the course and be correctly aligned with lines of latitude or longitude on the chart.

CHART WORK
Use a plotter or parallel rules to plot your course or position and dividers to measure distance. Use a soft pencil with a sharpener and eraser to hand.

COMPASS ROSE

Charts have one or more compass roses for use with a plotter or parallel rules. A rose points to true (geographic) north and also indicates the variation in magnetic north, which changes with location and time. The annual increase or decrease is displayed together with the year the chart was issued.

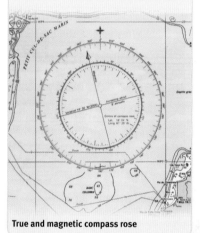

True and magnetic compass rose

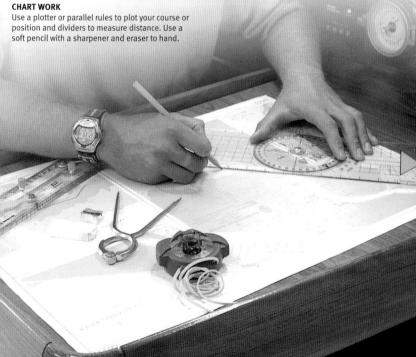

Position and course

Finding your position and plotting a route by chart, GPS, and compass are basic navigational requirements, which must be combined with an assessment of the effects of tidal streams and leeway in order for a skipper to steer the correct course.

FINDING YOUR POSITION

The simplest method of finding position is to take a latitude and longitude reading off the GPS – if it is working, the position will be accurate to within 15m (50ft). This data should always be double-checked. Dead reckoning is one method you can use, but it uses only course steered and distance travelled.

Estimated position (EP) is a more accurate method. It takes account of the effects of wind (leeway) and the direction (set) and rate (drift) of the tide. Tidal data may be obtained from a tidal atlas.

A more exact position can be obtained using a hand bearing compass to gain a three-point fix (*see below*) on prominent objects on land or at sea. If the bearings are accurate, you should obtain a very accurate fix. The three-point fix is also useful because the degree of accuracy of

WORK AHEAD
Always do as much navigation as possible in advance, particularly when calculating tidal effects or converting from a paper chart route to GPS waypoints.

the bearings is apparent in the size of the triangular "cocked hat" they produce on your chart. No triangle is most accurate.

Another method is to line up two landmarks to make a transit, producing a straight position line on the chart. Then take a bearing on a charted object at about 90 degrees to the line. The intersection of bearing and line will give your position.

EFFECTS OF TIDE AND WIND

Under sail, all yachts are pushed sideways by the wind, an effect called leeway, which is strongest upwind. When wind and tide are in the same direction, their effects combine. The sea should be fairly smooth, with evenly spaced waves, and the course steered will need to be markedly higher than the ground track (direct route). When wind and tide are opposed, their effects on course will partially cancel out and may create short, steep waves.

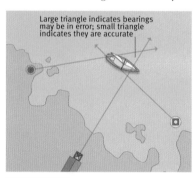

Large triangle indicates bearings may be in error; small triangle indicates they are accurate

THREE-POINT FIX
Locate three landmarks (such as church spires) or charted objects (such as buoys), each about 60 degrees from the next. Plot their bearings on the chart. The intersection of the bearings may form a triangle, or "cocked hat", that indicates your position.

SHAPING A COURSE

If leeway and tidal drift to windward cancel out, the course steered will match the ground track. If not, you will need to use a vector diagram to calculate how much to compensate for wind and tide. Tidal data can be obtained from a tidal atlas. You can assess leeway by taking a bearing on the wake of the yacht (*see below*). If leeway is 5 degrees, the water track (the course that will negate tidal effects) needs to be adjusted to windward by 5 degrees to produce the correct course to be steered.

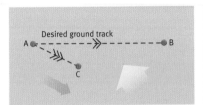

1 On the chart, mark your desired ground track from start point (A) to destination (B). Measure its length with the dividers and use the latitude scale on the chart to find the distance. Consult a tidal atlas and plot the direction of the tide from (A). Use dividers to mark the amount of drift in 1 hour (C).

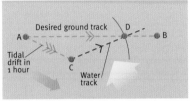

2 Open the dividers to measure the distance you expect to sail in the next hour. Place one point of the dividers on position C and mark where the other point intersects the ground track (D). Join points C and D to mark the water track – the course to follow to offset the effects of tidal drift.

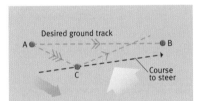

3 Once under sail, take a bearing on the boat's wake using a hand compass. The difference between this and the back, or reciprocal, bearing on the main steering compass is the amount of leeway. Adjust the water track to windward to allow for leeway, and you will have determined the course to steer.

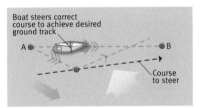

4 The helmsman follows the bearing of the course to steer, countering the effects of both tide and wind, and sails from A to B. Tide and wind should be monitored during a longer trip – every hour is about right, as the tidal atlas will supply hourly figures for the changing tide.

GPS WAYPOINTS

Waypoints are points along your route whose positions you can store in the GPS set. The equipment shows distance, bearing, and estimated time of arrival at the next waypoint and this data is fed to the chart plotter (if you are using one). Always double-check the distance and bearing of waypoints on a chart in order to avoid mistakes when inputting their positions into the GPS, particularly if using waypoints from a publication. Beware also of plotting a waypoint directly to a charted object in case you sail straight into it. Be aware that in busy areas, other yachts may be converging on the same waypoint. And remember that neither the GPS nor the chart plotter will warn you if there are headlands between two waypoints.

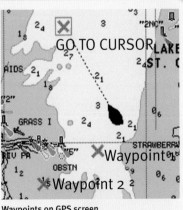

Waypoints on GPS screen

Buoyage and pilotage

When sailing by day, it is vital to identify buoys that provide a safe passage close to land. When sailing by night, lights with different colours and characteristics identify various lighthouses, buoys, beacons, and leading lights (which show the way into harbours).

BUOY GUIDANCE

The International Association of Lighthouse Authorities (IALA) operates two systems of buoyage, A and B, in various parts of the world. The main difference between the two systems is that the colour of the buoys identifying either edge of a channel, known as lateral marks, is reversed (*see below*). Lateral marks also indicate which of two channels is the preferred one. Cardinal marks identify a nearby hazard with safe water on one side. Isolated danger marks identify a specific danger, such as a small rock, with safe water all around. Safe water marks, also known as "fairway" marks, indicate safe water all around.

NIGHT LIGHTS

Navigational lights may be difficult to distinguish from shore lights, but each has a colour and flashing pattern, noted on the chart, to help you identify it. Never assume you have found the right light, always confirm: check the timing of flashes with a stopwatch to ensure you have identified the correct lights and use the hand bearing compass to check the light's position.

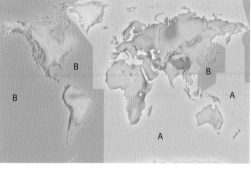

IALA BUOYAGE

IALA System A is used in Europe, Africa, Australia, India, and most of Asia. System B is used in the US, Central and South America, and parts of Canada, the Caribbean, and Southeast Asia.

IALA A-SYSTEM

When entering harbour, leave green lateral marks to starboard and red to port. When leaving, keep red marks to starboard and green to port.

IALA B-SYSTEM

When entering harbour, leave red lateral marks to starboard and green to port. When leaving, keep green marks to starboard and red to port.

PORT CAN

A red port "can" flashes red to mark the port side of the channel when you enter an IALA A-System harbour. Leave this lateral mark to starboard when leaving harbour.

CARDINAL MARKS

A cardinal mark warns of a nearby hazard. There are four types, one for each cardinal point of the compass, and each is clearly identifiable by its colour and top marks during the day and by a sequence of white-light flashes at night. Cardinal marks are identical in both of the IALA buoyage systems. They are either pillar- or spar-shaped and are topped by two cones, or top marks, arranged differently on the four types.

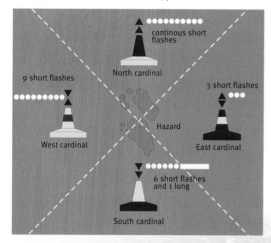

continous short flashes

North cardinal

9 short flashes

West cardinal

Hazard

3 short flashes

East cardinal

6 short flashes and 1 long

South cardinal

STARBOARD CONE
A starboard cone flashes green to mark the starboard side of the channel when you enter an IALA A-System harbour. Leave this lateral mark to port when leaving harbour.

CARDINAL MARKS AND LIGHTS
Cardinal marks are shown on charts, which will also identify the hazard they indicate. Always pass a cardinal in the direction indicated by its colours, top cones, or lights. Safe passage past a south cardinal is on the south side of the mark, past a west cardinal on the west, and so

Safe passage when lighthouse light is white

LIGHTHOUSE LIGHTS
Lighthouses may use coloured lights. The white sector indicates the safest route; coloured sectors indicate danger.

TREACHEROUS ROCKS
Lighthouses are among the most well-established means of alerting ships to a dangerous coastline. Their lights can often be seen from many miles away. This lighthouse is positioned on an obviously dangerous rocky promontory.

Sailing safely

Safety basics

Sailing is an extremly safe sport for all ages and abilities, in all types of boat. Most dangers can be avoided by allowing sufficient time to plan your trip, learning to use equipment correctly, and having basic knowledge of good sailing techniques.

SAFETY ON DINGHIES

Make sure you are properly clothed and equipped (*see* pp.54–55). Always wear a buoyancy aid; it will keep you afloat, and provide thermal protection. Sailing shoes are also important – bare feet are vulnerable on the beach and in the boat. Sailing gloves provide protection against rope burn. Beware of wind chill and wear plenty of clothing.

For dinghy sailors it is important to remember an offshore wind becomes considerably stronger as you sail away from the shore. In an onshore wind, extra care is needed launching and landing with breaking waves.

Once you are out on the water, be aware of potentially risky situations. The boom can cause head injury during an unexpected gybe. Brief the crew to watch the boom and stay low. Familiarize yourself and your crew with capsize drill to take the fear out of a real capsize,

SHARE YOUR SAILING PLANS
When possible, sail with safety boat cover. If none is available, tell a responsible person when you expect to leave and return, and where you will be sailing.

when panic is the greatest danger. Carry a folding sailing knife in the front pocket of your buoyancy aid – in an emergency it may be necessary to cut a line if someone gets tangled.

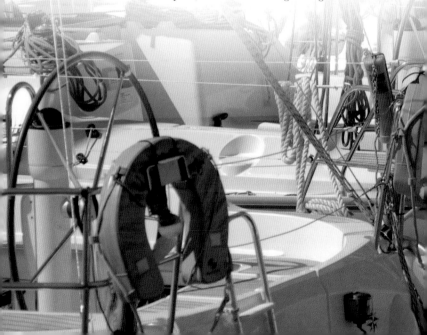

YACHT SAFETY

Safety on a yacht is ultimately the responsibility of the skipper (*see* Crew roles, pp.176–177). However, every individual on board also needs to consider the safety of others, as well as themselves. Plan your passage carefully, taking note of tides and weather forecast, and make a back-up plan in case the weather deteriorates. Brief the crew on safety equipment, and give everyone lifejackets and safety harnesses, adjusted to fit; these should be mandatory on deck in poor visibility or rough conditions. All the crew must have suitable protective clothing for rough weather. Watch for crew members feeling seasick or becoming too cold. Send them below, or be prepared to get them to a protected anchorage as soon as possible. Hands and feet are vulnerable. Always wear shoes and gloves when handling the anchor. Keep well clear when the rope or warp is dropping and do not let it run out of control. Show the crew where to find the first aid box, and brief them on the use of VHF in an emergency. People have been killed by unexpected gybes, hit on the head or back by the boom and knocked over

ROPE SENSE
Keep fingers away from winch drums, and beware of rope under tension. Learn to control the rope by taking turns round the winch and using the clutch.

the side. If you are sailing in difficult conditions downwind, fit a gybe preventer (*see* p.198) and steer more to windward to ensure the mainsail will not gybe. Brief the crew and make sure they stay low.

SAFETY EQUIPMENT
Make sure all safety gear on a yacht is in good working order for immediate use. Do not pile warps or fenders on top of life belts, which must be ready to be thrown.

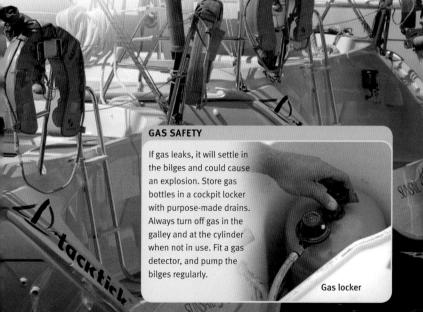

GAS SAFETY

If gas leaks, it will settle in the bilges and could cause an explosion. Store gas bottles in a cockpit locker with purpose-made drains. Always turn off gas in the galley and at the cylinder when not in use. Fit a gas detector, and pump the bilges regularly.

Gas locker

Communication

VHF radio, supported by specialist distress systems, may be vital to the safety of a yacht and its crew. Mobile phones can be used for social and non-emergency communications, while the traditional ship's horn still has a role to play when vessels are manoeuvring at close quarters.

MOBILE PHONES

A mobile phone is useful for coastal sailing, but its main role is to communicate non-essential messages, such as booking into a marina or restaurant, or calling up friends on shore. Its use in emergencies may be limited by poor signal at sea; more importantly, a mobile phone can communicate with only one number at a time, and will not provide a position or bearing for the information of a rescue team.

RADIO

VHF radio provides broadcast communication between yachts, other boats such as rescue craft or commercial shipping, and marine shore services. Most marine VHF uses "simplex" transmission, which means that communication is one-way at a time, with a transmit button determining whether the radio is sending or receiving. VHF procedure includes using Channel 16 only to establish communication, after which you should immediately change to a "working" channel. VHF transmission is possible only in "line of sight" – when transmitting and receiving aerials can

USING A MOBILE PHONE
Do not rely on a mobile phone for distress and safety calls. It is designed for use on land, and may not prove reliable in an emergency.

"see" each other. For instance, if you are on one side of a hilly island, your message may not reach a yacht on the other side. Transmission power varies between 1–24 watts, giving a maximum range of around 60 nautical miles if both aerials are tall enough. Aerials at sea level will have a range closer to 9km (5 nautical miles).

SOUND ALERTS

A horn is essential in fog (*see* p.259), but is also useful when manoeuvring in a large harbour, to inform nearby vessels what you intend to do next, and to understand their intentions.

USING A HORN
You can communicate your course by blasts of the horn in the following ways: one blast "altering course to starboard"; two blasts "altering course to port"; three blasts "going astern"; five blasts "your intentions are unclear".

Hand-held
waterproofed VHF
receiver

EMERGENCY BEACONS

Emergency position indicating radio beacons (EPIRBS) are an important feature of the Global Maritime Distress and Safety System (GMDSS).

EPIRB

An EPIRB transmits a one-way distress signal, activated manually or automatically. If a yacht sinks, an EPIRB with a hydrostatic release unit floats free, and automatically transmits a distress signal. An active EPIRB also enables a lifeboat or helicopter to take a direct radio bearing. An EPIRB must be registered with details of the yacht.

OTHER SYSTEMS

Search and Rescue Radio Transponder (SART) is a small, battery operated beacon which provides a homing signal on another vessel's radar screen.

The NAVTEX system displays search and rescue information, navigation warnings, and weather forecasts on screen or paper printout.

International Maritime Satellite Organization (INMARSAT) operates a global network of four communications satellites providing voice, text, telex, fax, and data transmission for yachts and shipping offshore.

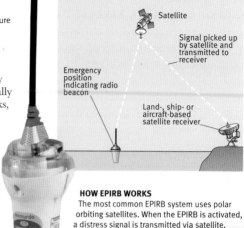

Satellite

Signal picked up by satellite and transmitted to receiver

Emergency position indicating radio beacon

Land-, ship- or aircraft-based satellite receiver

HOW EPIRB WORKS

The most common EPIRB system uses polar orbiting satellites. When the EPIRB is activated, a distress signal is transmitted via satellite, which calculates its position and transmits it to the nearest rescue centre.

VHF radio

COMMUNICATIONS EQUIPMENT

The basis of communications on a family-size yacht is VHF radio, which can be backed up by mobile phones or more specialized equipment. A nautical almanac or pilot guide provides details of VHF radio stations.

Radio procedures

All modern VHF yacht radios – fixed or handheld – should be compatible with the Global Maritime Distress and Safety System (GMDSS). This allows a Digital Selective Calling (DSC) distress alert to be transmitted, simply by pushing the red emergency button.

WHY VHF IS VITAL

A VHF radio should be used to maintain a "radio watch" at sea, using the recommended channels for calling, ship movements, and distress. Information about correct radio distress procedures and your yacht's call sign should be placed next to the radio. A DSC distress signal will activate DSC alarms in all radios within range, so that operators will listen on the distress channel for a subsequent Mayday call. The DSC signal also contains your yacht's MMSI number (*see below*), and GPS position.

VHF RADIO EQUIPMENT
VHF marine radios fitted with DSC allow a distress alert to be transmitted automatically every four minutes, with one push of the red button.

VHF REGULATIONS

A yacht fitted with VHF radio must have a valid licence, and nine-digit Maritime Mobile Service Identity (MMSI) number for DSC. The international qualification for using VHF with DSC is a Short Range or Long Range Certificate (SRC/LRC). An SRC qualifies you in VHF radio procedures. All crew should be taught how to operate VHF in an emergency, and how to avoid sending a false distress alert.

SPEAKING
Think what you are going to say, write it down if necessary, then speak slowly and clearly with your voice pitched higher (especially men) for maximum clarity.

EMERGENCY RADIO PROCEDURE

Summon help by alerting the coastguard, and other vessels, using emergency radio distress signals on Channel 16, as follows:
Mayday: Grave and imminent danger requiring immediate assistance.
Pan Pan: Urgent message concerning safety of crew member or yacht.
Sécurité: Safety of navigation.

HOW TO GIVE A DISTRESS MESSAGE

"Mayday, Mayday, Mayday.

This is Yacht *Dream*, *Dream*, *Dream*.

Mayday Yacht *Dream*.

MMSI (if known).

My position is (latitude and longitude, or bearing and distance from a landmark).

Yacht on fire and holed by a rock.

I have three crew.

I require immediate assistance.

Over."

CONTACTING THE MARINA

Marinas and harbour offices have their own VHF channels listed in the pilot book. VHF can be invaluable when you are about to enter the marina; you can talk directly to a dock master, who can direct you to a berth using a handheld VHF.

PHONETIC ALPHABET

A	Alpha
B	Bravo
C	Charlie
D	Delta
E	Echo
F	Foxtrot
G	Golf
H	Hotel
I	India
J	Juliet
K	Kilo
L	Lima
M	Mike
N	November
O	Oscar
P	Papa
Q	Quebec
R	Romeo
S	Sierra
T	Tango
U	Uniform
V	Victor
W	Whiskey
X	X-ray
Y	Yankee
Z	Zulu

Say numbers using the following pronunciation: zero, wun, too, tree, fow-er, fife, six, sev-en, ait, nin-er; 10 as wun zero; 22 as too too; 537 as fife tree sev-en; 2000 as too thousand.

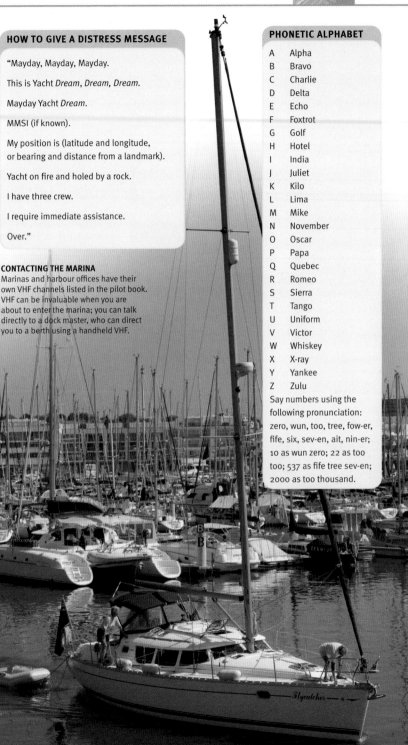

Sailing in poor visibility

Sailing at night or in poor visibility caused by torrential rain or fog increases the risk of collision. It is vital that the skipper and crew of a yacht should proceed with maximum caution, and have sufficient knowledge to take avoiding action if required.

SAILING BY NIGHT

Managing a yacht on a night passage requires additional skills. The crew need to work in a "watch" system, with two or three in charge of the boat for a specific period, while the rest of the crew are "off watch" and may choose to sleep down below. The traditional watch system of "four hours on, four hours off" can be modified to suit the crew and circumstances. On a one-night passage, a considerably shorter watch may be preferred. Before sailing into the night, the skipper should ensure that all crew are fed with a hot meal, have sufficient warm clothing for watch duty during the cold hours of the night, and that they will wear harnesses on deck at all times.

GREEN MEANS GO
This yacht is showing a green light on port tack. Any yacht approaching under sail on starboard tack will see "green for go" and can proceed cautiously.

WHITE LIGHT
A small dinghy – up to 7m (23ft) – under sail, oars, or motor must show an all-round white light when required, to ensure that they can be seen.

MASTHEAD TRICOLOUR LIGHT
A yacht of 7–20m (23–65ft) under sail must display coloured lights. A tricolour navigation light may be fixed at the masthead: red (port), green (starboard), and white (stern).

STERN AND COMBINED SIDELIGHTS
A yacht of under 20m (65ft) under sail may (as an alternative to the masthead tricolour light) have a separate white light at the stern, with red and green lights combined in one lantern at the bow.

IDENTIFYING LIGHTS AT NIGHT

Various combinations of lights are used to identify different craft, what they are doing, where they are heading, or whether they are still. Those illustrated below are examples of some of the many lights you may encounter when night sailing. Be sure to keep an authoritative reference on board for you to identify all the possible variations.

SMALL POWER VESSEL
Forward red light with white above: indicates the port side of power vessel less than 20m (65ft), under way.

LARGE POWER VESSEL
Red side light, white above: indicates port side of power vessel over 20m (65ft) long, under way.

TRAWLER
All-round green over white lights: indicates starboard side of fishing vessel, under way and trawling.

AT ANCHOR
Two all-round white lights: indicate vessels of over 50m (164ft) at anchor.

KEEPING WATCH AT NIGHT

Apart from sailing the yacht, and following the passage plan, the prime responsibility of the watch crew is to keep a good lookout. This should include scanning the horizon every five minutes. All lights must be identified and categorized as shore lights, such as street lights or car headlamps; navigational lights, such as lighthouses, channel markers, or harbour entrances; and other vessels, which may require avoiding action. All vessels over 7m (23ft) must display a minimum of red (port side), green (starboard side), and white (mast or stern) lights. Under power, a forward-facing white light must be shown above side lights. Lights are used in different combinations according to the size and type of vessel, which way it is heading, and whether it is sailing or motoring. Additional lights provide extra information. These navigation lights may appear confusing. The easiest way to ensure correct identification is to refer to a nautical almanac or pilot book.

FOG DANGER
Wait until fog lifts before you leave harbour. Motoring into fog makes it extremely difficult to be seen or to hear other motors.

SOUND SIGNALS IN FOG

A vessel that is out on the sea in fog should make regular sound signals to indicate its presence. Signals applying to vessels under 100m (328ft) are most relevant to yachts.

▬▬ ■ ■ **Under sail**	One long blast and two short blasts with the foghorn, sounded every two minutes.
▬▬ **Making way under power**	One long blast with the foghorn, sounded every two minutes.
▲▲▲ ▲▼▲▼▲ ▲▲▲ **Aground**	Three bells followed by rapid ringing for five seconds and another three bells, at one minute intervals.
▲▼▲▼▲ **At anchor**	Rapid ringing of the bell forward in the boat, at one minute intervals.

Key

▬▬	■	▲	▲▼▲▼▲
Long blast	Short blast	Bell	Rapid bell

Rough weather procedures

Modern yachts are extremely robust, and should prove safe and well-mannered in most rough weather situations. It is the duty of the skipper to be able to assess the situation, know how to manage the yacht, and decide what course of action to take.

HOW WINDY DOES IT NEED TO BE?

The best way to avoid rough weather is to check the forecast, consider the ability of your crew, and be cautious. Using wind speed as a guide is not enough. Rough weather is created by a combination of wind, waves, and tide. Force 4 is rated as a moderate breeze, but may prove extremely rough if you are beating with wind against tide, in shallow water, with a large swell and confused sea from the previous day's depression. Most yachts will need to be reefed in a Force 5 breeze, and should seek shelter before the wind reaches a near gale, Force 7. It is possible to continue sailing in a Force 8 gale, with deep-reefed mainsail and small headsail, but only when sea conditions are reasonable.

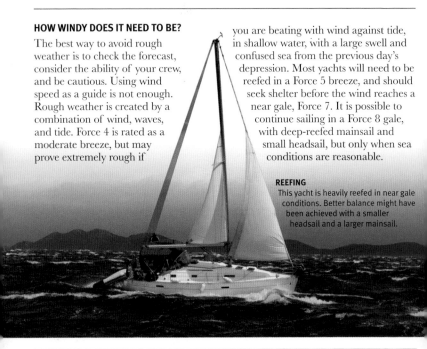

REEFING
This yacht is heavily reefed in near gale conditions. Better balance might have been achieved with a smaller headsail and a larger mainsail.

PREPARING FOR ROUGH WEATHER

If rough weather is expected, make sure all loose gear is securely stowed below, or secured on deck. Take particular care below, where it can be chaos if the contents of shelves and cupboards are flung across the saloon. Finalize navigation plans well ahead of time, and make sure you can refer to the chart or pilot book easily. Check that the mainsail and headsail are reefed or are ready for reefing if conditions demand it.

CLOSE HATCHES
Ensure that all hatches and windows are closed and locked. Check with the skipper before opening a hatch in rough weather.

WEAR LIFEJACKETS
Harnesses and lifejackets should always be worn in rough weather, on deck, and in the cockpit. They give security, and confidence.

HOOK ON
A harness does not serve any purpose if you are not clipped on. Clip on to a jackstay or strong fitting as you move forward.

SURVIVAL IN EXTREME WINDS

A yacht may be caught out at sea in conditions in excess of gale Force 8, when it may be too dangerous to approach land or attempt to reach an anchorage, and too difficult to sail. A skipper may choose to run before the wind with no sails, and trail a warp to slow the boat; or, if there is sufficient "sea room" (the distance the yacht will be blown to leeward), he may choose to ride out the storm.

Another option is to heave-to under deep-reefed mainsail and jib, with rudder locked so that the yacht lies close to the wind, while drifting slowly to leeward. If sea conditions become too bad, it may be necessary to "lie a-hull", with all sails down, and the rudder locked so that the boat tries to turn into the wind. Like this, the yacht will lie side-on to the wind, and be driven steadily to leeward. In extreme weather waves may break over the yacht. A sea anchor will hold the bow into the waves and slow travel.

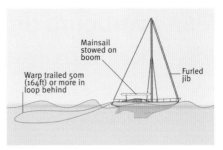

TRAILING A WARP

One tactic, if there is plenty of sea room, is to run downwind under bare poles. If the boat travels too fast, it may "broach", turning side-on to the waves. Trailing a long warp in a loop can be effective at slowing the boat.

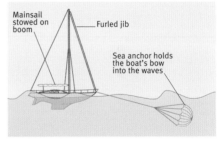

SEA ANCHOR

A sea anchor acts like a heavy duty parachute connected to the bow by a long, stretchy, nylon warp. It will hold the boat head to wind, which may be more comfortable than heaving to or lying a-hull, and slows downwind travel.

IN THE COCKPIT

This yacht is heavily pressed with the leeward deck digging under water. Reefing would bring the boat upright, providing a much more comfortable ride for the crew.

Man overboard drill

Falling over the side and becoming separated from the boat is a serious danger. It can be prevented by moving carefully around the deck, holding on at all times, and clipping on with a harness on deck or in bad weather. But if the worst happens, you must know what to do.

PRACTISING THE DRILL

The skipper should make sure the crew practise "man overboard" (MOB) drill regularly – ideally by day and night, in all sea conditions. A simple method is to choose an unexpected moment to throw a fender tied to a bucket over the side, while the yacht is sailing or motoring at full speed, and shout, "Man overboard!" All crew should wear lifejackets for the practice, in case anyone topples over the guard rails and turns the practice into a real man overboard situation. This is also a significant danger in a real accident. Always switch off the engine before you retrieve someone from the water or you could cause them serious injury. In a real man overboard accident, summon help by pressing the MOB button on your GPS (if you have one) at the same time as starting the rescue procedure.

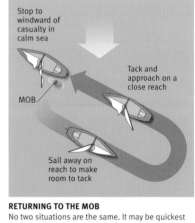

Stop to windward of casualty in calm sea

Tack and approach on a close reach

MOB

Sail away on reach to make room to tack

RETURNING TO THE MOB

No two situations are the same. It may be quickest to drop sails and approach under power, or tack or gybe under sail. You can aim to windward of the MOB in very calm conditions, but in stronger winds there is a risk of being blown into the person.

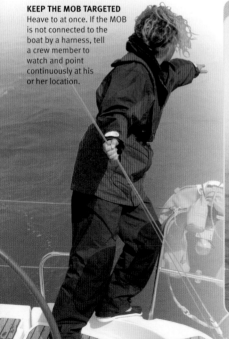

KEEP THE MOB TARGETED

Heave to at once. If the MOB is not connected to the boat by a harness, tell a crew member to watch and point continuously at his or her location.

MARKING THE SPOT

Throw the lifebuoy over the side immediately the "Man overboard!" alarm is given. It should be marked with the yacht's name, and reflective tape, and fitted with a drogue to prevent drifting, a whistle to attract attention, automatic light, and danbuoy with day-glo flag which flies 2m (6.5ft) above the surface. If the lifebuoy is deployed quickly it should be within reach of the casualty and will increase the chances of rescue.

1 **Getting the MOB back** on board may be hard, particularly if he or she is suffering from shock and cold. Use a boat hook to keep them alongside. A line looped under their armpits is an additional way of securing the MOB.

2 **In calm water** guide the MOB to the transom boarding ladder. In rough weather this could be dangerous, with the MOB getting pushed under the stern. Try hanging a loop of mainsheet over the side as a makeshift ladder.

3 **Make sure the engine** is not in gear with the propeller turning when the MOB is near the stern. Be prepared to help a weakened MOB climb the ladder. This can be extremely difficult in sea-sodden waterproofs.

4 **As soon as the MOB is back** on board, get him or her below and assess whether urgent medical attention is needed. To combat hypothermia, lie the casualty down in a berth, in dry clothes and a sleeping bag.

First aid

Most accidents when sailing are minor and related to being in an environment that is often cold and wet, and that keeps moving up and down. Common sense, and basic first aid skills, are all that is required to ensure that the crew remain fit and well in most situations.

GET TRAINING

The advice in this section is not intended as a substitute for a good first aid manual, still less proper first aid training; it is simply an introduction to the most common problems and how to deal with them. If you do not have first-aid expertise and are considering taking up sailing, particularly yachting, where you may be away from immediate medical help, it is highly advisable to sign up for a first aid course. This will help provide you with knowledge and confidence, which could prove a life-saver and will certainly help you to deal effectively with everyday injuries. First aid courses are widely available. You clearly won't become an expert, but you will be coached by a professional, who will demonstrate the limitations of what can be done when dealing with an accident on board, particularly when not to administer ill-advised measures, and the best course is simply to keep the person safe and summon emergency help. Specialist first aid courses tailored to dinghy and yacht sailors are available in many places, with particular emphasis on how to perform resuscitation and how to deal with hypothermia.

HYPOTHERMIA

Getting cold is miserable. It is also easy to avoid by wearing the right level of clothing – wetsuit, drysuit, or waterproofs with breathable layering, plus a thermal hat to prevent heat loss from your head. Getting hypothermia is dangerous. This conditions occurs if the body's temperature drops below 35°C (95°F). Symptoms are intense shivering and difficulty with speech. Further heat loss leads to physical and mental incapacity, with eventual loss of consciousness and death. A man overboard or capsized dinghy sailor without a wetsuit is extremely vulnerable to hypothermia – the colder the water, the greater the risk.

WARMING UP

Wrap the casualty in a blanket or sleeping bag and give him or her warm drinks and high energy foods. Seek medical advice if his or her condition does not improve fairly quickly.

FIRST AID BOX

On a yacht keep the first aid box readily accessible and ensure that all crew members know where to find it. Typical contents include: sterile dressings and gauze pads, adhesive dressings, a selection of bandages (with clips, tape, and safety pins), scissors, tweezers, sterile wipes, disposable gloves, painkillers, thermometer, and a first aid manual. Replace any items as soon as they are used.

TREATING CUTS

Small cuts are common afloat and are usually straightforward to deal with. Remember to wear disposable gloves if you are treating another person. The aim is to stop bleeding and prevent infection. If the wound is dirty, rinse the area with fresh water. Dry the area with a sterile swab and cover the wound with a dressing. If blood loss is severe apply pressure, and raise the injured part of the body above the level of the heart.

COVERING THE WOUND
Protect even minor injuries from infection. Use an adhesive dressing (small wounds) or a sterile dressing secured by a bandage (larger wounds).

DEALING WITH BURNS

Burns at sea are most likely to happen in the galley, or when working on a hot engine at sea, which is extremely inadvisable unless vital. The priority is to cool the burn, preferably with cold running water (but immersion in any cold liquid will do). Do not break any blisters that may form. Cover a serious burn with a lightly applied non-adhesive dressing (kitchen film can be used) and seek medical help as soon as possible.

COOLING DOWN
Cool burns in cold water for at least 10 minutes. Do not apply lotions or fats to the area as this may increase the risk of infection.

COPING WITH SEASICKNESS

Seasickness is unpleasant, but its effects normally disappear as soon as you reach shore. Seasickness medication can be effective and should be taken well before you start sailing. Possible side effects may include drowsiness. While many seasickness sufferers feel better above decks, it is important to avoid getting cold. A solution is to lie down with a warm sleeping bag in a comfortable berth. If you need to be sick, a bucket in the cockpit or cabin is safer and easier than hanging over the side. Eat dry toast, bread, or plain biscuits and drink water to offset dehydration.

FEELING SICK?
Many suffering from seasickness feel better in the fresh air where they can see the horizon. It may even help to take the helm for a while.

EFFECTS OF SUN

Excessive exposure to sun when sailing can cause a range of physical problems. Make sure all crew members use sunscreen, with hats and long sleeves providing extra protection. If anyone is sunburned, tell them to cover up and move into the shade. Burned skin can be cooled with fresh water. Apply aftersun lotion and drink plenty of water to offset dehydration. If you are sailing in very hot weather, it is vital to keep as cool as possible and drink water regularly. Heat exhaustion can be caused by excess loss of salt and water through sweating. Symptoms include headaches or cramps, pale and moist skin, fast and weak pulse, and slightly raised temperature. Treatment is to cool the victim and replace lost fluid and salt. Heatstroke can occur after prolonged exposure to high heat and humidity, which raises body temperature dangerously, producing headache, restlessness, dizziness, flushed and hot skin, and a fast pulse. Treatment is to cool the person as soon as possible by removing clothes, covering with a wet sheet, and using a fan.

CPR

Cardio-pulmonary resuscitation (CPR) is a vital technique to learn at a first aid course. It is a combination of chest compressions and rescue breaths, and involves giving 30 compressions on the centre of the chest at a rate of 100 compressions per minute, followed by two rescue breaths (*see* Drowning, *below right*).

RECOVERY POSITION

A casualty who is unconscious but breathing should be put in the standard recovery position. Roll the casualty on to their back, open the airway, and straighten their legs. Place the arm closest to you at right angles to the body, bring the other arm across the body, and hold the back of their hand against their cheek. With your other hand, pull up the far leg. Roll the casualty towards you on to their side by pulling the far leg, while keeping the hand pressed against the cheek. Check that the airway is still open. Bend the upper leg at the knee so that it supports the body.

KEEP WATCH

When a casualty is unconscious in the recovery position, keep checking their breathing and pulse until medical help arrives.

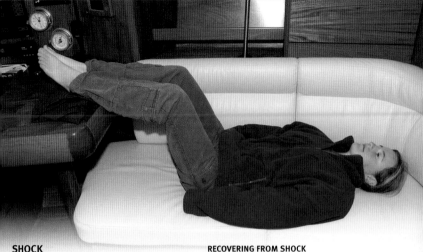

SHOCK

Shock, sometimes called circulatory shock, is caused by a dramatic fall in blood pressure. It can follow any serious injury, severe blood loss, dehydration (perhaps from diarrhoea or vomiting), and in rare cases it occurs as part of a serious allergic reaction. Symptoms include a rapid pulse, grey-blue lips, and a cold and clammy skin. Further symptoms may include weakness, giddiness, nausea, thirst, shallow and rapid breathing, and weak and rapid

RECOVERING FROM SHOCK
Watch a shock victim closely. Raise their legs above their heart and ensure they are kept warm with a fleece, blanket, or sleeping bag.

pulse. The recommended treatment is to keep the casualty warm and maximize blood supply to the heart and brain by raising their legs and loosening tight clothing. Do not leave the casualty or allow them any food or liquid – just moisten lips with water if required. Unless their condition improves rapidly, get medical help as soon as possible.

DROWNING

Drowning is among the most serious risks of an accident at sea. If you recover a person from the water who is unconscious, immediately open the airway and check breathing. If the casualty is not breathing, start CPR (*above left*) without delay. The instructions

for giving a rescue breath are as follows. Blow into the casualty's mouth and watch the chest rise, then remove your mouth and allow the chest to fall. Each breath should take about one second. Continue CPR until medical help arrives or until you are so exhausted you can no longer carry on.

OPEN THE AIRWAY
Tilt back the head, with fingers under the chin, before putting the other hand on the forehead.

BLOW INTO THE MOUTH
Pinch nostrils, take a deep breath, seal the casualty's lips with your lips, and blow in.

Emergencies on board

Most emergencies on board a yacht are caused by human negligence. Calling out the rescue services should be a last resort. Generally, you can keep yourself, your crew, and your boat safe by careful planning, and regular maintenance of the yacht's equipment and rigging.

PRINCIPAL EMERGENCIES

One of the most common reasons for call-outs to the rescue services is engine failure. Ensure you have enough fuel for a passage, and that the engine is serviced regularly. If the propeller becomes fouled by a piece of fishing net or discarded rope, the only way to clear it may be to dive underwater with a sharp knife, which is likely to be difficult and potentially dangerous at sea. Steering cables can fail if not maintained. An emergency tiller is supplied on modern yachts with wheel steering, attached to the rudder through a fitting at the back of the cockpit. Practise using this.

Leaking, which in some cases may lead to sinking, is another emergency. An older yacht may start leaking through a failed hull fitting, for example. If the yacht hits a rock, or is in a collision, it may start sinking. A hole below the waterline must be blocked as soon as possible with soft materials such as sails. This may help to stem the flow enough for bilge pumps to cope with the flooding. Yachts are occasionally dismasted due to rigging failure. The main danger is that pieces of mast that have gone over the side may smash a hole in the hull. Carry bolt cutters that can be used to cut the rigging free.

FIRE SERVICES
Fires can occur when moored. A fire in a marina will be attended by land-based fire services.

FIRE ON BOARD

Keep a fire blanket in the galley, and a foam or dry-powder fire extinguisher in the companionway. If you have a fire, do not enter the smoke-filled cabin. Get all crew on deck wearing lifejackets, taking fire extinguishers with you. Attempt to put out the fire by closing hatches to reduce the air supply. If the fire is in the engine compartment, do not open the inspection hatch; push the extinguisher nozzle into the emergency fire fighting hole (standard on modern yachts). Move crew and life raft as far as possible from the fire. Notify the emergency services.

HELICOPTER RESCUE

If a crew is seriously injured, helicopter rescue may provide the fastest transfer for medical attention. This is a highly specialized rescue technique, and you must follow instructions closely.

RESCUE AT SEA

If you are involved in a rescue by specialized marine services, such as lifeboat or coastguard helicopter, remember that they are the experts – follow their instructions, and do exactly as they say. If your rescuer is another yacht, you will need to assess if the skipper's skill at manoeuvring close by and providing assistance is sufficient for the job. Always advise an approaching boat of hazards such as ropes or sails in the water.

COLLISION DAMAGE
In reasonable conditions, a yacht may be able to reach port with a hole above the waterline. Below the waterline, it is possible to stem water flow for a short period with a sail braced against the hole.

GETTING A TOW
If you accept a tow from a commercial or private vessel, check if a fee is expected. Charitable rescue services, such as the UK's RNLI (pictured here), welcome donations.

A yacht that has engine failure may need to be taken in tow. As a precaution, carry an extra long, heavyweight warp. While you wait for rescue, make a plan for securing the tow line to your yacht, and choose fittings that are sufficiently robust to pull a great deal of weight through the water. On a small boat, for example, the base of the mast may be the best attachment point. Avoid using knots or loops that cannot be released under load, and protect the tow rope from chafing against a fairlead or bow roller.

RESCUE BY AIR

Helicopters play a major role in search and rescue operations to aid yachtsmen who get into difficulties. The helicopter provides a vital (but very expensive) alternative to a lifeboat since it can get to a rescue location quickly, take off crew in extremely hazardous sea conditions and transport them to medical facilities as fast as possible.

If you have summoned air rescue, use red or orange handheld flares as a signal to the helicopter if requested (orange smoke by day, and red by night). Do not fire parachute or mini flares, which can be dangerous to the aircraft.

WAITING FOR HELP
The crew of a dismasted yacht wait for help. The life raft has been prepared, but while the yacht is not in danger of sinking, it is best to stay on board (*see* Abandoning ship, pp.272–273).

Make sure you understand instructions from the approaching helicopter pilot on VHF, which will include the course and speed he wishes you to follow – hearing the radio will become impossible once he is overhead. A injured person being rescued is normally lifted by winch from the stern of the yacht. A winchman is lowered from the helicopter, who will secure, and be lifted with, the person. Allow the winch wire to earth in the sea before grabbing it. Never secure it to the yacht. If the person is conscious, ask him or her not to try to help; aggressive clinging on can make it more difficult for the winchman.

FLARES

Read instructions to familiarize yourself with firing methods before you need them. Attend a demonstration, organized by marine safety services, to see flares in action. Hand-held flares have a range of up to three miles, most effective by day. Parachute flares can have a range over seven miles, most effective at night. Fire flares to leeward so that smoke and debris blow away. Aim parachute flares clear of mast, rigging, and sails, downwind to achieve maximum height. Ensure all flares are in-date; dispose of old flares correctly.

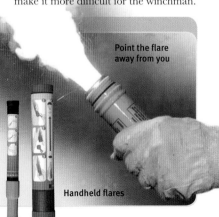

Point the flare away from you

Handheld flares

Abandoning ship

Never give the order to abandon ship unless it is absolutely vital – for instance, if the yacht is clearly about to sink or there is an uncontrollable fire. In most situations, staying on board a stricken yacht is likely to be safer for the crew than taking to the life raft.

LIFE RAFT CHOICE AND STORAGE

The number of crew on a yacht should not exceed the capacity of the life raft. It should be stowed ready for immediate launching – never below deck or beneath other equipment. Some yachts have a life-raft locker built into the transom, which ensures that launching will be straightforward. Other popular locations are strapped down on top of the coachroof, just behind the mast, or on the foredeck. From those positions the life raft can be lifted directly over the side. On some yachts the liferaft may

LIFE RAFT ON DECK
Ensure the life raft is secured in a position where it will be as easy as possible to throw it over either side of the yacht.

RACERS RESCUED
Yendys, skippered by Geoff Ross, sails to windward of a life raft containing the crew of the stricken *Skandia*, which lost her canting keel off the coast of Tasmania, during the 2004 Sydney–Hobart race. All crew were rescued and the yacht recovered.

DAWN AT PEMAQUID POINT LIGHTHOUSE
Since 1826, the headland dividing the John and
Muscongus Bays has been guarded by a lighthouse,
which now houses a fishermen's museum.

of Acadia and Mount Desert Island,
most of which is now incorporated into
the Acadia National Park.

Summer winds are mainly light,
although sea breezes make for good
sailing later in the day. It pays to keep
a close watch on the state of the tide.
Careless planning or navigation can
easily result in grounding or a long sail
to windward against a strong current
in one of the reaches.

OCEAN LIFE

The coastal waters of Maine are home to a
wide variety of marine wildlife, including
seals and birds. Among the most
frequently seen seals is the
common or harbour seal
(*Phoca vitulina*). This
mammal lives in
coastal waters and
feeds primarily on the
region's plentiful fish.

Common seal

Leeward Islands

EASTERN CARIBBEAN, ATLANTIC OCEAN

St. Martin
Antigua
St. Kitts and Nevis
Guadeloupe
Caribbean Sea
Dominica

The Leewards, the northern islands of the Lesser Antilles, stretch from St. Martin in the north to Dominica in the south. This is the Tropics of dreams: coral sand, crystal blue water, coconut palms, and the trades blowing at a steady 20 knots.

ESSENTIAL INFORMATION

CLIMATE Tropical: dry season in winter and wet season in summer.

WHEN TO VISIT December to May to avoid the hurricane season. The trade winds blow strongest from December to January.

DON'T MISS The Indian River trip on Dominica; Des Haies on Guadeloupe; the old dockyard in English Harbour on Antigua.

MOORING There are marinas on St. Martin, Antigua, and Guadeloupe. Elsewhere you will mostly be anchoring.

FAVOURITE ANCHORAGES Simpson Bay on St. Martin; Des Haies on Guadeloupe.

DON'T FORGET You will need clearance papers from the last island visited.

RICH DIVERSITY

The Leewards stretch for several hundred miles in a roughly north to south direction and include at least 14 sizeable islands. They are culturally and politically diverse, with eleven different governments; some are still colonies, others are independent. In the north, St. Martin, Anguilla, St. Barts, Barbuda, and Antigua are geologically older islands that have been worn down over time. Their peaks are too short to attract enough rain for rainforest growth. Less rainfall means more coral, and around Antigua and Anguilla some of the few coral reefs on the leeward side of the islands can be found. In the north, Guadeloupe and Dominica are younger islands with taller mountains, rainforest, and dramatic topography.

ISLAND WORLDS

The island of St. Martin encloses a large lagoon with marinas at the southern (Dutch) end and at the northern (French) corner as well as ample room to anchor all around the lagoon. Further south is the fashionable St. Barts and out on the eastern edge is the little-visited island of Barbuda, which has some of the finest beaches in the island chain, although you will need to wriggle in through the coral to get to the anchorages. To the south of Barbuda lies Antigua, which is one of the most developed yachting hubs in the Caribbean and home of Antigua Race Week. You will not want to miss English Harbour and Nelson's Dockyard, where there is a marina sitting just below the restored 18th-century buildings of the port. Farther on, there are anchorages all around the French island of Guadeloupe, including a particularly attractive one at Des Haies. There is a good marina at Point-à-Pitre, the island capital in the south, and there are also some wonderful anchorages positioned around the small island group of Les Saintes lying farther south. At the end of the chain, Dominica is the rough diamond of the Leewards, which has little in the way of facilities but possesses dramatic scenery and safe anchorages.

CLASSIC YACHT SAILING

The Leeward island of Antigua is famous for its yacht racing. In Antigua Classics Week, you can see everything from restored J-Class yachts, old schooners, and gaffers to modern classics engaged in some serious racing around the waters off Falmouth. After the classic yachts have run their races, boats sailed by local people, charter yachts, and some visiting cruisers come out for Antigua Sailing Week, where the competition on the water is fierce, and the celebrations ashore are legendary.

A classic yacht storms through the Atlantic swell off Antigua during Classics Week.

SHIRLEY HEIGHTS
Looking down from Shirley Heights over English Harbour and across to Falmouth on Antigua. This is the yachting hub of the Leewards and all visitors will pass through here at some time.

Windward Islands

EASTERN CARIBBEAN, ATLANTIC OCEAN

The Windwards are the southern chain of islands of the Lesser Antilles, stretching from St. Lucia in the north to Trinidad and Tobago off the Venezuelan coast in the south. These islands, with their high mountain peaks, let you get off the beaten track.

RICH HERITAGE

These popular islands offer wonderful trade winds cruising with easy passages and abundant anchorages. They offer the visitor a rich variety of local traditions with both French and English colonial influences. Martinique, at the northern end of the chain, has French heritage and provides good shopping. A short distance south lies St. Lucia. Its busy marina at Rodney Bay is the finishing line for the ARC (Atlantic Rally for Cruisers) and is popular with boats crossing from the Canaries.

MINI-ARCHIPELAGO

St. Vincent and the Grenadines form a mini-archipelago of islands and reefs and provide a remarkable cruising area. On the popular small island of Bequia, the anchorage at Admiralty Bay is often crowded with cruisers. The Tobago Cays are part of this area. Its emerald waters are protected from the Atlantic swell by a fragile barrier reef. If the atmospheric conditions are right, a green flash can be seen as the sun dips under the horizon.

Farther south lie Grenada and Trinidad. Grenada is a wonderful cruising area with a couple of small marinas and many protected anchorages. With its relatively muddy waters, Trinidad is mainly visited by yachts to lay up for the hurricane season in Chaguaramas Bay. Barbados, which lies about 160km (100 miles) farther out in the Atlantic than the rest of the group, is a favoured landfall for yachts crossing the Atlantic from the Canaries.

PETIT PITON, ST. LUCIA
Anchoring beneath one of the two distinctive pyramidal mountains on St. Lucia (Gros Piton is the other) is a cruising milestone.

ESSENTIAL INFORMATION

CLIMATE Tropical: dry season December to April, wet season June to October. Trade winds blow strongest from December to January.

WHEN TO VISIT December to May to avoid the hurricane season.

DON'T MISS The hurricane hole at Le Marin, Martinique; Soufrière, St. Lucia, under the twin peaks of the Pitons.

MOORING There are marinas at the main ports. In some bays there are laid moorings, but you will mostly use your own anchor.

FAVOURITE ANCHORAGES St. Pierre, Martinique; Prickly Bay, Grenada.

DON'T FORGET You will need the clearance papers from the last island visited.

Cuba

WESTERN CARIBBEAN, ATLANTIC OCEAN

Cuba, in the northwestern corner of the Caribbean, has some of the most pristine cruising areas in the region. Coral reefs extend as far as 16km (10 miles) offshore in places, and much of the best cruising is found inside the reefs.

HAVANA TO SANTIAGO

Cuba, the largest island in the Caribbean, is over 960km (600 miles) from end to end, but its jagged coastline is 3,700km (2,300 miles) in length. There are a number of marinas around the coast, the largest of which is Marina Hemingway just outside Havana in the north. However, the best sailing area is on the south coast, where there is enough cruising inside the main barrier reefs alone to keep you occupied for months, and more cruising beyond the reefs.

The Cubans are a friendly, effusive people, rivalling the Brazilians for style and sassiness. Getting something to eat and buying in provisions can be problematic in places, although the tourist dollar is often persuasive. The sea over the reefs is teeming with fish, and crayfish in particular are plentiful.

EASTERLY TRADE WINDS

The prevailing winds are the Atlantic trades, which blow from the east, pushing big seas along the coast beyond the reefs. When planning your itinerary, it is wise to take this into account. It is best to take an anticlockwise route around the island in order to take advantage of the longer navigable stretches within the reefs on the island's south side.

ESSENTIAL INFORMATION

CLIMATE Tropical: dry season December to April; wet season June to October. Trade winds blow strongest from December to January.

WHEN TO VISIT December to May to avoid the hurricane season.

DON'T MISS The wonderful architecture of Havana and Santiago; Isla de la Juventud.

MOORING Marinas at Havana, Cayo Largo, Santa Cruz, and Santiago, plus many anchorages and commercial harbours.

FAVOURITE ANCHORAGES Cayo Largo; Nueva Gerona on Isla de la Juventud.

DON'T FORGET First obtain a permit at a Port of Entry, giving a firm itinerary. Check in and out of major ports en route.

CASTILLO DEL MORRO
The 16th-century fort Castillo del Morro and its lighthouse, seen here across Havana Channel, dominate the entrance to Havana's old port.

Rio de Janeiro coast

BRAZIL, ATLANTIC OCEAN

BRAZIL
São
Paulo •
Rio de
Janeiro
Ilha
Grande
Parati
Atlantic Ocean

For many sailors Brazil is the ultimate destination. The country offers a combination of scorching sun, endless beaches, spicy food, and beautiful, friendly people. Just west of Rio de Janeiro lies one of the country's most attractive cruising areas.

WARM WATERS

Centred in the trade wind belt, breezes are steady and predictable along this coast, and violent storms are rare. Although there is much for the visitor to see in Rio de Janeiro, most people will want to cruise to one of the more tranquil areas along the coast, where it will be difficult to decide whether to relax in a café, bathe in the warm waters, or sail in the balmy breezes.

HIGHLIGHTS

A highlight for many locals, charterers, and visiting sailors is Baia del Ilha Grande, which is only two hours by road from Rio's international airport. With several nature reserves, hundreds of islands, and abundant anchorages, it provides fine sailing. The historic town of Parati, a proposed World Heritage Site, with its charming colonial Portuguese buildings, open air cafés, and restaurants, should be included in any exploration of the islands and waterways.

PARATI
In the 17th century, Parati was a major gold-shipping port. Its stunning scenery and beautiful waters make it a popular destination.

ESSENTIAL INFORMATION

CLIMATE Summer is hot and humid; winter is cooler and drier.

WHEN TO VISIT All year round, especially May to December.

DON'T MISS The historic town of Parati.

MOORING Free anchoring overall, several marinas in area.

FAVOURITE ANCHORAGES Baia de Parati; Praia dos Mangues, Ilha Grande.

FORMALITIES Some nationalities require visas. Customs, immigration, and port captain must be visited on entering and leaving every port. It may be advisable to complete formalities in Rio or São Paulo first.

As you glide through the clear waters, the changing shades of blue and green indicate depth almost as well as the charts and make for fascinating navigation. Polarized glasses are a great aid to judging depth and spotting coral when sailing in shallow water. During the prime sailing season, May to December, it is usually calm in the morning, with a moderate sea breeze setting in later to take the boat to its evening anchorage.

The Azores

PORTUGAL, ATLANTIC OCEAN

On the west to east Atlantic crossing, the logical landfall is the Azores, lying some 1,400km (900 miles) off the coast of Portugal. Most yachts make for Horta on Faial and, in fact, more visitors arrive at Faial by yacht than by ferry or plane.

SAILING PARADISE

Arriving in the Azores is like stepping back in time to a quieter and more gentle era. The small villages, with their old-fashioned Portuguese architecture on the edge of rolling green hills, have a rustic charm that leaves most sailors wondering why they did an Atlantic circuit when this little piece of sailing paradise was sitting on their doorstep.

ISLANDS OF PLENTY

The eight major islands that make up the Azores lie in a chain stretching some 500km (300 miles) across the northern Atlantic. The largest and most populated island is São Miguel to the east of the group. The imposing volcano on the central island of Pico is Portugal's highest mountain.

The islands are almost impossibly green and fertile, and the waters around them are a breeding ground for several species of whale – you will often sight schools of sperm and pilot whales when cruising around the archipelago.

SHELTERED HARBOUR
Horta resounds to cruisers celebrating a successful Atlantic crossing. Before you leave it is considered good luck to paint a mural on the harbour wall.

The islands are virtually self-sufficient in food, and the Portuguese-inspired cuisine using local produce is wonderful.

ESSENTIAL INFORMATION

CLIMATE Temperate: summer temperatures of 15–25°C (60–77°F).

WHEN TO VISIT April to September.

DON'T MISS Pretty harbours on Flores and Horta on Faial; Ponta Delgado on São Miguel (finishing line for UK "Azores and back" race).

MOORING Small fishing harbours and marinas on Faial, Terceira, and São Miguel.

FAVOURITE ANCHORAGES Horta on Faial.

DON'T FORGET All yachts, including EU-flagged yachts, must clear in and out at one of the Azores' three major yacht harbours on Faial, Terceira, or at Ponta Delgado.

Lofoten Islands

NORWAY, NORWEGIAN SEA

Norwegian Sea
Austvågøy
Borg
Hopen
Moskenesøy

Just north of the Arctic Circle, the island archipelago of Lofoten provides some of the most adventurous cruising in Europe. There are numerous safe anchorages for the sailor, many of them near colourful towns and villages.

VIKING WATERS

These islands run along the northwest side of an enormous fiord that contains a great variety of sea life. The islands rise almost vertically from the sea and make for a dramatic backdrop when cruising. Sailing is made easy by good charts, plentiful seamarks, and the midnight sun, which means that it never gets dark throughout the whole summer season.

FISHING AND FARMING

In Norway, sailing is a tradition that goes back to the Stone Age. These waters were home to the Vikings and their influence is clear in many of the traditional boats sailing there today. Fishing is a major industry here, but people also farm; the splashes of bright green fields, dotted with cheerful summer flowers, provide a contrast to the wide sea and skyscapes. Elk and deer can be seen grazing, there is a huge variety of sea birds, and several types of eagle soar above. When sailing, the chances of seeing whales are high. Summer winds alternate between southwest and north. Sailing tends

to be wild and wet on the windward side of the islands and gentle on the leeward sides. Autumn winds, which tumble down from mountain peaks, may blow very hard and come almost without warning, so it pays to watch how the winds play across the water and be ready to reef or drop sail at a moment's notice.

ESSENTIAL INFORMATION

CLIMATE Temperate, but may be surprisingly warm on a calm sunny day.

WHEN TO VISIT May to September (November, if you want to see killer whales).

DON'T MISS Whale-watching; the Viking museum at Borg.

MOORING Almost all towns have a public pontoon with guest berths at a reasonable charge. There are many well-sheltered free anchorages among the islands.

FAVOURITE ANCHORAGES Hopen, south coast of Austvågøy; Helle, Moskenesøy.

DON'T FORGET Reporting is not expected if arriving from other Scandinavian countries. Otherwise contact customs upon arrival.

PEACEFUL ANCHORAGE
A yacht lies at anchor in the tranquil waters off the south side of the Lofoten islands, under the mountains of Austvågøy at Storø.

Kiel and the Danish Islands

GERMANY AND DENMARK, BALTIC SEA

The north German port of Kiel is one of the world's finest yachting centres. Whether you are a local or have come through the Kiel Canal, it makes a fine stepping-off point for a trip to the roughly four hundred islands of Denmark.

A SAILING HUB

From the waters of Northern Germany, across Denmark to the west coast of Sweden and on into the Baltic, the cruising and facilities in these waters are world-class. Kiel, home to the hugely popular Kiel Week regatta (see p.326), has several major routes leading towards the Baltic or Copenhagen and the west of Sweden.

DELIGHTFUL DENMARK

Sailing in Denmark is so good that many Danes choose not to sail elsewhere. There is seldom more than a few hours' sailing between charming and welcoming old towns. Alternatively, anchor among the rural islands and pleasantly sheltered waterways, where windmills, lush pastures, and peaceful woodlands characterize the scenery. In the light to moderate winds, with no big seas or tidal currents, navigation and sailing are so easy that the crew just have to concentrate on the exhilaration of feeling their boat respond to the tiller and keep an eye open for other traffic.

SØNDERBORG, DENMARK
An easy day's sail from the busy waters of Kiel, Sønderborg lies on both sides of the Als Fiord. This pretty town welcomes yachts to tie up below bustling cafés and the stately Sønderborg Castle, which dates from medieval times.

ESSENTIAL INFORMATION

CLIMATE Temperate, but expect hot, dry weather from June to August.

WHEN TO VISIT Popular in July and August, but can also be beautiful in spring or autumn.

DON'T MISS Sønderborg Castle; the waterfront at Sønderborg; Viking Ship museum at Roskilde.

MOORING Guest berths in every port, only overnight stays are charged; many sheltered spots for free anchoring.

FAVOURITE ANCHORAGES Haderslev Fiord, west side of Little Belt; Roskilde Fiord.

DON'T FORGET Report to customs on arrival if coming from outside the EU. If coming from within the EU, check with customs, although formal clearance may not be required.

Cornwall

ENGLAND, ENGLISH CHANNEL, ATLANTIC OCEAN

Seafaring has been in the blood of the people of the wild and rugged coast of Cornwall for untold generations. Working boats or vessels based upon local designs, such as the Falmouth Quay Punts, have made sailing history all over the world.

NATURAL HARBOUR

Falmouth, one of the world's largest natural harbours, is Cornwall's main sailing centre, although many boats are also moored on the Helford or Fowey rivers. Most sailors favour the south Cornish coast, with its rocky scenery and easily approached harbours and rivers. The north coast is just as attractive but has fewer good harbours, and most ports lie up drying rivers with dangerous bars. If you have time, you can explore the Scilly Isles to the southwest, comprising more than 150 islands, many of which are nature reserves, offering a wealth of opportunities for wildlife enthusiasts.

CHALLENGING SAILING

Cornwall offers challenging cruising. The need for careful navigation and timing, to take advantage of tides and avoid the races off headlands, helps many sailors to perfect their sailing skills. A good plan is to sail west in short stages against the prevailing southwest winds. This may be a rough, wet thrash as the bow plunges into swells rolling in from the Atlantic. The homeward passage can be a refreshingly easy downhill run with a nice lift under the stern from swells that seem to be half the size they were on the outward leg. But beware of races off headlands, where even following seas can tumble over the decks and catch the unwary by surprise.

SHALLOW WATERS
Many of the north coast's picturesque ports, such as Port Isaac, have drying harbours. If you are staying over low tide, your boat should be prepared to "take the ground".

ESSENTIAL INFORMATION

CLIMATE Changeable; may be fine and warm in sheltered spots when cold and windy off the headlands.

WHEN TO VISIT April to early October; most popular between June and August.

DON'T MISS Falmouth Regatta, National Maritime Museum at Falmouth.

MOORING Marinas in major ports, berth to quay, or alongside fishermen in smaller ports; fees will be charged. Anchoring in rivers and among the Scilly Isles.

FAVOURITE ANCHORAGES The Helford River; port of Fowey, at the mouth of the River Fowey.

DON'T FORGET Non-EU boats report to customs on arrival. EU boats need not report.

Brittany

FRANCE, ENGLISH CHANNEL, ATLANTIC OCEAN

The Bretons often say, "If you can sail around the coast of Brittany, you can sail anywhere in the world." With its massive tides, tidal rips, and a coast studded with rocks and reefs, Brittany is a challenging but rewarding area in which to sail.

ANGRY WATERS

Brittany stretches from the Cherbourg peninsula around Cap Finistère and the angry waters of the Raz du Sein to the Golfe du Morbihan. Its rocky coast is one of the most picturesque in Europe. The waters around Brittany are exposed to gales coming in across the Atlantic, so some care should be taken, especially during spring and autumn. Fortunately, the Breton coast is also much indented and there are numerous safe harbours and anchorages all around it. The Golfe du Morbihan is a whole cruising area in its own right and is the home of the world-famous Glenans sailing school.

PASSION FOR SAILING

The Bretons are passionate about sailing and especially their traditional sailing craft. You will often see wonderful old wooden boats sailing around the coasts, equipped with surprisingly little in the

way of modern aids, but aided by a large helping of seamanship that enables them to safely negotiate their home waters. Ashore, Brittany offers a varied cuisine. In particular, you will find wonderful seafood – oysters and mussels figure prominently – as well as traditional pancakes (crêpes).

ESSENTIAL INFORMATION

CLIMATE Atlantic seaboard, settled summers.

WHEN TO VISIT May to September. Watch out for severe Atlantic depressions in spring and autumn.

DON'T MISS The Golfe du Morbihan dotted with islands; July's biennial Douarnenez Week festival.

MOORING Plenty of marinas and spectacular anchorages around the rocky coast.

FAVOURITE ANCHORAGES Douarnenez; Golfe du Morbihan.

DON'T FORGET EU boats need not report. Non-EU boats should report in and out.

ANSE DES SÉVIGNÉS, CÔTES D'ARMOR
A myriad of anchorages for use in calm weather are cut into the rocky foreshore along the savage Breton coast. In bad weather, head for a nearby harbour.

Balearics and Costa Brava

SPAIN, MEDITERRANEAN SEA

Lying between mainland Spain and the islands of Corsica and Sardinia, the Balearics are a convenient stepping stone on sailing routes through the western Mediterranean. On the mainland, the Costa Brava has the most spectacular coastline in Spain.

THE ISLANDS

The three largest islands, Ibiza, Mallorca, and Menorca, lie in an arc from west to east. Their coasts are visible from afar and have deep water, making them an easy landfall when on passage in the western Mediterranean. Ibiza is the "clubbing island", both famous and infamous for its clubs and rave parties. For peace and quiet, try the small island of Formentera a few miles away, where you can anchor off one of the long sandy beaches.

UNSPOILED BEAUTY

Mallorca, the largest and most developed of the islands, has marinas all around its coast and some wonderful *calas*, or coves, to tuck into. The island of Cabrera, off the west coast, is a marine reserve. You can get a permit to visit this oasis of calm and unspoiled beauty. The easternmost stepping stone, Menorca, is riddled with deep natural harbours and peaceful villages.

PALMA, MALLORCA
In Palma, you berth below the cathedral, often beneath the shadow of the superyachts that make this city their Mediterranean home.

FARTHER AFIELD

The Costa Brava, lying between the French border and the vibrant city of Barcelona, can be reached with an easy overnight passage. There are marinas and pretty harbours along the coast.

CADAQUES
Nestled between the sea and the mountains, the small harbour town of Cadaques on the Costa Brava was once home to the artist Salvador Dali.

ESSENTIAL INFORMATION

CLIMATE Typically Mediterranean, with spells of unsettled weather from Atlantic systems.

WHEN TO VISIT May to September.

DON'T MISS Superyachts at Palma Mallorca; the marine reserve at Cabrera; Mahon's wonderful natural harbour and good cuisine.

MOORING Numerous marinas – larger yachts should book in the summer; anchorages, some with moorings, around the islands.

FAVOURITE ANCHORAGES Mahon, Menorca; Andratx, Mallorca.

DON'T FORGET EU boats need not report, although customs will do spot checks. Non-EU boats should report at the first port of entry and out again when leaving Spain.

Southern Italy

ITALY, MEDITERRANEAN SEA

This coast is little cruised and yet offers sympathetic harbours and marinas, a spectacular coastline, and wonderful towns and villages. This area offers less than the north in terms of yachting facilities, but the friendliness and charm of the locals shines through.

THE COAST

From Amalfi the Campanian coast runs into the Gulf of Salerno before curving out to the rocky coast with the harbour of Acciaroli, Hemingway's favourite place in the Mediterranean, on the end. The coast runs down to Capo Palinuro before curving in again around Calabria like the inside of a large question mark. It is spectacular, mountainous country that is steeped in history, from Odysseus, to the Romans, and the medieval period. From the sea you can see hill villages clinging to the slopes that have changed little in a hundred years.

AEOLIAN COAST

Sail direct from the Amalfi coast to the Aeolian islands and you will miss out on some wonderful cruising. If you favour tranquillity, you will find much to keep you in places like Palinuro, Sapri, and Tropea, away from more crowded areas. In the summer, a southwesterly sea breeze blows from midday until sunset giving gentle sailing that at times may need a bit of help from the engine to get you to your next destination.

ESSENTIAL INFORMATION

CLIMATE Typically Mediterranean, with hot, dry summers.

WHEN TO VISIT May to October.

DON'T MISS Amalfi; the port of Acciaroli; Tropea, where you walk up 200 steps to the old town; the miniature harbour at Scilla, site of a large whirlpool in the past.

MOORING Marinas at Agropoli, Maratea, Vibo Valentia, and Tropea; elsewhere you will anchor and moor in small fishing harbours.

FAVOURITE ANCHORAGES Sapri; Acciaroli.

DON'T FORGET EU boats need not report, although customs will do spot checks. Non-EU boats should report at the first port of entry and out again when leaving Italy.

HISTORIC HARBOUR
Amalfi harbour is home to humble fishing boats as well as superyachts.

Corsica and Sardinia

SOUTHERN EUROPE, MEDITERRANEAN SEA

These two islands make up a vast and wonderful cruising area you will need months to fully explore. The Strait of Bonifacio, which separates the islands, is often described as the best cruising area in the western Mediterranean.

CORSICA

The granite coast of this mountainous island drops steeply off into deep water. The west coast is often exposed to strong westerlies, so you need to plan your cruising with care. Calvi, where you can berth in the marina under the shadow of a Genoese citadel or moor in the bay, is often the first stop for yachts on passage from France and Italy. You can mainly day-sail the rocky west coast using marinas or the numerous anchorages that cut into the rocky coast. The east coast has shallower water in places and

NEAR BONIFACIO
The picturesque harbour of Bonifacio is tucked inside a *calanque* – a deep, narrow inlet set back in a rocky cliff – concealed until you are almost there.

ESSENTIAL INFORMATION

CLIMATE Mediterranean: hot, dry summers.

WHEN TO VISIT May to October, although you can, with care, cruise for longer.

DON'T MISS Bonifacio's walled citadel; the savage seascape in the Golfe de Porto; the La Maddalena archipelago; Porto Cervo.

MOORING Many marinas and anchorages, some with moorings.

FAVOURITE ANCHORAGES Bonifacio, Corsica; Teulada, Sardinia.

DON'T FORGET EU boats need not report. Non-EU boats should report in and out.

the prevailing wind blows off the land, so the sea is flatter and the landscape less dramatic. In the south, the water is so clear you may think your keel will touch bottom when there is still clearance.

SARDINIA

Sardinia is the larger island of the two and, though mountainous, is less lofty than Corsica. Its west coast, like that of its neighbour, is exposed to strong westerlies and has marinas at Alghero, Oristano, and Carloforte on the old tunny fishing island of Sant Antiocco. In the north, the La Maddalena archipelago has been declared a marine reserve and though there are some restrictions, there are still numerous places to anchor around these wonderful islands. On the northeast corner on the Costa Smeralda, there is a cluster of very up-market marinas. At the southern end there are marinas at Cagliari and Teulada more suited to most wallets.

ALGHERO
The port of Alghero on the west coast of Sardinia has a definite Spanish flavour dating from the period when the island was ruled by the Spanish kingdom of Aragon.

Dalmatian Coast

CROATIA, ADRIATIC SEA

After a decade of conflicts in the former Yugoslavia, Croatia has become an independent state with most of the coastline. Investment in marinas is part of the onshore infrastructure that supports the wonderful cruising around the country's offshore islands.

ITALIANATE COASTLINE

Straggling down the eastern side of the Adriatic, the coast and islands of Croatia have so many anchorages you could conceivably never go into a harbour. But then you would miss out on the old cities and towns along the coast and on the larger islands, with their distinctive Italianate character. All of them have a harbour and many of them a marina. Much of this area was administered from Venice, and Venetian ways, such as an evening *passeggiata*, or stroll, and a coffee in an outdoor café, are an essential part of Croatian life.

SUPERB CRUISING

The entire coast offers superb cruising around the indented coastline and offshore islands, and there are some coastal areas not to be missed. The old walled city of Dubrovnik with the nearby islands of Korcula, Hvar, and Brac is justly popular – you could spend months exploring this region. Farther north the Kornati Islands and the mainland marinas at Zadar, Biograd, and Split make up another popular cruising area with good facilities in the main centres. Some of the islands are national parks, while others are virtually uninhabited.

THE BORA

The prevailing wind is a sea breeze that blows onto the coast from the west, but at times the dreaded *bora*, first cousin of the *mistral* in France, blows with some violence from the north. Then there is the *yugo*, a wind that blows from the south. If either wind threatens, stay tucked up in harbour.

VIEW OVER DUBROVNIK
The medieval city of Dubrovnik, is a "must-see" on the Dalmatian coast. Sail north and you are in Venice; sail south and you reach the Ionian Sea.

ESSENTIAL INFORMATION

CLIMATE Mediterranean: hot, dry summers.

WHEN TO VISIT Most visitors favour May to September, although you can, with care, cruise outside this season.

DON'T MISS Dubrovnik; the Krka waterfall, Skradin; Sucuraj harbour on Hvar.

MOORING Marinas on the mainland and islands; numerous anchorages.

FAVOURITE ANCHORAGES Dubrovnik; Korcula town harbour.

DON'T FORGET All boats must clear in and out at a designated port. A cruising permit will be issued.

Ionian Islands

GREECE, IONIAN SEA

The Ionian islands, off the west of Greece, have long attracted sailors. The area has a notably green aspect and, in common with other countries in the region, its older buildings have an Italianate feel, a legacy of Venetian rule from the 13th to the 16th centuries.

THE ISLANDS

The islands stretch in a ragged line down the west coast of Greece, from Corfu in the north to Zakynthos in the south. There are six sizeable main islands and many smaller ones, numbering about 40 in total. All of them, like the much indented mainland coast, have charming anchorages and harbours protected from the prevailing northwest winds.

GAIOS, PAXOS
Berthed off the town quay, you are literally in the middle of town with tavernas and cafés on your transom.

HISTORY

The Ionian region has a long history that involves the ancient Greeks, the Romans, the Venetians, the Turks, and even the British. The landscape is littered with the remains of past civilizations, ranging from the island of Ithaca, the home of Odysseus, and the ruins of Olympia in the Peloponnese mountains, to the castles and ancient olive trees of the Venetians, and the roads and fruit cake ("kek") bestowed by the British.

THE MAISTROS

The prevailing wind is the *maistros*, a less boisterous cousin of the *meltemi* in the Aegean. Between June and September, the wind blows from the northwest down throughout the whole area. It usually gets up about midday and blows hardest in the afternoon, at Force 4–6 (11–27 knots), before dying down in the early evening, allowing you to sail through the afternoon and get a good night's sleep in calm water. In early and late season, the

ZAKYNTHOS
St. George's Bay on the west coast of Zakynthos is a spectacular anchorage when the prevailing westerlies are not blowing hard.

maistros is less developed and some days it barely blows at all. If you are going north, you can start early in the morning and motor some of the way; alternatively, you can wait until midday and then beat your way north. This kind of sailing may at times be hard going, but it holds little menace when the sky is blue and the spray over the decks is warm.

FOLLOW THE CROWDS

It was inevitable that a sailing area as beautiful as this would become very popular, and so it has. There is a large charter fleet that includes both flotillas and bareboats, and at times the waters can feel busy. That said, this region features so many bays and coves that, with a little research and a bit of local knowledge, you can always find a harbour and anchorage that you can enjoy with just one or two neighbours.

CORFU
The Corfu channel with the Pindar mountains bordering one side, where Homer's "rosy fingered dawn" conjures up a landscape of haunting beauty.

ESSENTIAL INFORMATION

CLIMATE Typical Mediterranean with hot, dry summers and wet winters.

WHEN TO VISIT May to October. Peak season is July and August and best avoided because most of Europe is on holiday.

DON'T MISS The old town of Corfu; Kefallonia; ruins of Olympia at Katakolon.

MOORING There are two marinas and numerous fishing harbours and village quays. Otherwise there are anchorages everywhere.

FAVOURITE ANCHORAGES Kalamos Island; Platarias on the mainland; Sivota on Levkas.

DON'T FORGET All yachts must get a transit log on entry. Non-EU yachts must also get a cruising permit.

Gulf of Gökova

TURKEY, MEDITERRANEAN SEA

The Gulf of Gökova to the east of the Greek island of Kos runs inland for some 70km (45 miles). There are numerous anchorages and coves in its indented coast. The sides of the gulf are split by gorges and ravines, creating a spectacular landscape.

THE GULF

Heading into the gulf, the prevailing wind, known as the *meltemi*, tends to funnel into the bay from the west, giving you a downwind run in and a beat upwind as you come back out. Most yachts do a clockwise circuit to take advantage of the lighter winds on the southern side.

The coast is mountainous, with steep slopes covered in pine trees right down to the water's edge. In Cokertme and Sogut wooden jetties provide access to restaurants ashore, but in most other bays you'll need to anchor and take a line ashore to a convenient rock or pine tree, with just the occasional turtle and the chatter of cicadas for company.

The coast south and east of Gökova has several more large gulfs, including Hisaronu Korfezi and the popular Skopea Liman. Just across the water are the Greek Dodecanese islands.

HISTORIC SITES

The gulf is dotted with ancient sites from the Graeco-Roman period, enabling you to wander around the still-recognizable skeletons of ancient cities.

ESSENTIAL INFORMATION

CLIMATE Mediterranean, with hot, dry summers and wet winters.

WHEN TO VISIT April to October, but early and late season is also popular.

DON'T MISS The ancient sites at Kedreai and Knidos; the lively town of Bodrum.

MOORING Several marinas around the Bodrum peninsula; a small marina at Sogut; wooden jetties; numerous coastal anchorages.

FAVOURITE ANCHORAGES Sogut; Cati.

DON'T FORGET On arrival in Turkish waters all boats must go to a Port of Entry and report to customs, immigration, health authorities, and the harbour master.

Two thousand years ago, the gulf was the playground of Antony and Cleopatra and on the evocatively named Snake and Castle Islands there is still a small beach that Mark Antony is reputed to have laid out with sand imported from the Sahara.

ST. PETER'S CASTLE, BODRUM
Built by the Knights of St. John, this castle still guards the entrance to Bodrum harbour. A modern marina is tucked into its north corner.

Cape Town Area

SOUTH AFRICA, ATLANTIC OCEAN

Since the days of the Dutch East India Company, Cape Town has been one of the world's great sailing centres. This beautiful city is home to an enormous port that enthusiastically welcomes all visitors, from the largest cruise liner to the smallest yacht.

WARM HOSPITALITY

It is easy to get caught up in the conviviality of the Royal Cape Yacht Club, which puts itself out to greet the visitor. Remember that the Western Cape also has some pleasant cruising. Harbours such as Hout Bay, south of Table Mountain, and Saldanha 100km (60 miles) to the north also give a warm welcome to sailing boats.

ALL-SEASON SAILING

Summer can be very hot, and the strong winds that blow are often a great relief as well as making for exciting racing in Table Bay. With double-reefed main and a small jib, the sailing can be wild and wet, but is rarely cold. Winter is the time when flowers bloom and Southern Right Whales come inshore to give birth and raise their young. A coastal cruise at this time of year can be very rewarding. Yachts bound for the Caribbean are often built here, where prices are low and the skill level is high, before taking the gentle trade-wind passage across to Brazil and onwards to the Caribbean.

TABLE MOUNTAIN
The first sight as one approaches from seaward, Table Mountain National Park is a nature reserve right in the centre of this fine city. The harbour provides a wide range of facilities for yachts.

ESSENTIAL INFORMATION

CLIMATE Hot from November to April, warm temperate at other times.

WHEN TO VISIT All year round.

DON'T MISS Superb views of Table Mountain from the water, winter flowers, fynbos (unique, heatherlike, wild vegetation), and whale-watching.

MOORING There are a few possibilities for anchoring in Saldanha, otherwise berth in a marina; prices are very reasonable.

FAVOURITE ANCHORAGES Hout Bay; Port Owen on the south side of St. Helena Bay.

DON'T FORGET Report to customs and immigration (and also to the port authority upon departure). Customs clearance required when changing port and immigration must be notified if crew leave or arrive by air.

Seychelles

WESTERN INDIAN OCEAN

The Seychelles consist of two distinct island groups. The outer islands are coral atolls, the inner islands granite. Sitting just south of the equator, they have a unique tropical flora and fauna, including a large colony of giant tortoises on Ile Curieuse.

INNER GROUP

Mahé, Praslin, and La Digue, the main islands in the inner group, lie in a tight archipelago, with distances between the anchorages of little more than 40km (20 nautical miles). Victoria on Mahé is the main port and capital, and most yachts will head from here towards Praslin and La Digue.

GARDEN OF EDEN

Make sure to visit the Vallée de Mai on Praslin. You can take a bus from the anchorage at Baie Sainte Anne, then follow the marked trails through the rainforest. The main attraction here is the rare Coco de Mer palm. Its female seed was famed among sailors for its suggestive shape and is the largest of any plant in the world, weighing up to 30kg (45lb).

The Coco de Mer

ST. PIERRE ISLET, OFF PRASLIN ISLAND
All around Praslin there are idyllic anchorages where chunks of granite jut out of a turquoise tropical sea. St. Pierre Islet offers superb snorkelling.

ESSENTIAL INFORMATION

CLIMATE Tropical equatorial; temperatures are around 27–31°C (80–88°F).

WHEN TO VISIT All year round.

DON'T MISS The giant tortoise reserve on Ile Curieuse; the wonderful bays and sculpted rocks of La Digue; the Vallée de Mai.

MOORING Anchoring everywhere but Victoria on Mahé; around the Marine Reserves, use moorings to preserve the coral.

FAVOURITE ANCHORAGES Port Launay on Mahé; Ile Curieuse.

DON'T FORGET All boats must check in and out at Victoria on Mahé. Advise of arrival by radio and await instructions.

Langkawi

MALAYSIA, ANDAMAN SEA

Langkawi is an archipelago of about 100 islands off the west coast of Malaysia, just beneath the Thai border. This island group in the tropical Andaman Sea forms a wonderful cruising area that rivals the attractions of Thailand to the north.

THE ISLANDS

The main island, Pulau Langkawi, is riddled with inlets and bays, and many other islands are scattered around it. While locals say there are over 100 islands in the group, that total includes some very small landforms. The area is spectacular, with high limestone cliffs and steep slopes covered with thick jungle down to the edge of deep water.

JUNGLE CRUISING

Small, sandy beaches are locked in by the cliffs and you can anchor off your own beach and go ashore to explore. On the smaller islands there are mini-fiords draped in lush vegetation, where you can nose in and anchor with a line ashore to the cliffs. These tropical islands teem with wildlife: giant fruit bats, sea eagles, monkeys, and an impressive variety of venomous snakes. On Langkawi the main town is Kuah, with the marina and facilities of the Royal Langkawi Yacht Club on hand.

ESSENTIAL INFORMATION

CLIMATE Tropical; dry season in winter and wet season in summer.

WHEN TO VISIT November to April.

DON'T MISS The Maiden's Lake anchorage on Pulau Dayang Bunting; the night market and local restaurants at Kuah.

MOORING Marinas on Langkawi at Kuah, Rebak, and Pantai Kok; many spectacular anchorages around the archipelago.

FAVOURITE ANCHORAGES Fiord anchorage on Pulau Gabang Darat; Kuah.

DON'T FORGET All boats must go to a Port of Entry, register at the Marine Department, then report to immigration, customs, health, and finally the harbour master. Breaking drugs laws here carries severe penalties.

PANTAI BEACH, LANGKAWI ISLAND
Pantai Beach sweeps alongside the Andaman Sea, on the fringe of the Indian Ocean. In the bay's north corner is the Pantai Kok marina and anchorage.

Phuket

THAILAND, ANDAMAN SEA

Thailand's jungle-covered limestone islands rising out of a warm, blue, tropical sea are alluring enough. Take account of the gentle Thais, an exotic cuisine and culture, and a light monsoon wind, and you have one of the best sailing destinations possible.

PHUKET AND ISLANDS

The hub of yachting in Thailand is the island of Phuket, which has three marinas and a number of well-sheltered bays such as Ao Chalong. It is home to the King's Cup, a week of racing, and the Andaman Sea Rally, which offers you a rare chance to sail in company from Phuket to the Andaman Islands to the northwest.

East and south of Phuket peninsula is an archipelago of islands peppering the sea. To the east is Phang Nga Bay, with the two large islands of Ko Yao Noi and Ko Yao Yai, and the smaller but better known Ko Phi-Phi Don. Scattered in between are countless smaller islands, many uninhabited except for occasional passing sea gypsies, who live all year on their small groups of boats catching fish and diving for coral. The limestone

TON SAI BEACH, KO PHI-PHI DON
One of the most beautiful islands in the world, Kho Phi-Phi Don is a day's sail from Phuket and is usually the finish for one of the races in the King's Cup.

ESSENTIAL INFORMATION

CLIMATE Tropical; dry season in winter and wet season in summer.

WHEN TO VISIT The winter northeast monsoon period from December to March is the favoured time.

MOORING Marinas around Phuket at Yacht Haven and Boat Lagoon; anchoring in shallow bays and coves around the archipelago.

FAVOURITE ANCHORAGES Ko Lipe; Nai Harn.

DON'T MISS Exploring the *hongs* in Phang Nga Bay; the King's Cup in early December.

DON'T FORGET Call in at a Port of Entry within 24 hours of entering Thai waters. Most boats clear in at Ao Chalong. Report to immigration, customs, and the harbour master.

WESTERN PHUKET
The anchorages on the west coast of Phuket can be used during the favoured northeast monsoon blowing off the land.

islands are spectacular, fantastic jutting pillars covered in thick jungle down to the water's edge. The area features *hongs* (lagoons accessible only by sea caves), rock tunnels, caves, and chimneys eroded from cliffs, which may be explored by dinghy or kayak. The water is milky green and you must take care over your navigation in shallow waters. Farther south the water is clearer and it is easier to see the coral and rocks around the islands.

SOUTH OF PHUKET

From Phuket south to the border with Malaysia is a lesser known – but no less scenic – area with numerous islands to cruise around. Do not neglect the much indented coast, where there are small fishing villages. Offshore some of the islands are inhabited and in this area you will be likely to see families of sea gypsies. The water in this area is clearer for snorkelling and diving, although if you want really clear water, you will need to sail around the outside of Phuket and northward to the Similan Islands.

Tonga

PACIFIC ISLANDS, WESTERN PACIFIC OCEAN

A kingdom with strong links to Britain, Tonga has three main island groups and numerous outliers, all offering superb cruising. Sunshine, steady breezes, and golden sand under waving palm trees are all to be found in this enchanting group of islands.

VAVA'U

The Vava'u Group, the northernmost collection of islands, forms the centre of Tonga's sailing activity, which is based in the main town of Neiafu. Sailing in sheltered and clear waters, you can explore blue lagoons, wooded islands, and low coral reefs. There are long, sandy beaches and intriguing underwater caves that can be reached only by diving. As much or as little company as desired can be found in the numerous anchorages. Local colour can be found in Neiafu's streets and market or by joining in one of the popular traditional feasts.

GETTING THERE

Unless you are chartering, Tonga is best reached by sailing directly from New Zealand or as a port of call while crossing the South Pacific, by those lucky enough to be making that journey. Facilities for

VOLCANIC SHORES
Heavy surf along the coastline of Vava'u, the largest island in the volcanic Vava'u Group, a chain that contains 40 smaller islands.

private boats are less well developed in Tonga than in Fiji, where boats can be left at various marinas. The islands are at risk from cyclones during the summer, so the main sailing season runs from May to November, when the weather is pleasant, dryish, and cool. Trade winds provide almost constant easterly winds, interrupted by half-day westerlies.

SNORKELLING
Warm, crystal clear waters, flourishing coral reefs, and multitudes of colourful fish are found in virtually every anchorage.

ESSENTIAL INFORMATION

CLIMATE Tropical, with cooling breezes.

WHEN TO VIST All year, but May to November is the preferred time.

DON'T MISS On Vava'u, dive into a cave lit from below through tropical waters.

MOORING Anchorages are plentiful and free in both areas.

FAVOURITE ANCHORAGES Kenatu islet, Vava'u.

DON'T FORGET Notify customs and immigration on arrival.

Fiji

PACIFIC ISLANDS, WESTERN PACIFIC OCEAN

Ranging from towering mountains to tiny coral strands, this huge group of islands offer a wonderful variety of cruising experience. They are deservedly popular with sailors. The traditional way of life is strong and gives a thoroughly charming atmosphere.

ISLAND HOSPITALITY

Fiji has a well-deserved reputation for hospitality and colour. The main hazards that visiting sailors might encounter are excess sun and the fine local rum. These islands contain bustling modern towns and villages, where people live in traditional grass homes along a coral strand. There are two large islands and several groups of smaller, tropical gems sprinkled across the blue Pacific. The fishing and diving here are unparalleled and many places, some rarely visited by yachts, offer superb anchorages and a warm welcome. Sailors tend to congregate around Suva, the capital, at Malololailai on the west coast of Viti Levu, and at the friendly marina in Savusavu on the south coast of Vanua Levu. The towns all have large markets selling colourful clothing, tropical fruits, and Indian spices.

THE SOUTH PACIFIC EXPERIENCE

The southeast trade wind is predominant in this region, and the sailing can vary from running in the open ocean to exploring mangrove swamps. Outlying islands tend to have the most translucent water, and here the traditional culture is best preserved. The crew of a visiting yacht bringing gifts are often welcomed into the life of a south sea village – and that is an unforgettable experience.

ESSENTIAL INFORMATION

CLIMATE Tropical; trade winds provide almost constant easterly winds.

WHEN TO VIST All year round, but May to November is the best time, avoiding the cyclone season.

DON'T MISS Kava (gift-giving) ceremony.

MOORING Anchorages are plentiful and free. There are marinas at Savusavu, Suva, and Malololailai.

FAVOURITE ANCHORAGE Viani Bay, southeast side of Vanua Levu.

DON'T FORGET Notify customs and immigration on arrival.

SAVUSAVU BAY

With its friendly and helpful marina, this is an excellent place for cruising boats to enter Fiji and from which to explore the coast of Vanua Levu.

Whitsunday Islands

EASTERN AUSTRALIA, PACIFIC OCEAN

The Great Barrier Reef is over 2,000km (1,250 miles) long and provides sanctuary for an enormous variety of sea life. One of the island pearls inside the reef is the Whitsunday Islands, a group of about 30 islands, where you can enjoy tropical heat and steady breezes.

BEACHES AND RESORTS

Whitsunday Island, the largest of the group, and its neighbours form the eastern boundary to Whitsunday Passage, a 30-km (20-mile) stretch of sheltered waterway. The area offers many enticing anchorages both for a restful night and for exploring the beautiful coral reefs and sea life. There are also sophisticated resorts and marinas. Ashore, much of the land is National Park and offers a good opportunity to view Australia's unique wildlife.

GREAT BARRIER REEF

The waters are a meeting place for long-distance cruising sailors, Australian yachtsmen and women, and the charter fleet. Despite its popularity there still

SANDY BEACHES
Miles of sandy beaches line the coast of Whitsunday Island. Swim ashore and wander along the miles of sand, and you may meet wallabies out for a stroll.

seems to be room for everyone. Hook Island, at the northern end of the group, offers one of the best selections of cruising anchorages. The Great Barrier Reef lies about 80km (50 miles) offshore and can be visited by private yacht or with one of the local tour operators.

ESSENTIAL INFORMATION

CLIMATE Tropical heat, pleasantly cooled by onshore winds.

WHEN TO VISIT Best from May to November, avoiding the cyclone season.

DON'T MISS Diving on the reef.

MOORING Anchoring is free, though in some places it is prohibited in order to protect the coral, so moorings must be used.

FAVOURITE ANCHORAGES Butterfly Bay, north side of Hook Island; Cataran Bay, north side of Border Island.

DON'T FORGET Prior notice of arrival must be given from departure port. Expect to be overflown by customs on approach. Report upon arrival at a Port of Entry.

SNORKELLERS' PARADISE
These waters are famous for their underwater life, with plentiful brightly coloured fish and fantastically shaped coral visible just beneath the keel.

Bay of Islands

NEW ZEALAND, PACIFIC OCEAN

The wooded islands, blue waters, and sandy beaches of this area in the north of New Zealand's North Island continue to delight sailors. It was an early base for the Maoris, who arrived here first, to be followed by explorers, whalers, and European colonizers.

EXOTIC DESTINATION

With sheltered anchorages, a subtropical climate, and pleasant breezes, the Bay of Islands is idyllic. Hundreds of long-distance cruising boats flock here every year to escape the South Pacific cyclone season. Opua is the hub from which charter boats, local yachts, and ocean voyagers cruise. Nearby Russell, the first capital of New Zealand, is a charming old town where sailors like to congregate.

DESERTED BEACHES

Out on the water, you can navigate up winding rivers and inlets, float past green, hilly islands, pick mussels, or dive for scallops, and end the day choosing a snug anchorage off a deserted, sandy beach. There are great opportunities for walking, swimming, and diving. Summer is busy, winter more peaceful, but the sailing is just as good.

ROBERTON ISLAND
Roberton Island, in the foreground, is a favourite anchoring spot. Many other lovely beaches and bays are to be found on the islands lying behind.

ESSENTIAL INFORMATION

CLIMATE Warm all year.

WHEN TO VISIT All year round; November and Febuary are often the best months.

DON'T MISS Tall Ships Race; whale-watching; Waitangi Treaty Grounds.

MOORINGS Marina at Opua; marina at Kerikeri with short-term visitors' berths; anchorages are free and plentiful.

FAVOURITE ANCHORAGE South side of Roberton Island; Whangamumu Harbour, south of Cape Brett.

DON'T FORGET Report upon arrival, preferably by radio in advance.

MAORI CULTURE

Ashore, the rural New Zealand countryside offers a range of attractions, from walks in the native forest to wine-tasting at a vineyard. Maori culture abounds on land and sea, and many artists and craftspeople have settled here.

Sea of Cortez

MEXICO, PACIFIC OCEAN

Made famous by the novelist John Steinbeck, who cruised here in 1940, the Sea of Cortez draws sailors from the north to its unique maritime environment, hot climate, and golden beaches. This area deserves greater fame with cruising sailors the world over.

RUGGED COASTLINE

Californians are blessed with one of the world's finest cruising grounds right on their doorstep. The Sea of Cortez is nearly 1,100km (700 miles) long and its shores are fringed with wonderful anchorages that offer the choice of lonely wilderness or sophisticated resort. Many think that the area on the west side of the sea between La Paz and Puerto Escondido provides the finest cruising. Sightings of orca, dolphins, and turtles are commonplace, and the waters are warm and clear, with superb snorkelling. Many bays are well-protected and the scenery ashore is awe-inspiring in its dry and rugged grandeur.

FERTILE WATERS
The stark contrast between the arid, desert-like terrain on shore and the abundant life underwater is one of the chief attractions of this colourful coast.

MIXED WEATHER

The best way to cruise here is to sail off for the winter or longer. Many cruisers become semi-permanent residents, returning year after year. For those returning to San Diego, the prevailing wind direction makes for a hard beat back, but you can always sail home by way of Hawaii.

The area is both challenging and relaxing. Sailing is generally easy, with warm, gentle breezes. During winter, however, cold northerlies occasionally blow down from California, making for rough and even dangerous conditions. Between June and October, hurricanes are possible. If conditions do turn nasty, the pilot books will help you find plenty of safe anchorages.

ESSENTIAL INFORMATION

CLIMATE Very hot in midsummer, cool in midwinter.

WHEN TO VISIT All year, but there is a risk of tropical storms in summer; spring and autumn are the best times.

DON'T MISS Swimming with manta rays and sea lions.

MOORING Marinas in main centres and a wide choice of free anchorages.

FAVOURITE ANCHORAGES Partida Island, north of La Paz; Puerto Escondido.

DON'T FORGET Clear in with immigration, port authority, and port captain. Each crew member must buy a fishing licence unless absolutely no fishing gear is carried on board.

Isla Chiloé

CHILE, PACIFIC OCEAN

The waterways of Chile are a sailor's paradise. From the stormy waters of Cape Horn and the glaciers of the Beagle Channel to the gentler waterways of Chiloé, this land is made for sailors, and the people welcome them with open arms.

STEPPING BACK IN TIME

Chiloé, a large island off Chile's southern coast, has a mild climate and fertile soil. The language and traditions of the friendly people hark back to an earlier day. In one of countless sheltered anchorages on a sunny evening you might find apple-laden carts drawn by oxen to a wooden cider press and fishermen offering fresh fish and oysters. There are colourful traditions of music and dance and a great variety of good food and wine. Besides the magnificence of the Andes, there is beautiful rainforest and pastoral farming scenery.

FIORDS AND PEAKS

Chiloé shelters a fine archipelago from Pacific swells, and breezes are usually steady and moderate. Good charts, pilot books, and weather forecasts make the cruising in Chiloé no more challenging than that in popular cruising grounds elsewhere. Small boats are a way of life here and sailors instinctively feel at home. You can sail out to a rural island, or in half a day sail to the dramatic fiords that lie at the feet of the Andes, the volcanic peaks that are hardly ever

ESSENTIAL INFORMATION

CLIMATE Temperate; often hot in summer and it never snows in winter.

WHEN TO VISIT Summer is most popular but it is pleasant all year round.

DON'T MISS Summer festivals with traditional customs, music, dance, and food; World Heritage wooden churches.

MOORING The only marinas are on the mainland at Puerto Montt; otherwise you will need to anchor.

FAVOURITE ANCHORAGES Castro, Isla Chiloé; Isla Mechuque; Puerto Pindo, Isla Quehui.

DON'T FORGET Puerto Montt is the Port of Entry. Formalities are handled by the Armada (navy). Call them on arrival and afterwards visit customs and immigration.

out of sight. Then, when the skipper and boat are fully prepared, you can sail south into the fiord-like channels that entice the boat towards Cape Horn.

BOATS AT ACHAO, CHILOÉ
Under the snowcapped Andes, colourful ferries carry produce and passengers from island to island, and fishing boats are found everywhere.

World
of racing

The America's Cup

VENUE AND TIMING SET BY HOLDER

The America's Cup is the world's longest-running international sports competition, pre-dating the modern Olympics by 45 years. It is sailing's pinnacle event, in which two yachts from different nations compete in a best-of-nine duel.

SPORT'S LONGEST WINNING STREAK

The America's Cup dates back to 1851, when a US syndicate challenged Britain's Royal Yacht Squadron (RYS) to a race around the Isle of Wight. The United States won the cup and held it against challenges from Canada, Britain, and Australia for a staggering 132 years. Eventually, the 12-Metre class *Australia II*, skippered by John Bertrand and owned by businessman Alan Bond, took the cup in an enthralling match in 1983. Since then it has gone back to the United States, then to New Zealand, and in 2003 was won by Switzerland.

CHALLENGES

The holder of the cup names the date, venue, and conditions for its defence. In the run up to a new challenge, teams from major yacht clubs worldwide develop new boats to offer as a challenger. These boats then compete in a tournament for the Louis Vuitton Cup, a prestigious trophy in itself, to select the final challenger for

LOUIS VUITTON CUP
Boats in action during the Louis Vuitton Act 9 to decide the challenger for the 32nd America's Cup. It was won by 2003 America's Cup winner *Alinghi*, off the Sicilian port of Trapani, southern Italy in 2005.

the America's Cup itself. In 1988, New Zealand and America exploited loopholes in the existing 12-Metre class, producing a mismatch between the 36-m (120-ft) giant monohull *KZ1* and the 20-m (65-ft) catamaran *Stars and Stripes*. As a result, the America's Cup Class (ACC) was introduced prior to the 1992 race and keeps the monohull boats close to 23m (75ft) overall length.

THE DUEL

The duel comprises the best of a series of day races "around the buoys" and provides some of the most exciting close racing in the sport. It remains one of the most closely fought and treasured challenges in yachting.

CLOSE CHALLENGE
Team BMW Oracle Racing's *USA 87* sails the 11th and last match race against Italian yacht *Luna Rossa* during the Louis Vuitton Act 10 of the 32nd America's Cup, in Valencia, Spain.

ALINGHI IN ACTION
The Swiss Alinghi Team (*see opposite*) made changes for the 2007 defence. Instead of a gap of three or four years with no racing, the defender raced the challengers at various venues in fleet and match races.

HISTORIC TROPHY

The trophy is a silver gilt ewer – a large jug with a wide mouth – bought by the Royal Yacht Squadron for the first race in 1851. Over the years two silver plinths have been added, to make room for more names. In 1997, while the cup was in New Zealand, it was attacked with a hammer by a protester. The damage was severe, but the London silversmiths who originally made it went to considerable trouble to repair the cup, free of charge, because of the history of the trophy and the esteem in which it is held worldwide.

The trophy and the 2003 winning crew of the Swiss boat Alinghi

RACE SUMMARY

EVENT TYPE	"Round the buoys" match racing
FREQUENCY	Every three or four years
CREW	Fully crewed
BOAT	America's Cup Class

RACE FACTS

After a controversial 1988 victory by the United States, the win was overturned in court and awarded to New Zealand, then returned to the United States on appeal.

Chicago–Mackinac Race

UNITED STATES, LAKE MICHIGAN

No ocean race has a heritage which goes back this far, to 1898, the organizing Chicago Yacht Club dating from 1875. Remarkably, the Chicago–Mackinac Race even managed to continue through most of World War I and all through World War II without a break.

OCEAN RACING IN FRESH WATER

Lake Michigan is so vast that the Mackinac can properly be called a freshwater "ocean" race. After the inaugural 1898 event, the next race was not held until 1904 and then it ran annually to 1916. There was another hiatus until 1921, but since then it has not missed a beat.

The prevailing wind direction means that the race most often starts under spinnaker, within a mile of downtown Chicago, the course being straight to Mackinac Island, some 540km (290 nautical miles) away. The race usually requires two nights at sea, and crews choose between shores in order to find the best breeze. A fleet of about 300 boats is common, which Lake Michigan's vast size can accommodate comfortably.

RACE SUMMARY

EVENT TYPE 540-km (290-nautical mile) freshwater "ocean" race

FREQUENCY Annual

CREW Fully crewed

BOAT Grand-prix, cruiser-racers

RACE FACTS In 1937, only eight out of 42 starters finished the race after the lake was struck by an unusually ferocious gale.

There are two choke points: the picturesque Manitou islands; then the Greys Reef channel, busy with the Great Lakes commercial traffic. The Chicago skyline is visible for the early part of the race, and the giant Mackinac bridge dominates the finish.

ANNIVERSARY RACE

Part of the fleet of nearly 300 yachts ready themselves for the start of their class against the backdrop of the Sears Tower, Chicago, 12 July 2003. The race marked the 105th anniversary of the world's longest annual freshwater yacht race.

Key West Race Week

UNITED STATES, GULF OF MEXICO

Key West Race Week, first held in 1987, has proved that starting a regatta in an area with no real tradition of yacht racing can work if the ingredients are right. In recent years about 300 boats have competed in four course areas off the town of Key West.

SHORT RACES

Previously the event that held primacy in Florida was the Southern Ocean Racing Conference. The Conference "Circuit" comprised the St. Petersburg–Fort Lauderdale Race (rounding Key West) over 644km (348 nautical miles) plus the Miami–Nassau race over 281km (152 nautical miles). There were also shorter day races off Fort Lauderdale, Miami, and Nassau. The event provided a wonderful variety of locations and races but it took over three weeks and was a logistical headache. Hence the idea to start a one-week regatta of day races, at the southernmost of the Florida Keys. This event would offer short, competitive races in turquoise waters and warm winds – a recipe that appealed not just to yachtsmen from the northern United States but from Europe too. In short, it fitted the time-pressured lifestyles of most racing yachtsmen. They could fly in and out for a short but intense week of fun, competitive racing.

AT THE WINDWARD BUOY
Farr 40 class boats round a windward mark during the final race of Key West Race Week, January 2004. The regatta attracted a fleet of 301 boats.

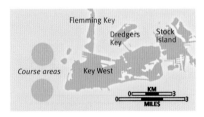

Flemming Key
Dredgers Key
Stock Island
Course areas
Key West

KM
0 3
0 3
MILES

RACE SUMMARY

EVENT TYPE Multi-event regatta

FREQUENCY Annual

CREW Fully crewed

BOAT Grand-prix, cruiser-racers

RACE FACTS In 2006 there were 285 regatta entrants from a record 37 American states and 14 nations.

Bermuda Race

UNITED STATES TO BERMUDA, ATLANTIC OCEAN

If any race can claim to have kick-started the new sport of racing yachts offshore, it is the Bermuda Race. Only three yachts competed in the first race in 1906, which was run from Gravesend Bay, Brooklyn, New York, out into the Atlantic to the remote islands of Bermuda.

US AND BRITISH COOPERATION

The 1906 race start was organized by the Brooklyn Yacht Club but it did not find its current home of Newport, Rhode Island until 1936, having also moved to New London on the shore of Long Island Sound for a time. Since 1923, the finishing club has been the Royal Bermuda Yacht Club, the third oldest yacht club outside the British Isles to hold a royal warrant. Each club member was asked to contribute £2 to the finishing celebrations, cementing the club's reputation as one of the most hospitable at which to finish a long race. The race has been a biennial event since 1926.

GULF STREAM CHALLENGE

The Gulf Stream is a powerful Atlantic current, like a warm, swift river in the ocean, that produces Bermuda's tropical climate. It also has a profound effect on race strategy because the course takes the fleet directly through the stream. Today's sailors make use of extensive computer modelling of the stream, but for decades navigators relied on a thermometer to judge if they were in the northeast-going stream or one of its eddies. Being in the open north Atlantic, the race can also be subject to heavy weather, such as anticyclones and tropical storms. Outlying reefs and poor visibility are a dangerous combination, but electronic position-fixing aids have made Bermuda a less treacherous landfall.

2006 RACE
Yachts in St. David's Lighthouse Division class 7 line up at the start of the Centennial Newport–Bermuda Race 2006 in Newport, Rhode Island.

RACE SUMMARY

EVENT TYPE 1,175-km (635-nautical mile) ocean race

FREQUENCY Biennial

CREW Fully crewed or two-handed

BOAT Racers, cruiser-racers, cruisers

RACE FACTS In 1932, the schooner *Adriana* caught fire, and one of the crew was lost.

Antigua Sailing Week

LEEWARD ISLANDS, CARIBBEAN SEA

Sublime tropical conditions, a picturesque island, great sailing, and even better parties, with rum punches and steel bands: the Antigua event is the Caribbean regatta par excellence and is the standard by which all other regattas are judged.

RACE AND REGATTA SERIES

From small beginnings, the regatta has developed into the concluding stage of the Caribbean Big Boat Series. Leg 1 starts in St. Maarten, with the Heineken Regatta in early March, followed by the British Virgin Islands Spring Regatta a month later. Then comes Antigua Sailing Week. The regatta has over 200 entries each year but in fact there are even more yachts afloat, as many non-competing vessels accompany those racing and partying. Racing is from Dickenson Bay, Falmouth Harbour, and down the west coast; each evening there are parties wherever the yachts finish racing. There is a lay-day (a day with no sailing) halfway through the regatta but, far from being a rest, there are more festivities in Nelson's Dockyard. The week concludes with the English Harbour Race. The finale is the day after, when the locals come out and carnival on Dockyard Day.

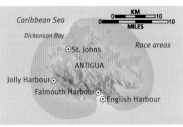

Caribbean Sea

Dickenson Bay

St. Johns

Race areas

ANTIGUA

Jolly Harbour

Falmouth Harbour

English Harbour

KM

MILES

RACE SUMMARY

EVENT TYPE	Fun regatta
FREQUENCY	Annual
CREW	Fully crewed
BOAT	Yachts of all kinds

RACE FACTS Now one of the most popular regattas in the world, Antigua Sailing Week began in 1967 with only 10 boats starting.

FLEET RACING SPECTACLE
A downwind leg brings out multi-coloured spinnakers to glimmer in the Caribbean sunshine in the 2004 event, creating a true racing spectacle in carnival colours.

Route du Rhum

FRANCE TO GUADELOUPE, ATLANTIC OCEAN

The Route du Rhum is a French single-handed transatlantic race, following a mainly downwind course with a finish in the Caribbean. The "rhum line" is the direct route from start to finish; the monohulls sail a fairly direct course while the faster multihulls sail a longer course.

NOVEMBER GALES AT THE START

Starting in November's autumnal conditions in St. Malo, on the Brittany coast of France, the race finishes at Pointe-à-Pitre in Guadeloupe. The Route du Rhum's reputation was sealed in the first race, in 1978, by one of the all time great finishes in solo racing. Canadian Mike Birch was leading in the trimaran *Olympus Photo* as he approached Guadeloupe. As the wind became lighter, Michel Malinovsky, in the cigar-thin monohull *Kriter V*, passed Birch. But when they had the line in view, *Olympus Photo* gained pace and Birch won by 98 seconds.

MONOHULL RECORD BREAKER
Skipper Steve Ravussin of Switzerland sailing to the first mark in the 2002 Route du Rhum in his trimaran *TechnoMarine*, which later capsized.

The 2002 race was also dramatic. Trouble hit less than 24 hours from St. Malo and continued in the following days in the stormy Bay of Biscay. Of the 18 multihulls that started, 15 were abandoned, and only three finished.

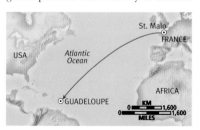

RACE SUMMARY

EVENT TYPE 6,500-km (3,510-nautical mile) transatlantic race

FREQUENCY Every four years

CREW Solo

BOAT 12.1–18.2m (40–60ft) mono- and multihulls

RACE FACTS The first Route du Rhum race in 1978 was marred by the mysterious loss of the French yachtsman Alain Colas and his trimaran *Manureva*.

Tour de France à la Voile

FRANCE, ENGLISH CHANNEL, ATLANTIC OCEAN, MEDITERRANEAN SEA

There can be no better insrpiration than one of the world's truly great sporting events: the Tour de France. In 1978, Bernard Decré set about replicating the contest in sailing by asking local authorities to fund teams of identical yachts to race under the name of their town or region.

A BIG BOOST FOR FRENCH YACHTING

The first Tour de France à la Voile was a success and made a huge impact on cruiser-racing in France. The race provides inshore round-the-buoys racing, plus coastal and overnight competition. The boats chosen traditionally fall into the 9–12m (30–40ft) range. Venues on the coasts of the English Channel, the Atlantic, and the Mediterranean provide a wide range of sailing conditions. Entries now come from all over the world. The sailing Tour is a huge logistical exercise requiring training, financial controls, crew selection, accommodation, food, and transport in some 20–30 different places. The Tour is held in July each year, and provides a month of racing. The towns involved erupt into popular fetes as the race reaches them. Some 25 years after it was created, there are now fewer offshore legs but distances are longer. To give maximum experience for training crews, the Tour has settled into a three division event: professionals, amateurs, and students.

RACE SUMMARY

EVENT TYPE Team racing, multi-event and multi-venue

FREQUENCY Annual

CREW Fully crewed

BOAT One-design

RACE FACTS Since its foundation in 1978, the race has involved over 100,000 crew members from many countries.

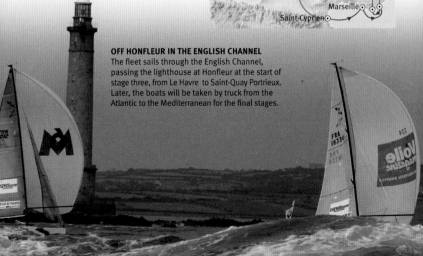

OFF HONFLEUR IN THE ENGLISH CHANNEL
The fleet sails through the English Channel, passing the lighthouse at Honfleur at the start of stage three, from Le Havre to Saint-Quay Portrieux. Later, the boats will be taken by truck from the Atlantic to the Mediterranean for the final stages.

Vendée Globe

ROUND-THE-WORLD

Philippe Jeantot created the Vendée Globe as a direct successor to the BOC Challenge, which he won in 1982/3 and 1986/7. This was the first non-stop solo circumnavigation race since the Golden Globe of 1968/9, and competitors were to receive no assistance en route.

A RACE FOR THE TOUGHEST

Vendée Globe is a French-based race, starting and finishing on the Côte Vendéenne at Les Sables d'Olonne. The loss of life and number of rescues by fellow competitors experienced in this race bear testament to the daunting, not to say brutal, nature of the challenge offered by the event to even the most experienced sailors.

Eric Tabarly, the famous French yachtsman, fired the starting cannon of the first race in late November 1989. Four weeks later, as the leaders were in the south Atlantic, preparing the arcing turn to the west and entering the Southern Ocean, Philippe Poupon's *Fleury Michon X* capsized and lay on her side. Loïc Peyron was the first of three

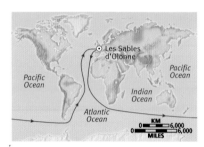

rivals to reach Poupon. Remarkably, Peyron was able to sail close enough and slowly enough to throw a line that Poupon could make fast. The tug of the line as Peyron's yacht sailed on was enough to right *Fleury Michon X*.

Tragedy struck the second race even before the start. American Mike Plant and his yacht *Coyote* were lost en route to the start from the United States. Then, four days after the start, Nigel Burgess

DESIGNED FOR ONE
France's Patrice Carpentier and *VM Materiaux* soon after crossing the line of the 2004 start. Open 60 yachts like this are specifically designed for single-handed sailing.

TRAINING FOR THE EVENT

Meticulous training that enables competitors to become confident with every aspect of managing their craft is essential to enable them to cope with the huge challenges of the event in an infinite variety of sailing conditions. The gale-raked seas of the Bay of Biscay in autumn can be as tough as the Southern Ocean.

French sailor Marc Thiercelin training off Les Sables d'Olonne for the 2004 event.

lost his life. From 14 starters, only seven boats finished. The third race was no less eventful. Former British Royal Marine, Pete Goss, made a heroic rescue of Frenchman Raphaël Dinelli, while Tony Bullimore and Thierry Dubois were both the subjects of dramatic rescues in the remote Southern Ocean by the Australian navy. Of 16 starters, only six finished the race. Tragically, another life was lost as French Canadian Gerry Roufs was lost at sea, although his boat was later found off the coast of Chile. The Vendée Globe is the toughest of tough races and is full of stories of remarkable resilience.

SETTING OUT AROUND THE GLOBE

On 7 November 2004, 20 sailors from six countries started the fifth Vendée Globe sailing race at Les Sables d'Olonne on France's Atlantic coast.

RACE SUMMARY

EVENT TYPE Non-stop round-the-world ocean race

FREQUENCY Every four years

CREW Solo

BOAT Open 60 class monohull yacht

RACE FACTS Carbon-fibre Open 60 yachts are among the fastest and safest sailing boats, having the ability to right, with the aid of the skipper, following a capsize.

Transat Jacques Vabre

FRANCE TO BRAZIL, ATLANTIC OCEAN

Two-handed racing evolved from single-handed racing rather than the other way round as might be expected. The Transat Jacques Vabre, which starts from the French maritime city Le Havre, is a case in point: having begun as a solo race in 1993, it became two-handed in 1995.

FRANCE'S COFFEE RACE

The first four races finished at Cartagena in Colombia, but from 2001 the finish was relocated to Salvador da Bahia in Brazil, a more developed city better suited to the expanding event.

The change of destination made a fundamental change to the race, for instead of being able to rely on tradewinds from south of the Iberian peninsula more or less all the way to the finish, the sailors now found the Doldrums interrupting the course, providing more varied conditions in which to test their racing skills. There were 13 entries in the first race, split between monohulls and

RACE SUMMARY

EVENT TYPE Ocean race; 10,000km (5,400 nautical miles) for multihulls, 7,960km (4,300 nautical miles) for monohulls

FREQUENCY Biennial

CREW Two-handed

BOAT Monohull and multihull classes

RACE FACTS Over 40 boats now enter this race along the old commercial sailing routes.

multihulls, with Frenchmen Yves Parlier and Paul Vatine the first to finish in their respective classes, with times of 16 and 19 days. The third race saw entries climb to 18, the monohulls and multihulls starting on different dates, with the faster multihulls sailing a longer course. By 2001, entries had bulged to 33 boats, and both monohulls and multihulls had become subdivided into two classes.

FAMILY RACING
Father and daugher Bob Escofffier and Servane Escoffier racing off Le Havre in their monohull *Adecco* in the 2003 Transat.

South Atlantic Race

SOUTH AFRICA TO BRAZIL, ATLANTIC OCEAN

The Cape Town to Brazil race across the South Atlantic is known by its traditional shorthand name, the "Cape-to-Rio", but because of the frequently changing destination, it has been renamed by its South African organizers as the South Atlantic Race.

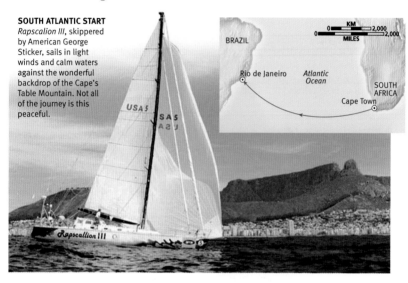

SOUTH ATLANTIC START
Rapscalion III, skippered by American George Sticker, sails in light winds and calm waters against the wonderful backdrop of the Cape's Table Mountain. Not all of the journey is this peaceful.

CHANGING ROUTES FOLLOW THE WIND

The Cape-to-Rio has been the only regular transatlantic race in the southern hemisphere since it was first staged by the Royal Cape Yacht Club in January 1971. It was long at some 6,670km (3,600 nautical miles), taking yachts around the eastern flank of the South Atlantic high pressure system to Rio de Janeiro via Isla da Trinidade. The race has also been run to the Uruguayan resort of Punta del Este at the entrance to the massive River Plate estuary. In 2006, the finish was moved to Salvador da Bahia, where the greater consistency of winds in the final stretch was a key attraction, as well as the city's top-level yachting facilities. The race's name changed to the South Atlantic Race at the same time.

HIGH INTERNATIONAL INTEREST

The second race was staged in 1973 and by 1976 the race had become the last leg of the Gauloises Triangle, backed by the French cigarette brand that was active in yachting sponsorship at the time, bringing in more international entries. The three-year cycle was broken in 1999 when the race was held back a year to mark Brazil's quincentenary, with a fleet of 80 yachts competing. American Bob McNeill's maxi *Zephyrus IV* set a new course record of 12 days 16 hours and took handicap honours too, the first yacht to do the double since Kees Bruynzeel's *Stormy* in 1973 (*see below*).

RACE SUMMARY

EVENT TYPE 6,670-km (3,600-nautical mile) ocean race

FREQUENCY Usually every three years

CREW Fully crewed

BOAT Monohulls up to 30.5m (100ft)

RACE FACTS Despite three heart attacks the year before, Kees Bruynzeel, aged 72, took 1973's line and overall handicap honours.

Fastnet Race

ENGLAND AND IRELAND, ENGLISH CHANNEL, ATLANTIC OCEAN, AND IRISH SEA

First run in 1925, the Fastnet is one of the world's classic ocean races. Run in August from Cowes, Isle of Wight, to the Fastnet Rock off southwest Ireland, and back to Plymouth via the Scilly Isles, it is tactically demanding. It can be dangerous too, as the 1979 race proved.

HISTORY

Having sailed in the 1924 Bermuda Race (*see* p.312), Englishman Weston Martyr recognized the "skill, courage, and endurance" needed for the sport of yacht racing. Martyr then joined E.G. Martin, who had bought the French Le Havre pilot yacht *Jolie Brise*, and *Yachting World* magazine's editor, Malden Heckstall-Smith, in organizing

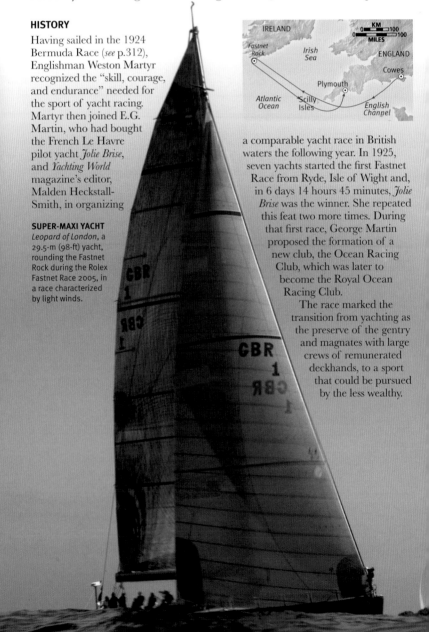

SUPER-MAXI YACHT
Leopard of London, a 29.5-m (98-ft) yacht, rounding the Fastnet Rock during the Rolex Fastnet Race 2005, in a race characterized by light winds.

a comparable yacht race in British waters the following year. In 1925, seven yachts started the first Fastnet Race from Ryde, Isle of Wight and, in 6 days 14 hours 45 minutes, *Jolie Brise* was the winner. She repeated this feat two more times. During that first race, George Martin proposed the formation of a new club, the Ocean Racing Club, which was later to become the Royal Ocean Racing Club.

The race marked the transition from yachting as the preserve of the gentry and magnates with large crews of remunerated deckhands, to a sport that could be pursued by the less wealthy.

1979 DISASTER

The 1979 race saw 15 lives lost. The subsequent inquiry noted lessons about the inverted stability of yachts, the problems of inadequately secured batteries, cookers, and hatchboards, and of the difficulty of navigating with poor fixing aids and sodden charts. VHF radios become mandatory for the 1981 race and all electronic aids were allowed two years later. Qualification requirements were also brought in.

Helicopter rescue during the 1979 Fastnet Race

The start is now traditionally from Cowes, with 250–300 yachts competing in six or more classes.

ATLANTIC DANGERS

Before the 1979 tragedy (*see above*), the 1927, 1930, 1949, and 1957 races were all very tough. Only 12 of 41 starters finished in 1957, testament to how fierce waves can be as Atlantic low-pressure systems rake across the continental shelf.

This was why the 1979 race saw so many lives lost. With 303 boats, it was the biggest-ever fleet, a concentration of small yachts in the path of a particularly vicious depression. American Ted Turner, founder of CNN, swept through to win in *American Eagle* as the bigger boats escaped the worst of the storm. Willie Ker's Contessa 32, *Assent*, came through to win Class V and to prove that smaller boats can also be seaworthy.

The Fastnet Race has an unshakable position as the keenest challenge for offshore crews in UK waters. Boats must now meet numerous requirements that specify stability characteristics for hulls and high levels of safety equipment. Varying percentages of the crew must have prequalified aboard the yacht and trained in communications, first-aid, and sea safety.

All entries are eligible for the prime trophy: the Fastnet Challenge Cup. The numerous other trophies include one for the oldest boat to complete the course, and another for the galley slave of the yacht with the greatest elapsed time.

RACE SUMMARY

EVENT TYPE 1,126-km (608-nautical mile) offshore race

FREQUENCY Biennial

CREW Fully crewed or two-handed

BOAT Grand-prix, cruiser-racers

RACE FACTS The course monohull record of 2 days 5 hours 8 minutes was set in 1999 by New Zealand's Ross Field in the 24-m (80-ft) Maxi *RF Yachting*.

Cowes Week

ENGLAND, THE SOLENT, THE ENGLISH CHANNEL

Having reached its 200th anniversary, Cowes Week remains the most enduring regatta in the world. It takes place in the Solent, the stretch of water separating the south coast of England from the Isle of Wight. Cowes lies dead centre of the island's northern shore.

SMALL BEGINNINGS

Cowes Week regatta traditionally runs for eight days in the first week of August. Seven yachts took part in the first regatta in 1826, when the first prize of a gold cup was awarded by King George IV of Great Britain, an avid yachtsman. Later that week there was a ball, a dinner, and fireworks, setting the pattern for the next 200 years. Since the 1950s, Cowes has been a thoroughly modern regatta open to all, and by 2001 the regatta received over 1,000 entries for the first time.

THE RACES

The Solent is characterized by strong double tides, making for challenging sailing for even the most experienced crew. Each day of racing sees about

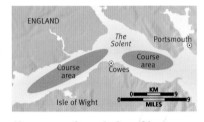

40 races, one for each class of boat, including cruiser-racers, one designs, and small boats. More than 30 different courses, which are typically about 30km (15 nautical miles) long, are raced each day by amateur sailors competing

DOWNWIND SPECTACLE
The 29.7-m (98-ft) Class 0 *ICAP Maximus* (NZL) is seen here during its successful 2006 attempt on the Round The Island monohull record, which it achieved in 3 hours 20 minutes 9 seconds.

RACE SUMMARY

EVENT TYPE Multi-event regatta

FREQUENCY Annual

CREW Fully crewed

BOATS Small dayboats, cruiser-racers, grand-prix boats

RACE FACTS The Solent is one of the busiest commercial stretches of water in the world, and during race week it gets even busier as about 8,000 sailors compete each day.

A ROYAL AFFAIR

Cowes Week has a long tradition of patronage by the British royal family. The first race here in 1826 was organized by The Royal Yacht Club, now the Royal Yacht Squadron, and George IV presented a gold cup for that race. The Prince of Wales, later Edward VII, raced here in the 1890s in the yacht *Britannia*, as did George V in the 1920s. Of the modern royal family, Prince Philip has been a regular participant for over 30 years, along with Prince Edward and the Princess Royal.

King George V racing at Cowes

alongside Olympic and World Champions. During the Week, a total of about 1,000 boats and some 8,000 crew compete, watched by thousands of spectators on land and sea.

A SOCIAL EVENT

Cowes is routinely referred to as the "Mecca of Yachting" and remains a massive draw for non-sailing spectators. Besides the racing, the Week is filled with evening parties and balls, the highlight being the famous fireworks display held on the final Friday, which attracts an audience of over 170,000 people both on the water and the shore.

Gotland Runt

SWEDEN, BALTIC SEA

The Swedish Gotland Runt and the Danish Sjælland Rundt are among the largest keelboat races in the world, in terms of the number of participants. In 1984, a massive 2,072 yachts started the Danish event at Helsingor, the highest number ever recorded for any race.

ISLAND RACE

Gotland Runt evolved out of the Visby Race, which took place in the 1920s and 30s. The yachts left Sandhamn, an island off Sweden's east coast, for Visby on the island of Gotland in the Baltic Sea, then returned. By 1937, the year of its formal inauguration, the race had become a Round Gotland affair, involving various routes in different years. Since 1969, it has been an annual July race over 640km (350 nautical miles) from and to Sandhamn, rounding Gotland in a clockwise direction since 1979. The heart of the fleet is made up of cruiser-racers and family crews, for whom the race is often their sole race of the season. Entries are now in the 400–500 range, the biggest contingent coming from Finland.

DANISH RACE

The Sjælland Rundt race loops around the Danish island of Sjælland, on which the capital Copenhagen is sited. The

A FAMILY AFFAIR
Hundreds of family-crewed yachts are packed into Sandhamn Island harbour, preparing to start the Round Gotland race in the Stockholm Archipelago.

race starts and finishes at Helsingor on the northeastern coast and has been an annual event since 1947. The track is 410km (220 nautical miles), and the race is open for yachts ranging from grand-prix boats down to small dayboats, helping to account for the huge entry.

RACE SUMMARY

EVENT TYPE 640-km (350-nautical mile) offshore race

FREQUENCY Annual

CREW Fully crewed

BOAT Cruiser-racers, grand-prix boats

RACE FACTS In 2002, Knut Frostad set a course record of 26 hours 12 minutes with the 18-m (60-ft) multihull *Academy*.

Velux 5 Oceans

ROUND THE WORLD

In the Velux 5 Oceans round-the-world race, one of sailing's greatest challenges, solitary sailors take to the seas every four years in yachts expressly designed for solo racing, competing over many months to cover a distance of about 56,000km (30,000 nautical miles).

GLOBAL CHALLENGE

The 2006 course of the highly dangerous Velux 5 Oceans (formerly the BOC Challenge and Around Alone) began in Bilbao, Spain. The first leg ended in Fremantle, Western Australia, the second in Norfolk, Virginia, United States, followed by a sprint back to Bilbao.

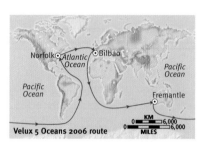

Velux 5 Oceans 2006 route

The 1982 and 1986 races were won by France's Philippe Jeantot, an extremely fit former deep-sea diver, in the superbly designed *Credit Agricole I* and *II*. The first race pioneered the use of the ARGOS satellite plotting beacons, allowing yachts to be tracked from land while in mid-ocean. In 1983, ARGOS enabled British competitor Richard Broadhead to sail 590km (320 nautical miles) to rescue Frenchman Jacques de Roux from his flipped yacht *Skoiern III* in the Southern Ocean. Unlucky French sailor Isabelle Autissier's EPC11 was dismasted in 1994 and her PRB capsized in 1999.

RACE SUMMARY

EVENT TYPE Round-the-world ocean race

FREQUENCY Every four years

CREW Single-handed

BOAT IMOCA Open 60 class yachts

RACE FACTS Two men have been lost at sea in the Southern Ocean: Frenchman Jacques de Roux in the 1986 race and Briton Harry Mitchell in the 1994 race.

FINISHING LINE
Briton Emma Richards sails *Pindar* into Newport, Rhode Island on 4 May 2003, finishing fifth in the Around Alone race, which began in New York City on 15 September 2002. Today the race is called the Velux 5 Oceans.

Kiel Week

GERMANY, BALTIC SEA

Kiel Week stands proud as northern Europe's biggest regatta and one of the world's great festivals. At its core is serious racing, including one of the biggest Olympic class events in the world, based at the 1972 Olympic harbour. Ashore there is carnival and culture in abundance.

Baltic Sea

Course areas

Kiel Canal

GERMANY

KM

Kiel⊙

MILES

BALTIC SAILING
Competitors in the 420 class sailing over the Baltic Sea near Kiel harbour, Germany, in 2005.

IMPERIAL BEGINNINGS

In 1891, the German Kaiser, Wilhelm II, purchased the unsuccessful British challenger for the America's Cup of 1887, the 33-m (109-ft) cutter *Thistle*. He renamed the yacht *Meteor* and she became the first of five yachts to bear the famous name. Ambitious, and wanting to race in Germany's own regatta, he offered his patronage in 1895 to an annual sailing and rowing event held each June on Kieler Fiord, which had been running since 1882. So Kiel Week was born, and the Kaiserlicher Yachtclub (Imperial Yacht Club) was formed. Over three million people now visit the festival, from 70 different countries, for a nine-day

FAST FAVOURITES
Italians Pietro and Gianfranco Sibello trapezing on their 49er at Kiel in 2006.

programme of events in June each year. All manner of music events and performance art take place ashore. The festival also includes diplomatic and scientific meetings and presentations. The fleet is mainly dinghies but includes cruiser-racers. Nine courses are used for the Olympic, International, and National classes – which range from Optimists to H-Boats – while cruiser-racers are set offshore courses. The festivities culminate with the "Windjammers' Parade" of Tall Ships.

RACE SUMMARY

EVENT TYPE Combination of sailing regatta and shoreside festival

FREQUENCY Annual

CREW Fully crewed

BOAT Dinghies, keelboats, cruiser-racers

RACE FACTS During Kiel Week, about 5,000 sailors compete in 2,000 boats, including about 250 cruiser-racers.

Copa del Rey

MALLORCA, SPAIN, MEDITERRANEAN SEA

Spain has several Copas del Rey – King's Cups – in sports including soccer and basketball. At the annual sailing regatta held in Palma de Mallorca, King Juan Carlos frequently competes and has won the cup several times himself, in boats based at a palace just outside Palma.

GOOD ISLAND SAILING CONDITIONS

The regatta has outgrown its 1982 origins as a local Mediterranean event. Of the 58 boats in the first event, only 35 were Spanish. This mirrored the expansion of the island of Mallorca as a summer destination for yachtsmen from all around Europe. The Bay of Palma is one of the best course areas in Europe in the summer season, the wind and sun producing optimum sailing conditions.

Like other event organizers, the Real Club Nautico has been subject to pressures from the changing rating rules used for big boat racing. When the International Offshore Rule (IOR) petered out in the early 1990s, the club embraced wholeheartedly the International Measurement System (IMS), and for more than a decade Spain

RACE SUMMARY	
EVENT TYPE Regatta	
FREQUENCY Annual	
CREW Fully crewed	
BOAT Grand-prix, cruiser-racers	
RACE FACTS This event was originally part of the Mediterranean International Championship and the Balearic Sailing Week.	

was the hotbed of top level IMS competition, with entries regularly topping 120 boats. Special efforts have also been made to include classes for more affordable cruisers, and locally designed boats. The event is now used as a round in various season-long championships. In 1990 it was part of the Maxi Yacht World Championship and in 2006 it was a stop on the Transpac52 class MedCup circuit. The patronage of King Juan Carlos of Spain has aided the event's growth.

Palma de Mallorca

MALLORCA

Course areas

Mediterranean
Sea

KM   9
MILES   9

DOWNWIND LEG
Yachts sailing in the first stage of the Copa del Rey in Palma de Mallorca in August 2004. Many of the yachts entering this prestige event are backed by commercial sponsorship.

Les Voiles de Saint-Tropez

FRANCE, MEDITERRANEAN SEA

Classy, showy, glamorous, it is hard to know whether this regatta was made for Saint-Tropez or whether Saint-Tropez was born to host the regatta. Rather like the humble town itself, before it was propelled to super-chic status, the event burst from simple origins.

A CLASS REGATTA
By 2006 there was a waiting list of yachts, their owners dreaming of taking part in this classic and glamorous event.

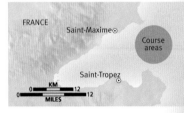

FRANCE
Saint-Maxime⊙
Course areas
Saint-Tropez⊙
0 — KM — 12
0 — MILES — 12

LA NIOULARGUE

From a private race in 1981, out to La Nioulargue shoal (a shallow water area) in the Bay of Pamplonne, an event of world renown was born. A Saint-Tropez beach club owner recognized just what a successful regatta could do to extend Saint-Tropez's season, and marketed the event intensively as La Nioulargue. By 1983, 65 yachts had entered.

Soon entries were capped at 200 as the small port filled to overflowing with innovative racers, classic yachts, and modern production cruiser-racers. Later, the limit was raised to 300. Always, the finest yachts were found space to moor stern-to on the quay, where their gleaming superstructures and hulls could be admired by the throng in the smart bars and restaurants.

1995 was a pivotal year. A fatality occurred when *Mariette*, a 1916 Herreshoff-designed (*see* p.28) schooner, collided with the much smaller 6-Metre class yacht *Taos Brett IV*. For three years, no regatta was run while lawyers' liability claims were contested. When the event was restarted in 1999, it could no longer be called by its old name and became Les Voiles de Saint-Tropez. The event is without equal in sailing. Trophies are awarded for innovation, and a "concours d'élégance", as well as for racing.

RACE SUMMARY

EVENT TYPE Local racing and "concours d'élégance"

FREQUENCY Annual

CREW Fully crewed

BOAT Grand-prix, cruiser-racers, classic yachts

RACE FACTS The first La Nioulargue race was to settle a private bet.

Giraglia Race

ITALY AND FRANCE, MEDITERRANEAN SEA

From modest beginnings, the Giraglia has become the self-proclaimed "Fastnet of the Mediterranean", using the off-lying rock of Corsica's northern coast as its emblematic turning mark. It is the culmination of a series that starts with three inshore races in the Gulf of Saint-Tropez.

MISTRAL INFLUENCE

From a single race back in 1953, by 1998 the event had grown into a week-long series of races based in the south of France at Saint-Tropez and finishing in Genoa, or sometimes Portofino, in Italy. The long-distance finale is the Giraglia Race itself. Nowadays, the series is called the Rolex Giraglia Cup. The *mistral* – a strong, northerly wind characteristic of the region – has a major bearing on race results and often forces retirements. In 1962, there were only 35 finishing boats from 58 starters.

Three clubs join forces to run the event. The Yacht Club Italiano in Genoa is the Mediterranean's oldest yacht club,

RACE SUMMARY

EVENT TYPE 450-km (243-nautical mile) offshore race

FREQUENCY Annual

CREW Fully crewed

BOAT Grand-prix, cruiser-racers

RACE FACTS In 1976 the winds were so light that one boat took 84 hours to complete the race, which normally takes 35–45 hours.

founded in 1879 under the patronage of King Umberto II. The club's first race was held in 1880 and attracted 177 yachts for a race in the Gulf of La Spezia. Saint-Tropez's Société Nautique may be even older, with records going back to 1866, though the club was formally established in 1899. The third participator is the Yacht Club de France.

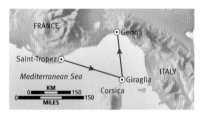

THE DAY BEFORE THE RACE
The Italian Pier Luigi Loro Piana in *My Song* follows *Magic Jena*, skippered by Italian Domenico Cilenti, in Saint-Tropez bay, preparing for the Giraglia Race.

Middle Sea Race

MALTA AND SICILY, MEDITERRANEAN SEA

The Middle Sea Race is a Mediterranean offshore classic that was founded in 1968. It undoubtedly has one of the world's most beautiful race courses, starting and finishing in Malta and taking its competitors close to several islands and an active volcano.

RIVALRY

The race was founded in 1968 by the Royal Malta Yacht Club and the London-based Royal Ocean Racing Club. It came about due to a friendly challenge between Maltese brothers Paul and John Ripard and Englishman Jimmy White. John Ripard won the 1968 race with *Josian*. Since then, its late-season scheduling and unique course have continued to attract a high-quality international field.

ISLAND ROUTE

Starting from Malta's capital Valletta, the fleet sails anticlockwise, heading north along the eastern coast of Sicily to the Straits of Messina between Sicily and the Italian mainland. It then heads north to the Aeolian Islands, and the active volcano of Stromboli, before turning west to the Egadi Islands, south to Pantelleria and Lampedusa, then northeast on the final leg to Valletta.

HIGHLIGHTS

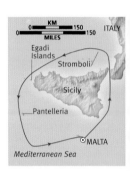

Famous competitors in the Middle Sea Race include the Englishman Sir Francis Chichester, the first man to sail single-handed around the world. In 1978, Briton Bob Whitehouse Vaux set a course record in *Mistress Quickly* that stood until 1999, when Italian skipper Andrea Scarabelli demolished it in *Riviera di Rimini*, knocking over six hours from the time. In 2000, American Bob McNeil knocked a further eight hours off the record in *Zephyrus IV*, crossing the finish line after 2 days 16 hours 49 minutes.

THE FLEET LEAVES MARSAMXETT HARBOUR
In 2005, only 9 of the 58 starters – seen here leaving the harbour beneath the Royal Malta Yacht Club – finished. Most of the others ran out of time due to light winds.

RACE SUMMARY

EVENT TYPE 1,125-km (607-nautical mile) offshore race

FREQUENCY Annual

CREW Fully crewed

BOAT Grand-prix, cruiser-racers

RACE FACTS Past competitors include noted French yachtsman Eric Tabarly and eminent German conductor Herbert von Karajan.

Auckland–Suva Race

NEW ZEALAND TO FIJI, CORAL SEA, PACIFIC OCEAN

Sailors have definite migratory tendencies, and when the southern hemisphere winter arrives, the lure of the blue waters of the tropical Pacific islands is compelling. The Auckland–Suva Race, from New Zealand to Fiji's capital, provides the perfect destination.

THE FLEET SAILS OUT
The fleet of 37 starting the 2005 race, which saw maxi *Konica Minolta* smash the race record.

EARLY DAYS

Many regard the Pacific races of the 1960s as the finishing school for a generation of Kiwi sailors who went on to enjoy phenomenal success in the 1970s and 80s, winning the Ton Cups, Sydney–Hobart, Kenwood Cup, and Admiral's Cup. These wins provided the momentum for New Zealand's America's Cup triumphs in 1995 and 2000. New Zealand's Royal Akarana Yacht Club organized the first Auckland–Suva Race in 1956, when the yachts did not exceed 11m (36ft). Some 13 yachts started the 2,100-km (1,140-nautical mile) passage, and four of these retired. At the time, navigation relied on dead reckoning and sights. In contrast, *Konica Minolta* crossed the line first in heavy rain in 2005 relying solely on computer navigation.

In the rugged 1966 race, Ray Haslar's *Tartariki* sank. The wooden dinghy lashed to her cabin top to act as a life raft had its bottom blown out by air trapped inside the sinking yacht. Life rafts became compulsory from then on.

RECORDS

In 1956, *Wanderer* took 11 days 12 hours to finish first. In the 2005 50th anniversary race, Stewart Thwaites' 30-m (98-ft) maxi *Konica Minolta* smashed *Future Shock*'s 1989 record of 4 days 14 hours in 3 days 10 hours, adding the Auckland–Suva to its Auckland–Noumea record.

RACE SUMMARY

EVENT TYPE 2,100-km (1,140-nautical mile) ocean race

FREQUENCY Annual

CREW Fully crewed

BOAT Grand-prix, cruiser-racers

RACE FACTS At the time of the 1956 race, radio equipment was not mandatory, although some yachts carried World War II vintage "Gibson Girl" hand-cranked distress radios.

Melbourne–Osaka

AUSTRALIA TO JAPAN, PACIFIC OCEAN

The 120th anniversary of the opening of the port of Osaka was the trigger to create this race from Melbourne in 1987. It is one of the longest races, apart from round-the-world events, at 10,200 km (5,500 nautical miles) and presents challenging conditions.

REVERSE SEASONS

During the 30–35 days this race usually takes, the crews experience three seasons and demanding conditions. The fleet sets off from Melbourne, Australia in the southern hemisphere's autumn, sailing through the Bass Strait, where wind and sea conditions may be severe. The boats head through the tropics, picking their way through the Solomon Islands of Micronesia and encountering the unpredictable Doldrums before taking in summer across the equator. Beyond that, the yachts nose into the east-to-west flowing North Equatorial Current from the Philippines to Taiwan. A final hurdle lies in wait in Japanese waters, where there is a chance of tropical cyclones before they reach Osaka, Japan, in spring.

CORE COMPETITORS

Since the inaugural race in 1987, which had 64 starters from seven nations, entries have gradually declined. By 1999,

RACE SUMMARY	
DISTANCE 10,200-km (5,500-nautical mile) ocean race	
FREQUENCY Every four years	
CREW Two-handed	
BOAT Shorthanded race boats, cruiser-racers	
RACE FACTS Australians G. Wharington and S. Gilbert hold the record of 26 days 20 hours.	

numbers had flattened out at about 20 starters from four nations. This may have been due to the challenging nature of the course, the race duration, and the fact that only two-person crews may compete, meaning that some boats must be specialized for a crew of two. First home in both 1987 and 1991 was *Nakiri Daoi*.

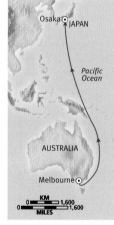

PACIFIC CONTEST

At a gruelling 10,200km (5,500 nautical miles), the Melbourne–Osaka race is one of the longest ocean races in the world and provides a Pacific alternative to the established shorthanded events in the Atlantic.

Sydney–Hobart

MAINLAND AUSTRALIA TO TASMANIA, PACIFIC OCEAN

The southern hemisphere's most famous ocean race, first run in 1945, is a national event in Australia, its Boxing Day start drawing huge holiday crowds to Sydney Harbour's beaches and promontories to see the fleet head off for Tasmania.

ICON OF AUSTRALIAN SPORT

The Sydney–Hobart race attracts both amateur crews in small yachts and professionals in the world's longest and fastest monohulls. The spectacular start is in Sydney Harbour, where thronging crowds, spectator boats, and media helicopters buzzing overhead heighten the drama. The fleet sails out into the Tasman Sea, heading down Australia's southeast coast to the Bass Strait, which divides the mainland from Tasmania. The sailing here can be dangerous – the combination of shallow waters and strong winds may produce steep and difficult seas. The fleet then heads down the east coast of Tasmania towards Tasman Island and turns right into Storm Bay. Here the yachts can falter in the complex of currents. The final stretch is up the Derwent River to Hobart.

DISASTER

Mast-high seas savaged the fleet in 1998 and six lives were lost. The survivors were fortunate that the storm struck while they were within range of the coast, allowing a huge air-sea rescue operation to take place.

RACE SUMMARY

DISTANCE 1,160-km (628-nautical mile) ocean race

FREQUENCY Annual

CREW Fully crewed

BOAT Grand-prix boats, cruiser-racers

RACE FACTS Bob Oatley set the 2005 record of 1 day 18 hours 40 minutes in *Wild Oats XI*.

CLOSE PURSUIT
New Zealand's *Alfa Romeo* pursues Australian arch rival *Wild Oats XI* down Australia's east coast in the 2005 race.

KM
0   800
0   800
MILES

AUSTRALIA   Sydney

Hobart

Transpac Race

LOS ANGELES TO HONOLULU, PACIFIC OCEAN

One of the great ocean races, the Transpac, or Transpacific, was first held in 1906 in the wake of the famous San Francisco earthquake, which caused its start to be moved to Los Angeles. It is now recognized as one of the great downwind races.

DOWNWIND CHALLENGE

The winner of the first Transpac was the the 26-m (85-ft) *Lurline*, which took 12 days 5 hours to complete the 4,120-km (2,225-nautical mile) voyage. Her owner, Clarence MacFarlane, had suggested the race in the first instance. It wasn't until 1934 that the fleet size began to build significantly, with 12 entries in three classes. The finish line is off Diamond Head, Honolulu. Since 1991, the starts have been phased, with the smaller yachts leaving earlier in a bid to bring all the entries into the finish celebrations at the same time.

Better meteorological understanding of the Pacific High (an area of high pressure and light winds) after World War II saw navigators forsake the direct course in order to pick up the bottom of the High and bring the wind direction aft. This cemented the Transpac's reputation as a downwind race and created the design phenomenon of the West Coast "sled" style yachts of light displacement and big downwind sail plans.

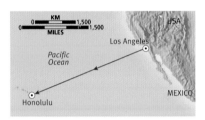

RACE SUMMARY

EVENT TYPE 4,120-km (2,225-nautical mile) ocean race

FREQUENCY Biennial

CREW Fully crewed

BOAT Grand-prix, cruiser-racers

RACE FACTS In 2005, German Hasso Plattner made a monohull record time of 6 days 16 hours 4 minutes in *Morning Glory*.

CENTENNIAL START
Division I and II competitors getting off to a typically close-fought start in the 2005 Transpac Race off Point Fermin near San Pedro, Los Angeles.

Newport to Ensenada Race

SOUTHERN CALIFORNIA TO MEXICO, PACIFIC OCEAN

Newport Beach, Los Angeles, is the starting point of the annual race to Ensenada, Mexico. It is a short race, at just 240km (130 nautical miles), and is a candidate for the world's most popular international ocean race, regularly attracting an entry of over 450 boats.

CELEBRITY COMPETITORS

The Newport to Ensenada Race is organized by the Newport Ocean Sailing Association (NOSA). The race's friendly nature, short distance, and exotic destination have attracted a diverse array of sailors. Actor Humphrey Bogart competed, as did television news icon Walter Cronkite, while Roy Disney, former president of Disney Pictures, has been an avid and frequent participant.

Disney's maxi *Pyewacket* set the monohull course record in 1998 in just 11 hours 54 minutes. Then, in 2003, Disney broke the record again in a newer *Pyewacket*, in 10 hours 44 minutes. The fresh, consistent winds in 1998 also saw American sailing, ballooning, and aviation record-setter Steve Fossett set the multihull record in 6 hours 46 minutes. Fossett was sailing one of the two 18-m (60-ft) *Stars and Stripes* catamarans built for Dennis Conner's America's Cup defence of 1988. Back in 1983, an all time record of 675 yachts entered the race.

RACE START

A bowman calls the final few seconds for his helmsman at the start of the 2005 Newport to Ensenada Race. It is the shortest of several races heading to tropical Mexico from the vast Los Angeles conurbation. Others finish in Puerto Vallarta and Manzanillo.

RACE SUMMARY

EVENT TYPE 240-km (130-nautical mile) offshore race

FREQUENCY Annual

CREW Fully crewed

BOAT Grand-prix, cruiser-racers

RACE FACTS Actor Humphrey Bogart led the 1947 race in *Santana*. When he mistook truck headlights for the race searchlight, he nearly hit the rocks, but still finished third.

Volvo Ocean Race

ROUND THE WORLD

The 1960s feats of solo sailors raised a question: if one person could sail around the world, could full crews race around it? The first such race was organized by Britain's Royal Naval Sailing Association and sponsored by brewing company Whitbread.

A PIONEERING RACE

Three hundred and twenty four crew on 17 diverse yachts responded to the call for the first race. It was staged in 1973–74 and set the pattern for many subsequent round-the-world races: an autumn start from northern Europe timed to bring the fleet through the Southern Ocean during the southern hemisphere summer.

With stops in Cape Town, Sydney, and Rio de Janeiro, the first race also created the concept that a round-the-world race should embrace the three great capes: Good Hope (South Africa), Leeuwin (Australia), and Horn (South America). Cape Horn in particular – with the preceding stages through the Roaring Forties, Furious Fifties, and Screaming Sixties – established this type of racing as one of the most extreme sports in the world.

Three lives were lost in this first race, and lessons were learned in the cruellest way about the use and effectiveness of safety harnesses and man overboard recovery techniques. Information was gained, too, about the properties of stainless steel in extreme cold conditions, such was the pioneering nature of this racing circumnavigation.

The route has been altered from time to time in response to changing world circumstances, and the race has enhanced or made the reputations of many yachtsmen and women.

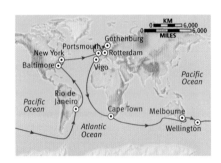

VOLVO OCEAN RACE STAGES 2005–06

STAGE	APPROXIMATE DISTANCE
Vigo–Cape Town	11,850km (6,400nm)
Cape Town–Melbourne	11,300km (6,100nm)
Melbourne–Wellington	2,700km (1,450nm)
Wellington–Rio de Janeiro	12,400km (6,700nm)
Rio de Janeiro–Baltimore	9,250km (5,000nm)
Baltimore–New York	750km (400nm)
New York–Portsmouth	6,000km (3,200nm)
Portsmouth–Rotterdam	2,800km (1,500nm)
Rotterdam–Gothenberg	900km (500nm)

INNOVATION IN YACHT DESIGN

Since 1997–98, the race has used only class boats unique to this race: first the Whitbread 60, utilizing water ballast to boost power, which was first designed for the 1993–94 race. Following a change of sponsor in 2001–02 to Volvo, the new and extremely powerful Volvo Open 70 class with canting keels was introduced in 2005.

IN-PORT RACE

In 2005–06, in-port racing was introduced between long-distance legs, to give spectators the opportunity of seeing these racing machines in action from close up.

RACE SUMMARY

EVENT TYPE Round-the-world ocean race

FREQUENCY Every four or three years

CREW Fully crewed

BOAT Volvo Open 70

RACE FACTS In May 2006, Dutchman Hans Horrevoets was swept overboard from *ABN Amro Two* and died in 5-m (15-ft) waves in the Atlantic during Leg 7.

OFF THE ISLE OF WIGHT
In the foreground is *ABN Amro One*, winner of the 2005–06 race. Sailing behind is sister ship *ABN Amro Two*, which during the race set a monohull 24-hour world record of 1,042km (563 nautical miles).

Olympic Racing

WORLDWIDE

Introduced in 1900, sailing is one of the oldest sports in the modern Olympics. The classes raced change over time, and future classes will reflect rising participation by women and greater athleticism of sailors. A continuing trend is towards smaller boats with fewer crew.

Olympic racing is based on short events about 30–75 minutes in duration, with a one-design fleet racing a course that offers a variety of different sailing angles under the International Sailing Federation (ISAF) Racing Rules. There are heats for each event, so that the final fleet for each is not too crowded. Points are awarded according to the finishing position in each race, with the lowest accumulated scores throughout the competition winning the medals.

The courses for Olympic races are mainly set on the day of the race and

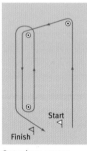

Outer loop course

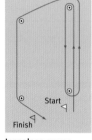

Inner loop course

SINGLE-HANDED GLORY
Ben Ainslie of Great Britain competes at the 2004 Olympics in Athens, Greece, in the Finn Heavyweight dinghy class in which he won the Gold Medal. The sail windows help to avoid collisions in close racing.

may have to be changed during the day, depending on the wind direction. The emphasis is on upwind and downwind sailing, with smaller amounts of reaching. The diagrams above show conventional "loop and sausage" courses:

OLYMPIC CLASSES

The ISAF selected these classes for 2008:
One-person dinghy, men (Laser)
One-person dinghy, women (Laser Radial)
Two-person dinghy, men (470)
Two-person dinghy, women (470)
Heavyweight dinghy, mixed (Finn)
Skiff, mixed (49er)
Multihull, mixed (Tornado)
Keelboat, men (Star)
Keelboat, women (Yngling)

the start is always directly into the wind, so that tacking to the first mark spreads the fleet. A good race depends on a good course having been laid. In the Olympic Games, the combination of short courses, closely matched boats, and unmistakable identification of competitors makes the sailing exciting for spectators as well as the competitors.

From the 1960s onwards, dinghy and keelboat design has moved towards smaller, lighter, and mass-produced boats. This has made boat purchase less expensive and therefore less exclusive – the result is a truly international entry in modern Olympic sailing events. Separate women's events were introduced in 1988.

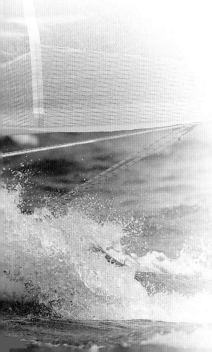

SMALL BOAT, BIG SAIL AREA
The 470 is a well-established Olympic class for both men and women. A trapezing crew keeps the light, planing hull level in the water.

EXTREME BOAT
High-performance 49ers jostle on the start line, each needing to make the best start possible. The lead boat will have the huge advantage of clean air.

TORNADO CLASS
Brazilians Maurico Santa Cruz Oliveira and Joao Carlos Jordao in the open multihull Tornado finals in Athens in 2004. This is the fastest Olympic class.

YNGLING
Fighting for position on the start line, the Yngling – the women's keelboat – made its debut as an Olympic-class boat at Athens in 2004.

Glossary

Aft Towards the stern.

Amidships At the centre of the boat.

Astern Backwards; behind the *stern*.

Backstay Wire support leading from the *masthead* to the *stern*.

Beam Widest point of the boat.

Bear away Turn the boat away from the wind.

Bearing Direction of an object from the boat, or between two objects, measured in degrees relative to north.

Beat To sail to *windward* on a *close hauled* course, zig-zagging towards a given point.

Berth (1) Place assigned for leaving a boat alongside a quay, or pontoon, or in a marina. (2) To manoeuvre a boat into a berth. (3) A bed on a boat. (4) Sufficient distance from other boats or objects for the boat to manoeuvre.

Bilge (1) Rounded parts of the *hull* where the sides curve inwards to form the bottom. (2) Area under the cabin, where water collects.

Bilge keels Twin keels, used on boats designed to dry out sitting upright.

Block Pulley through which a rope is passed.

Boltrope Reinforcing rope along a sail's edge.

Boom Horizontal spar, to which the foot of a sail is attached.

Boom vang Metal strut between boom and mast that holds the boom down.

Bow Forward end of a boat.

Bow line Mooring *warp* running from the *bow* to shore, ahead of the boat.

Bowline Knot used to make a loop in the end of a rope, or to tie it to a ring or post.

Breast rope Mooring *warp* running at right angles to the boat, from *bow* or *stern*.

Bridle (1) Wire span for attaching *forestay* to hulls on a catamaran. (2) Rope span sometimes used to secure the lower *mainsheet block* on dinghies that do not use a mainsheet *traveller*.

Bulkhead Below-deck partition separating one part of a boat's interior from another.

Burgee Small flag flown from the top of a mast, as an indicator of apparent wind; also used as an identifier of club or other affiliation.

By the lee Sailing *downwind*, with the wind tending to blow from the wrong side of the sail.

Cap shroud Outer shroud.

Cardinal mark Form of buoyage, used to indicate a large or individual hazard.

Catamaran Boat consisting of two narrow hulls connected by two beams and a trampoline or rigid deck.

Centreboard Movable *foil* to resist *leeway*. that pivots around a pin inside a centreboard case.

Chain plates Strengthened metal deck fittings on each side of a boat, and at the *bow* and *stern*, to which the *shrouds*, *forestay*, and *backstay* are attached.

Cleat (1) Fitting for securing a rope; a clam cleat, or jamming cleat, secures it between two movable, toothed jaws; a horn cleat has two prongs projecting from a central base, round which the rope is wound. (2) To secure a rope on or in a cleat.

Clew Lower aft corner of a sail.

Close hauled Sailing as close to the wind as possible, with the sails pulled in tightly.

Coachroof Raised cabin roof in the middle of a yacht deck.

Cockpit Working area, usually towards the *stern*, from which the boat is steered.

Companionway Steps leading down from *cockpit* to cabin.

Crew (1) Either all on board, or all except the *helmsman*. (2) To work as a member of the crew (including the helmsman), or to work alongside a helmsman with your own tasks.

Cringle Metal or plastic eye sewn into a sail.

Cunningham Control line for adjusting tension in the *luff* of a sail.

Daggerboard Movable *foil* that slides vertically inside its case, to be lowered below the *hull* to resist *leeway*.

Depth sounder Electronic device for measuring distance from the seabed to the instrument's transducer.

Displacement Weight of water displaced by the submerged part of the *hull*.

Dodgers Weather cloths laced along the guard rails for added protection in the *cockpit*.

Dorade Ventilator that feeds air to the interior while keeping water out.

Downhaul Rope for hauling down sails, or for controlling a *spar*.

Downwind (or offwind) With the wind blowing from *aft* of the *beam*.

Ebb tide Tide moving (ebbing) from high water to low water.

EPIRB Emergency position indicating radio beacon that transmits distress signals to satellites that are part of the *GMDSS*.

Fairlead Ring or loop, for guiding a rope.

Fender Cushioned protector hung over the side, between boat and pontoon or other vessel.

Fiddle Raised lip on a horizontal surface below decks, such as a table or shelf, to prevent objects falling off when the boat heels.

Fin keel Single, central, fixed, ballasted *keel*.

Flood tide Tide moving (flooding) from low water to high water.

Foils Collective term for *keel/centreboard/ daggerboard*, *skeg*, and *rudder*. May also refer to sails when describing aerodynamic forces.

Fore Towards the *bow*.

Forestay A *stay* leading forward from the *mast* to the *bow*.

Foul tide Adverse tidal stream.

Freeboard Height between deck and waterline.

Galley Boat kitchen.

Genoa Large *headsail* that overlaps the mast.

Gimbals Fittings that allow an object such as a galley stove to swing, so as to remain upright when the boat heels.

GMDSS Global Maritime Distress and Safety System: set of standards for modern radio and satellite communication systems.

Gnav *Boom vang* that is attached to the *mast* above the *boom*.

Gooseneck Universal-joint fitting fixed to a *mast*, for attaching the *boom*.

Goosewinging To set the *headsail* on the opposite side to the *mainsail*, when sailing *downwind*.

GPS Global Positioning System receiver, using information from a network of satellites to determine position accurately.

GRP Glass-reinforced plastic (fibreglass).

Guard rail Safety rail or wire fitted around the deck edge, supported by stanchions.

Gunwale Top edge of the side of the *hull*.

Guy Rope that controls a traditional *spinnaker* on the windward side.

Gybe To turn the *stern* through the wind.

Halyard Rope or wire used to hoist a sail, flag, *burgee*, or other signal.

Hand-bearing compass Portable compass for taking *bearings*.

Hank Metal or plastic hook used to secure a sail to a stay, such as a *jib* to the *forestay*.

Head (1) Top corner of a triangular sail, or top edge of a four-sided sail.

Headboard Reinforced top corner of a sail, to which the *halyard* is attached.

Heading Direction in which you are steering the boat, measured by compass.

Heads (1) Sea toilet (2) Compartment containing the toilet and washing facilities.

Headsail Sail set forward of the *mast*.

Head to wind With the *bow* directly into the wind, and sails *luffing*.

Heave-to To bring a boat to a controlled halt by *trimming* the sails.

Heel (1) To lean over to one side. (2) Fitting at the bottom end of the *mast*.

Helm *Tiller* or wheel, and by implication also the *rudder*, by which the boat is steered.

Helmsman Person who steers the boat.

Hike out To sit out on the sidedeck secured by *toestraps*, to keep a dinghy level.

Hoist To raise a sail or flag.

Hull Main body of a boat.

IALA International Association of Lighthouse Authorities; responsible for buoyage systems.

In irons Stuck *head-to-wind* with sails *luffing*, and no steerage.

ISAF International Sailing Federation; the international governing body of sailing.

Jackstay Webbing or wire line that runs the length of the sidedeck, to which *crew* attach their *lifelines* when working on deck.

Jib Triangular *headsail*.

Kedge (1) A light, auxilliary anchor. (2) To pull the boat along by hauling the cable of a kedge anchor that has been dropped some distance from the boat, for example, to refloat a boat that has grounded.

Keel Ballasted plate fixed below the *hull* of a sailing boat, to resist *leeway* and provide righting moment.

Kicking strap Multi-purchase rope tackle from *boom* to *mast*, to hold the boom down.

Knot Unit of speed at sea; defined as one nautical mile per hour.

Lazyjacks Restraining lines rigged from *mast* to *boom* to retain the *mainsail* when it is lowered and stowed on the boom.

Lee helm Imbalance between sails and rudder that tends to turn the boat to *leeward* when you let go of the *helm*.

Leech *Aft* edge of a sail.

Lee-oh Call made by the *helmsman* when executing a tack.

Lee shore Shore on to which wind is blowing.

Leeward Away from the wind.

Leeway The sideways drift of the boat to *leeward* caused by the effect of the wind.

Lifeline Tether of a safety harness worn by yacht crew that is attached to points, such as *jackstays*, on the boat.

Lift Wind shift; when the wind moves *aft* you are "lifted".

Luff (1) Forward edge of a triangular sail. (2) To turn towards the wind. (3) To make the forward edge of a sail shake and lose wind, by sailing too close to the wind, or with the sail insufficiently *sheeted* in.

Lying a-hull Drifting with all sails stowed, usually in heavy weather.

Mainsail Principal *fore-and-aft* sail.

Mainsheet Sheet controlling the *mainsail*.

Mast Vertical pole to which sails are attached.

Mast gate Point where the *mast* passes through the deck of a dinghy or small keelboat.

Masthead Top of a *mast*.

MAYDAY Internationally recognized radio distress signal, for use when a ship is in grave and imminent danger.

Mizzen mast Smaller, *aft* mast on a boat with two masts.

Mooring (1) Permanently laid arrangement of anchors and cables, to which a boat can be secured. (2) The process of securing a boat in a *berth* or to a mooring buoy.

Nautical almanac Annual reference book giving information, such as tidal and port data, for a wide area.

Nautical mile Unit of distance at sea; defined as one minute (1′) of latitude, standardized to 1,852m (6,076ft).

Navigation lights Signal lights shown by a boat to indicate relative course, position, and status such as sailing, motoring, fishing, towing.

Neap tide *Tide* with the smallest range between high and low water, occurring at the first and last quarters of the moon.

Offshore / onshore wind Wind blowing off/on to the land.

Outhaul Rope that pulls something out, such as the *clew* outhaul to adjust tension in the foot of the *mainsail*.

Painter Rope attached to the bow of a dinghy or small boat, used for *mooring*.

PAN PAN Internationally recognized distress signal that takes priority over all except a MAYDAY message.

Passage Journey between two ports.

Pile moorings Large wooden or metal stakes (piles) driven into the seabed, with fittings to which *mooring warps* are tied.

Pinch To sail too close to the wind.

Pitchpole To capsize *stern* over *bow*.

Plane To use speed to lift part of the boat on to the surface of the water, which further increases speed by reducing drag.

Pontoon Floating platform.

Port Left-hand side of boat, looking forwards.

Prop walk Paddlewheel effect of a turning propeller. Prop walk pushes the *stern* sideways in the direction that the propeller rotates.

Pulpit/pushpit Elevated, rigid metal rail around the *bow/stern* of a boat.

Quarter Boat's side between *beam* and *stern*.

Rake Amount that a *mast* leans *aft*.

Ratchet block Pulley containing a ratchet that permits motion in one direction only, to prevent the load slipping when *crew* release pressure on the rope.

Reach To sail with wind blowing from the side.

Ready about Phrase used to warn *crew* that the *helmsman* is about to tack.

Reef To reduce sail area when the wind becomes strong.

Rig (1) Configuration of sails, *spars*, and *masts*. (2) To *step* the mast and attach the sails.

Rigging System of wires and ropes used to keep the *mast* in place and work the sails. Standing rigging includes all fixed *shrouds* and *stays* that support the mast. Running rigging includes all moving lines, such as *sheets* and *halyards*, used in setting and trimming of sails.

Roller-furling Mechanical system to roll up and stow *jib* or *mainsail*.

Roller-reefing System for reefing a *headsail* or *mainsail*, by rolling it on to a *spar* or *stay*.

Rudder Movable underwater blade used to steer the boat, controlled by *tiller* or wheel.

Run To sail directly *downwind*.

Seacock Valve that can be shut to close a through-*hull* fitting.

Shackle U-shaped link with a closing pin, used to connect ropes and metal or wire fittings.

Sheet Rope attached to the *clew* of a sail, or to a *boom*, to adjust the sail.

Shroud Wire support either side of the *mast*.

Skeg Downward-projecting foil at the *aft* end of the *hull*, smaller than the *keel*, which supports the *rudder*.

Slab reefing Traditional method of reducing area of *mainsail*, by partially lowering the sail and tying up the loose fold (slab) of sail created.

Sleeved sail Sail that has a sleeve at the *luff*, which wraps around the *mast*.

Slot Gap for airflow between the *leech* of the *jib* and the *luff* of the *mainsail*.

Spar General term for *masts* and *booms*, etc.

Spinnaker Large, light, *downwind* sail set forward of the *forestay*.

Splice To join two ropes or wires by interweaving their strands.

Spreaders Small poles extending sideways from one or more places high on the *mast*. *Shrouds* run through their outer ends, to distribute mast support as broadly as possible.

Spring *Mooring warp* led astern from the *bow*, or forward from the *stern*, to prevent a moored boat moving ahead or *astern*.

Spring tide *Tide* with the largest range between high and low water, occurring at or just after the new moon and full moon.

Stanchion Upright post supporting guard rails.

Starboard Right-hand side of boat, when looking forwards.

Stay Wire running *fore* or *aft* from the masthead, to support the *mast*.

Steerage way Speed through the water that is necessary in order for the boat to be steerable.

Stem Main upright or sloping structure at *bow*.

Step (1) A recess or fitting into which the base of the *mast* is fitted. (2) The process of fitting the mast in position.

Stern Rear of the boat.

Storm jib Very small, heavyweight *headsail* used in strong winds.

Tack (1) Forward lower corner of a fore-and-aft sail. (2) To turn the *bow* of a boat through the wind. (3) Course of a boat sailing to *windward*, expressed as port tack (wind from the *port* side), or starboard tack (wind from the *starboard* side).

Tell-tales Light strips of fabric, sewn or glued to sails to show wind-flow and best sail *trim*.

Tender Small boat used to ferry people and provisions to and from a larger boat.

Thwart Seat fixed across a small boat.

Tidal atlas Set of small-scale charts showing tidal stream directions and rates of flow.

Tide Regular rise and fall of the sea's surface, and the associated horizontal streams, caused by the gravitational pull of the moon and sun.

Tide tables Predictions of the times and heights of high and low water for every day of the year, based on a specific location. New tables are calculated for each year.

Tiller Rod by which the *rudder* is controlled, for steering.

Toestraps Straps of webbing under which a dinghy crew hook their feet when *hiking out*.

Topping lift Rope running from masthead to *boom* end, used to support the boom when the *mainsail* is not hoisted.

Trampoline Strong nylon mesh stretched between the *hulls* of a *catamaran* or *trimaran*.

Transom Flat vertical surface of the *hull* across the *stern* of a boat.

Trapeze Wire used in high-performance dinghies, to enable the crew to place their weight farther outside the boat than they would if just *hiking out*.

Traveller Slider that travels along a track, used for altering *sheet* angles.

Trim To let out or pull in *sheet*, to adjust a sail.

Trimaran Vessel with three *hulls*.

Trip To release a rope quickly.

Trot Line of *mooring* buoys.

Uphaul Rope for adjusting the height of a *spar*.

Upwind To *windward*.

Vang Metal strut between *boom* and *mast* that holds the boom down.

VHF Very High Frequency radio, used for ship-to-ship and ship-to-shore transmission and receiving of communications.

Wake Waves or track generated *astern* by a moving vessel.

Warp Any rope used to secure or move a boat.

Washboards Wooden or plastic shutters that close off the *companionway*.

Watch (1) Division of *crew* into shifts. (2) Time each watch has duty.

Waypoint Position, in latitude and longitude, of an important point along a route. Usually for programming into an electronic navigational system.

Weather helm Imbalance between sails and *rudder* that causes the boat to turn to *windward* when pressure on the *tiller* eases.

Weather/windward shore Shore from which the wind is blowing.

Whip To bind the ends of a rope with thin twine, to prevent strands unravelling.

Whisker pole *Spar* for holding out the *jib* when *goosewinged*.

Winch Device to provide mechanical advantage for pulling in *sheets* and *halyards*.

Windage Drag caused by parts of the boat and *crew* exposed to the wind.

Windlass Mechanical device used to pull in heavy cable or chain, such as that attached to an anchor.

Windward Towards the wind.

Useful Resources

ASSOCIATIONS AND RULING BODIES

The website of the International Sailing Federation (ISAF) has information on the organization of world sailing (mostly racing) and links to all the national authorities for sailing:

www.sailing.org

For information on disabled sailing:

www.disabledsailing.org.uk
www.sailing.org/disabled

The websites of the national associations of the UK, Ireland, Australia, New Zealand, South Africa, the US, and Canada carry details of clubs, sailing schools, and courses. Each body oversees competitive and recreational sailing:

www.rya.org.uk
www.sailing.ca
www.sailing.ie
www.sailing.org.za
www.ussailing.org
www.yachting.org.au
www.yachtingnz.org.nz

Useful sites for learning about the rules that govern all types of sailboat racing:

**www.sailingbreezes.com/sailing_breezes_current/
    articles/BS05/Rules.htm**
www.sailingcourse.com/racing_rules.htm

GENERAL INFORMATION

These sailing portals and news sites offer lots of useful sailing content:

www.boats.com
www.sailinganarchy.com
www.sailingscuttlebutt.com
www.sailtrain.co.uk
www.sailworld.com
www.thedailysail.com
www.themainsail.com
www.voilesnews.fr
www.yachtsandyachting.com

RACING

Whether you aspire to sail at the highest level or just enjoy following the major competitions, these are the sites for some of the world's top ocean races (www.sailing.org, mentioned earlier, has links to these and other races):

http://rolexsydneyhobart.com
www.rorc.org/fastnet
www.routedurhum.org
www.skandiacowesweek.co.uk
www.velux5oceans.com
www.vendeeglobe.fr./uk
www.volvooceanrace.org

BOATS AND EQUIPMENT

By no means an exhaustive list, but here are the sites of some of the popular classes:

www.laserinternational.org (lasers)
www.lasersailing.com (lasers)
www.ldcracingsailboats.co.uk (RS dinghy range)
www.hunter707.org.uk (Hunter 707)
www.sailing.org/classes/classlist.asp
www.toppersailboats.com
www.uksonar.info (International Sonar keelboat)

WEATHER INFORMATION

The national weather centres of the UK, Ireland, Australia, and United States are good starting points for finding online weather information, and there are others worth trying:

www.bom.gov.au/weather
www.met.ie
www.meteo.fr
www.meto.gov.uk
www.nws.noaa.gov
www.weather.org.uk/charts/thumbs.html
www.weatheronline.co.uk/sail.htm
www.westwind.ch
www.windguru.cz

The US Coastguard and the British RNLI websites contain useful information:

www.rnli.org.uk
www.uscg.mil

Index

Acknowledgments

AUTHORS' ACKNOWLEDGMENTS

Jeremy Evans would like to thank all the staff at Minorca Sailing Holidays (www.minorcasailing.co.uk), who sailed some of their fantastic range of dinghies to perfection to provide a massive amount of help with this book. Also to Dan Jaspers and his trusty crew at Sunsail Yacht Sailing Schools in Port Solent (www.sunsail.co.uk) who did brilliant work on the yachts and were able to cope with our every whim and demand. Plus Alan, Richard, and Andrew Taylor who did a great job for the catamaran section with their trusty Hobie 16 Spi, while giving up a lot of time to dodge and dive in some truly appalling weather – we particularly appreciated that voluntary pitchpole! Having previously worked on their Sea Safety Guidelines, I would like to give a big vote of thanks to the Royal National Lifeboat Institution for providing so much knowledge on safety issues (www.rnliseasafety.org.uk). A special thanks to Bryony Hackett-Evans, who was an excellent RIB driver and also helped provide useful advice for this book, and finally to Cathy Meeus and Hugh Schermuly who turned out to be great people to work with on a difficult, time-challenged project.
Rod Heikell would like to thank Lu Michell, John Goode at *Sailing Today*, Willie Wilson, and Katrina Sewell.

PUBLISHER'S ACKNOWLEDGMENTS

Dorling Kindersley and Schermuly Design would like to thank the following for their invaluable help with this book: Lynn Bresler for proofreading and indexing; Sunsail Yacht Sailing Schools and Minorca Sailing holidays for generously providing facilities for the photography; Bryony Hackett-Evans for helping to organize the dinghy sailing shoot, for modelling, and for expert dinghy-sailing advice; Dan Jaspers for skippering, modelling,

and sharing his knowledge; Dale Birrell, Anthony Bisset, Katie Bushnell, Ruth Fentiman, Andrew and Richard Glover, Samantha Grieve, Nicholas Marshall, Christopher Miller, Arron Mullen, Helen Reid, Anna Renz, Becky Shuttleworth, Matt Staniforth, and Alex Stone for acting as models. We would also like to thank all the manufacturers who kindly supplied images: Garmin Ltd, Jeanneau, Plastimo UK, and Raymarine Inc. Valuable advice on First Aid was provided by Dr Vivien Armstrong.

PICTURE CREDITS

The publisher would like to thank the following for their kind permission to reproduce their photographs:

(Key: a-above; b-below/bottom; c-centre; f-far; l-left; r-right; t-top)

1 Getty Images: (tc). 4-5 Corbis: (c). 6 Getty Images: (c). 7 ©Jeremy Evans: (c). 8-9 Getty Images: (t). 10 Alamy Images: (br). 11 Corbis: (br). 12-13 DPPI: (b). 13 DPPI: (cra). 14 ©Jeremy Evans: (cla). 15 Corbis: (c). 16-17 Corbis. 18-19 Corbis. 20 Corbis: (bc) (cla). 21 Corbis: (ca) (clb). 22 Corbis: (cl). 23 Corbis: (cra) (b) (clb). 24 Kos Picture Source: (bc). 25 Corbis: (bc) (ca). 26 Corbis: (bc). 27 Corbis: (br). Getty Images: (ca). 28 Alamy Images: (bc). © Mystic Seaport, Rosenfeld Collection, Mystic, CT: (tc). 29 Corbis: (cra). Van de Stadt Design: (br). 30 Corbis: (bl) (cra). 31 Corbis: (c). Getty Images: (clb). 32 Alamy Images: (ca). 32-33 Corbis: (bc). 33 Alamy Images: (cra). 34 Alamy Images: (ca). 35 Corbis: (bc). 39 Getty Images: (ca). 40-41 ©Jeremy Evans: (tc). 41 Th. Martinez: (cra). 42 ©Jeremy Evans: (clb). 42-43 ©Jeremy Evans: (tc). 43 Jeanneau: (br). ©Jeremy Evans: (clb). 48 Action Images: (c). 49 Action Images: (c). Corbis: (cla). Kathy Mansfield: (tl). © Mike Good/Dorling Kindersley: (fcra). 60-61 Getty Images: (c). 66 ©Jeremy Evans: (crb). 67

©Jeremy Evans: (bc). 69 ©Jeremy Evans: (ca). 70-71 Jeanneau: (c). 82-83 ©Jeremy Evans: (c). 84-85 ©Jeremy Evans: (c). 94 ©Jeremy Evans: (cra). 95 ©Jeremy Evans: (cb). 96 ©Jeremy Evans: (bl). 96-97 RS racing: (br). 97 ©Jeremy Evans: (cla). 108-109 ©Jeremy Evans: (c). 134-135 Corbis: (c). 137 Getty Images: (fcra). 140 ©Jeremy Evans: (cra). 148-149 Corbis: (c). 152 Alamy Images: (cra). ©Jeremy Evans: (bc). 153 Corbis: (br). 154 Corbis: (c). 155 ©Jeremy Evans: (c). 158-159 Corbis: (tc). 159 Skandia Team GBR/ Richard Langdon: (fcrb). 160-161 RS racing: (c). 167 ©Jeremy Evans: (c). 172 Steve Sleight: (tl). 174 ©Jeremy Evans: (ca). 174-175 Jeanneau: (bc). 175 Alamy Images: (cra). 178-179 Corbis: (c). 193 Corbis: (tl). 204-205 Corbis: (c). 214 ©Jeremy Evans: (cra). 214-215 ©Jeremy Evans. 216 Corbis: (clb). 218 Cathy Meeus: (c). ©Jeremy Evans: (br) (bl). 220-221 Alamy Images: (c). 222 Corbis: (cra). Jeanneau: (bc). 224-225 Corbis: (c). 227 Alamy Images: (bc) (cra). 230 Alamy Images: (bl). 231 Science Photo Library: (c). 233 Alamy Images: (bc) (c). 236 Plastimo/Navimo UK Ltd: (ca). 238-239 Admiralty Leisure: (c). 240 © Mike Good/Dorling Kindersley: (bc). Raymarine plc. : (ca). 241 Raymarine plc. : (fclb) (tc) (fcr). 242 ©Jeremy Evans: (bl). 243 ©Jeremy Evans: (fbr). 244 ©Jeremy Evans: (crb) (fcrb). © Mike Good/ Dorling Kindersley: (fcra). 245 Imray-Iolaire: (cra). 246 ©Jeremy Evans: (cra). 247 Raymarine plc. : (br). 249 Corbis: (br). 252 ©Jeremy Evans: (fcra). 254 © Mike Good/Dorling Kindersley: (bl). 255 McMurdo Ltd : (ca). 256 © Mike Good/Dorling Kindersley: (bc). Raymarine plc. : (crb). 257 Alamy Images: (c). 258 Corbis: (bc). 259 Alamy Images: (clb). 260 ©Jeremy Evans: (c). 261 Corbis: (bc). 264 © Mike Good/Dorling Kindersley: (br). 265 © Mike Good/Dorling Kindersley: (fcr) (fcra). 266 © Mike Good/Dorling Kindersley: (fcra) (bl) (br). 267 © Mike Good/Dorling Kindersley: (bc/recovery) (ca). 268-269 Corbis: (bc). 270 Getty Images: (bc). 270-271 Alamy Images: (tc). 271 Getty Images: (c). Royal National Lifeboat Institute: (br). 272 Getty Images: (bl). 274 Cathy Meeus: (tl). 274-275 Corbis: (c). 276-277 Getty Images: (br). 277 Getty Images: (ca). 278-279 Corbis: (bc). 279 Getty Images. 280 Getty Images: (bl). 281 Corbis: (bc). 282 Getty Images: (bc). 283 Corbis: (ca). 284 Andy O'Grady/Ulla Norlander: (fcra). 285 Andy O'Grady/Ulla Norlander: (bc). 286 Alamy Images: (bc). Getty Images: (bl). 288 Corbis: (bl). Kos Picture Source: (fcra). 289 Corbis: (bc). 290 Alamy Images: (fcra). Getty Images: (fbl). 292 Cathy Meeus. 292-293 Getty Images: (bc). 293 Corbis: (cra). 294 Corbis: (bc). 295 Getty Images: (ca). 296 Getty Images: (ca). 297 Corbis: (bc). 298-299 Corbis: (bc). 299 Getty Images: (fcra). 300 Corbis: (fclb) (ca). 301 Getty Images: (bc). 302 Getty Images: (ca). 303 Getty Images: (bc). 304 Getty Images: (fcr). 305 Corbis: (bc). 306-307 Getty Images: (c). 308 Corbis: (cra) (bc). 2006 Tim Wilkes/www.timwilkes.com: (ftl). 309 Getty Images: (cla) (c). 310 Getty Images: (bc). 311 Getty Images: (ca). 312 Action Images: (fcra). 313 Alamy Images: (bc). 314 Action Images: (ca). 315 DPPI: (bc). 316-317 Corbis: (bc). 318 Kos Picture Source: (bc). 319 DPPI: (ca). 320-321 Kos Picture Source: (c). 321 Getty Images: (fcra). 322-323 Corbis: (cb). 323 Corbis: (fcr). 324 Alamy Images. 325 Corbis: (br). 326 Corbis: (fclb). Empics Ltd: (fcla). 327 Getty Images: (bc). 328 Will Jones: (fcr). 329 Getty Images: (bc). 330 Kos Picture Source: (bc). 331 Chris Lewis Photography Ltd: (ca). 332 Kazi Publishing: (bl). 333 Getty Images: (br). 334 UnderTheSunPhotos.com: (bc). 335 UnderTheSunPhotos.com: (ca). 336 Action Images: (bl). 337 Action Images: (c). 338-339 Getty Images: (bl). 339 Getty Images: (fcra) (fcra/Women's 470) (fcrb) (fbr)

Maps on pages 276–305 and 308–336 are Mountain High Maps ® copyright © 1993 Digital Wisdom, Inc.

Every effort has been made to trace the copyright holders. The publisher apologizes for any unintentional omissions and would be pleased in such cases to place an acknowledgment in future editions of this book.

All other images © Dorling Kindersley
For further information see: **www.dkimages.com.**

THE ELLEN MACARTHUR TRUST

Launched in 2003 the Ellen MacArthur Trust was set up to enliven and empower the lives of children suffering or recovering from cancer or leukaemia. The main activity of the Trust involves taking the kids out sailing around the south coast of the UK. "Meeting the challenges of sailing at sea, the children gain confidence and are reminded that there is life beyond their illness. At the same time they meet friends suffering from the same disease, which reminds them they are not alone in their struggle."

THE Ellen MacArthur TRUST For more information please log onto: **http://www.ellenmacarthurtrust.org** or email: **frank.fletcher@ellenmacarthurtrust.org.**